Missouri Taxpayers

1819-1826

by
Lois Stanley
George F. Wilson
Maryhelen Wilson

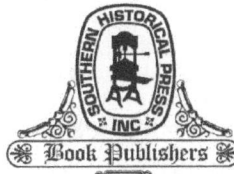

Southern Historical Press, Inc.
Greenville, South Carolina

Please direct all correspondence and orders to:

www.southernhistoricalpress.com
or
SOUTHERN HISTORICAL PRESS, Inc.
PO BOX 1267
375 West Broad Street
Greenville, SC   29601
southernhistoricalpress@gmail.com

ISBN #0-89308-434-4

Printed in the United States of America

This is the first listing ever made of documented male residents of
Missouri on a state-wide basis at the time its first census would have
been taken -- 1820-1825. There are approximately 14,000 names.

When Missouri became a state in August, 1821, the estimated popu-
lation was about 60,000. That figure represented about 10,000 adult men
(based on the generally-assumed six-persons-per-household).

By the first federal census of the state -- 1830 -- thousands of
them had died, moved, or simply disappeared. As a result, researchers
often look in vain for the name of their settling ancestor.

But there are excellent sources for the names of early Missourians.
First, the tax lists; an astonishing number have survived, some from the
territorial days, many more from the earliest years of statehood. The
known lists cover 15 counties in existence before 1826; there are lists
of delinquents for eight more. And there are valuable lists for all
counties in the State Archives -- taxes on writs, deeds, executions,
convictions, etc., and year after year,licenses to sell goods, run a
ferry, deal in groceries or "spirits." These have been combined here.

With them we have included names of others (who may or may not have
paid taxes) from an excellent secondary source: newspapers. These are
names which appeared in legal or other notices, the detailed "taking up"
of strays, the Annual Statements of counties. Newspapers also published
delinquent-taxpayer lists not found elsewhere.

One list from this period not available for publication is the 1821
Ray County Assessor's list. The original has disappeared, but a copy was
made and can be found in Woodruff and Hodges' excellent Missouri Pioneers
series, Volume II.

Dates of the Lists

When possible the years 1820 through 1825 were used. If at least two such
lists were unavailable one was added from 1819 or 1826. When none of
these could be found delinquent lists were used. Example: the only known
listing for Scott County is the 1826 delinquent. On the other hand, we
included all years from 1819 through 1825 for Montgomery, a difficult-to-
research "burned" county.

When available tax lists and secondary data for the same county were
compared there was a high percentage of duplication. So it seems reasonable to assume that many of the secondary listings would have appeared
as taxpayers on the lost lists.

Location of the Lists

Most of those included here are from the Missouri Historical Society, St.
Louis. The 1821 Ste. Genevieve is from the State Archives of Missouri,
Jefferson City. The 1821 Lincoln is from that county's 1878 Atlas.

Newspapers

All available newspapers for the period were checked. They include the
Missouri Gazette-Missouri Republican and the Enquirer, St. Louis; the St.
Charles Missourian; the Herald and the Independent Patriot, Jackson (in
Cape Girardeau County) and the Intelligencer, Howard County. These can
all be found at the Newspaper Library, State Historical Society of Mo.,
Columbia. The first three are also at Mo. Historical Society, St. Louis.

Explanations

Asterisk * -- this person paid a "poll" tax only and was probably young
and single (though a very old man might pay the same small
tax). This information not available in all counties.

Double asterisk **
Double ++   -- indicates incorrect alphabetical order.

Triple asterisk*** or more **** -- footnotes.

NOTE: the same person may appear in two or more counties. This may
indicate large landholdings in some instances; in others, the county line
may have changed or the person actually moved.

IN APPRECIATION

We thank Mr. Gary W. Beahan, State Archivist of Missouri and his staff
members Patsy Luebbring and Amy Thrash; Mrs. Alma Vaughn, Librarian, and
her staff, Newspaper Library, State Historical Society, Columbia; and Mrs.
Kathleen Schoene, Librarian, Catherine Barbour, Associate Librarian, and
Grace Morledge and Beth Wilson, Assistant Librarians, Missouri Historical
Society, St. Louis, for their help in this compilation.

CONTENTS

Missouri Taxpayers 1819-1826

iii

ABBOTT, George
ADAMS, James
ADKINS, Robert
 Roland
AGIN, Thomas
ALDEMATH, Benjamin
ALEXANDER, Joshua
ALFORD, Isaac
 Kemp
ALLEN, Elijah
ANDERSON, Henry
 John
 Nell R.
 Thomas
ANTHONY, Louis
AUSTIN, Benjamin
 David
 Isaac
 Isham
 Joel
 John
 Joseph
 Josiah
 Peter
 Robert

BAKER, Jane
 John
 John H.
 Robert
BALLINGER, Edward
 ("Neddy")
BALL, Allen
BALTELL, Obediah
BANES, John S.
BARBER, Jonathan
BARCKER, Amos
BARCLAY, Robert
BARGER, Abraham
 Gasper
 Henry
 James
 Philip
BARNES, Amos
 Aquilla
 Benjamin
 Elizabeth
 Henry
 "Big James"
 "Little James"
 John
 Nancy
 Philip
 Richard

BARNES, Shaderick
 William
BARNETT, Adam
 Hutchings
 Jesse R.
 John
BARR, Robert S.
BARTON, John
 Jonathan
 Joshua
BASS, Lawrence
 Peter
BATES, Isaiah
 William P.
BATTERTON, Enoch
 John
 Moses
 Ransom
 Samuel
BAW, William
BEATY, Samuel
BEAZLEY, Thomas
BECK, Willis
BECKER, John Sr.
BECKETT, John R.
BELCHER, Isaac
 Isham G.
 John Sr.
 John Jr.
BENNETT, James
 Joseph
 Sur
 Thomas
BERRY, John
 Milton
 Thomas
 Tyree
 William G.
BETTLE,
 BITTLE Jacob
BIDDICK, Edmund*
 Jonathan
BISHOP, Elias
BISWELL, Jeremiah
 Thomas
BITTLE,
 BETTLE Jacob
BLACK, Reuben D.
BLACKBURN, Jesse
 John
BLEDSOE, Anthony
 Gaven
 Isaac
 John

BLEVINS, Ausburn
 Joseph
BOHANNAN, Charles
 Larkin
BOLES, Elam*
BOON, William
BOSTON, Sarah
BOUNDS, Josiah
BOYD, Jesse
 John
BOYER, George
BRADLEY, Squire
BRADY, John A.
BRAM, Joseph
BRIMAGER, David
BRINK, Ephraim
 Hibert L.
 John
BROOKS, James
 Thomas
BROWN, Baswell
 Meredith
BRUNER, Stephen
BRYANT, Benjamin
 Hiram
 Hughram
BUFORD, Francis
BULLARD, John
 Martha
BURDINE, Benjamin
 Betty
BURK, William
BURKELOW, Samuel Van
BURLISTON, Hilka
BURNS, Charles
BUTTERWORTH, Alexander*

CALDWELL, Samuel
CALLAHAN, Dennis
 William
CALLAWAY, James
CALLEW, Henry
 John Sr.
 Robert
CALLIT, John
CAMPBELL, William
CARNEY, Peter *
CARTER, Arusted
CAVE, Catherine
 Henry Sr.
 Henry Jr.
 John
 Reuben
 Richard Sr.

1

CAVE, Richard Jr.
    William
CHALLAS, Hugh
CHAPMAN, Stephen
CHARLESS, Hezekiah
CHEVIS, Thomas*
CHISUM, Benjamin
CHRISTIAN, Adam
    John
CLARK, Lewis
CLEMENS, Garland
COAPLAND, John
COCHRAN, see
    CORKRAM
COCK, John
COLEMAN, John
    Strother
COLLETT, John
COLLIER, Peyton
COLLINS, Bartlett
    James
    Lewis
COLVIN, Alexander
    Benjamin Sr.
    Benjamin Jr.
    Garland
    Henry
    Jeremiah
CONLEY, Francis
CONYERS, Thomas W.
COOK, John
COOLEY, William*
COPHER, David
    Jesse
COPPAGE, Isaac
    Simeon
    Thomas
COPPER, Thomas
CORKRAM, Robert
CORLEW, John
    John Jr.
    Robert
    William*
COYL, Elizabeth
    Luman
CREASON, Elijah
    James
    Peter
    Walter
CREWS, Hiram
CROCKER, Hugh
CROCKETT, Samuel
CROUCK, William
CROUSON, Thomas
CROW, John

CRUMP, Anderson
    Daniel
    George
    John
    Joseph
    Patrick
CUNNINGHAM, James
CURRY, John
    William B.
CURTIS, Fielding

DALE, Benjamin
    Elijah
    George C.*
    Jesse
    Robert
DALEY, Michael
DAVIS, Abner
    Anderson
    Anthony J.
    Bayler
    Benjamin
    Briscoe
    Clay
    Elijah
    Henry C.
    Hugh
    Isaac Sr.
    Isaac Jr.
    James
    John
    Joseph
    Joshua
    Moses*
    Samuel
DEAVENPORT, Abraham
    John
DE JARNETT, Josiah
DILLON, John
DIXON, James
DODDS, John
DOIEL, David
DOUGLAS, Alexander
    Hugh B.
    John
    William
DULEY, Thomas
DUNN, William H.*
DUSKEY, James

EATON, William G.
EASLEY, Will
EAST, Herbin
EASTIN, Pressena
EDMONDSON, Thomas
EDWARDS, Presley
ELLINGTON, Alexander M.

ELLIOTT, Eppy
    Reubin
ELLIS, Peter
ELLISON, Alexander
    Thomas
ELSTEN, Elias
    Jemima
ENGLEHEART, George
ESHAM, Joseph
ESTES, Ambrose C.
    Richard
ESTIL, Benjamin
ETHELL, Benjamin
    James
    John
    Willis A.
EVANS, Pleasant
EVINS John

FALKNER, John
FAUBUSH, James
FORBUSH
FENTON, Caleb
    James E.
FERICE, John
FEUGIT, John
FICUS, Adam
FINDLEY, David
FINLEY Philander
FINNEY, John
FLAKE, Philip*
FLEMON, James
FOLEY, Abram
    Elijah
FORBUS, James
FOSTER, Elijah
    John L.
FOUNTAIN, Peter
    Joseph
FOWLER, John W.
    Captain John
    Robert
FREEMAN, John
    Joshua
FRENCH, Hugh
    Lewis
FULCHER, Jefferson
FULKUSON, Richard
FURGESON, Benjamin

GALAWAY, Samuel
GARVER, Samuel
GAUSLIN, William
GENTRY, Bartlett
    Benjamin
    Elizabeth

GENTRY, Henry
    Nicholas
    Richard
    Zachariah
GIDDEN, Daniel
GILLUM, Joshua
GIVIN, Matthew
GLASGOW, Allen
    Nathan
GLASS, Michael
GLENN, Hugh
    Joseph
    William
GOFORTH, James
GOLDIN, Richard
GOOD, Robert
GOODHUE, Marie
GOODIN,
GOODWIN Alexander
    Amos
    Benjamin
    Joshua
    Robert
GORDIN, George W.
GOSLIN, see
  GAUSLIN
GRAHAM,
GRAYUM John*
    John
    Jonathan
    William
GRANT, Daniel
    Daniel Jr.
    George
    John
    Thomas
GRAVES, John
    Francis*
GRAY, John Esq.
    John*
    Seaven
    Thomas
GREEN, Benjamin F.
    John
    William
GREENHALGH, John
GRIFFITH, Robert
GRINDSTAFF, Abraham
    Michael
GRUBBS, William
GUTHERY, James

HACKNEY, Hightower
HADDICK, Charles
HAINES, Samuel
HALDANE, David

HALEY, Matthew
HALL, Jeremiah
    William
HALLEN, John B.
HAMB, George
    Silas
HANNA, Andrew
    Esam
HANSLEY, Anthony
HAPPEN, John
HARDIN, Charles
HARDY, John
HARK, Thomas
HARRIMAN, Hugh
    John
HARRINGTON, William
HARRIS, David R.
    Hickerson
    James
    Overton
    Ook (sic)
    Tyre
    Tyre Jr
    Wiggerson
HARRISON, George
    James
    John
HART, Thomas
HATFIELD, Abram L.
HATTEN, Benjamin
    Charles B.
    Michael R.
    Reuben
    William (Wm. P.)
HAUSINGER, Jacob
HAWKINS, James
    John
    Willis
HAZLERIG, Charles
HAYDEN, William
HEAD, Agness
    Alfred
    Moses
HEADEN, William
HEARN,
HERN James
    Joel
    Clayton
HECKMAN, David
HEME, Allen
HENDERSON, John
HENDRICKS, Andrew
    James
    Peter
HENSINGER, Jacob

HENSLEY, Ichabod C.
    William
HENSON, Thomas
HIBBARD, Samuel
HICKHAM, John
    Joseph
HICKS, Absalom
    Elizabeth
    James
    Young E.
HIGH, James
HILL, Archibald
    Catherine
    William (Wm. Y.)
HINCH, Michael
HINTSUCK, John
HODGEN, Daniel
    Samuel
HOGGS, Daniel
    Samuel
HOLIDAK, Thomas
HOLMES, George
    Silas
HOOKING, Jacob*
HOPSON, John
HOWARD, J. B.
HUBBARD, Daniel
    Devett
    Durrell
    Eusebus
HUDSON, Loderick*
    Richard
HUGH, Charles
HUGHES, Allen
    Charles
    John
HUGHSTON, William L.
HUME, George
    Lewis
HUNTSUCKER, John
    William
HUSH, George
HUSK, Isaac
HUSTON, John M,
    Robert*
HUTSON, Ferguson

INARD, David

JACKSON, David
    Elijah
    Zachariah
JAMES, Henry
JAMISON, Harrison
    John
    Peyton*
    Samuel

3

JEFFRY, Isaac T.
JENNINGS, James
    Royal
JEWELL, George
    William
JONES, Christopher
    Henry
    James
    John B.
    Levi
    Lewis
    Mosias
    Robert
    Thomas
    Tyre H.
    William Sr.
    William Jr.
    William B.
    (3 Williams, 1825)
JONSEN, Thomas
    William
JONSTEN, George
    Samuel

KAVANAUGH, Jane
    Nicholas
KEETON, John Sr.
    John Jr.
    William
KELLY, Benjamin
    John
    William
KELSOE, John G.
KENNAN, John
    Thomas
KETCHUM, James
KITCHIN Solomon R.
KILLGORE, Isham
    Johnson
    Thomas
KING, Daniel
    Jamerson
    James Jr.
KINKAID, David
    (Davis?)
    John
    Joseph L.
    Lewis
    Matthew
    William
KINMAN, Hiram
KIRTLEY, James
    Sinclair
KISER, John W.

KOYLE, John
KUYKENDALL, Jacob

LAMBERS, Samuel
LAMPKIN, Daniel
    John
LANHAM, Richard
LAUGHLIN, Charles
    James*
    Polly
LAUGHN, Charles
LAWRENCE, George
LAWLESS, Bird
    Martin
LEMMON, John
    Robert
    Samuel
    William S.
LEWIS, Daniel
    Ira
    Jesse
    Stewart
    William
LIENTZ, William (two)
LIFFLER, John
LIPSCOMB, Francis
LITTLE, Hiram
    Joseph
LONG, Jesse
LOWRY, James S.
LUNSFORD, Littleton
LYNCH, David
    John
LYNES, Joseph
    Mary
    William
    William* 1825

McBANE, Elizabeth
    Turner
McBRIDE, Jacob
    Priestly
    Thomas
McCARTY, Ezekiel
    James
    John
    William
McCLAINE, Thomas
    William
McCLELLAND, James
McCLINTOCK, John
McCOY, Elizabeth
    Joseph C.
McCUBINGS, Nicholas

McDANIEL, Absalom
    Francis
    John
    Joseph
    Samuel
    Sarah
McDOW, Charles
    John
    Robert
    Thomas
McFARLAND, George
McGEE, David
    Wal (?)
McGILL, John
McGUIDIE, David
McGUIRE, Levi
McHANEY, Andrew
McINTIRE, Charles
McKAY, Joseph C.
    Walter
McKINNEY, Enoch
    Stephen
McKINZIE, John
McMICLE, John
McMULLIN, Aaron
    John
    Michael
McNEAL, Archibald*
McPHEETERS, Addison
McQUITTY, Andrew
    David Sr.
    George
McSWAIN, Daniel

MACEY, Walter
MARCH, Rudolph
MARCUM, Lucy
MARNEY, Amos
    Jonathan
MARS, Samuel
    Stephen
MARSHALL, Joseph
MARTIN, Foster
    James
    Samuel
    Tyre
    William
MATHIS, Sarah
MATTHEWS, W.E.
MAUPIN, John
    Thomas
MAYO, James Sr.
    James Jr.
    John

MEEK, John B.
MILLER, James
MINOR, John
MINTER, William
MITCHELL, Stephen
       William
MOODY, John
MOONEY, James
MORDECAI, Solomon
MORRIS, Werner
MOSLEY, Shedrick
MOSS, James W.
    James C.
    John
    Mason
MOTHERSHEAD, Benjamin
MULLINS, William
MURPHY, Jesse

NASH, Ira P.
    Ord
NEAL, Daniel
    Miner
NEALEY, John
NELSON, John
    Robert
NESBIT, Joseph
NEWLAND, Isaac
NICHOLS, James
    John
    Robert
    Samuel B.
NOLAND, Smallwood W.
NOWLIN, William
NUTTING, Samuel* 1821

OGAN, Alexander
    John
    William
OSBON, Jeptha
OREAR, William
ORR, William
OUSLEY, Anthony

PACE, Samuel
    Jonathan
PAGE, Mann
PARK, Jehiah
PARKER, John
    Oliver A.
PARUT, David
PASLEY, Henry
PATTON, Hugh
    John
    Thomas
    William

PAUL, John
PAVY, Jesse H.
PAYNE, Ballinger
    George
    Isaiah
    Isam
    James
    John Sr.
    Noah
    William
PEARSON, James
    Nathaniel
    William
PEDEN, John
PERCEL, McCune
PERKINS, John
PERSINGER, Joseph
PETTUS, Dabney
PHILIPS, Ellen R.
    George
    Henry
    Hiram
    Jesse
    John
    John G.
    John Sr.
    John Jr.
    Thomas
    William*
PIGG, Renard
PINKIN, Jesse
PIPER, George
    William*
PIPES, William
POAGUE, John
POLK, Andrew
POTTS, Frederick
    John
POWERS, David
PRATT, Joseph R.
PROCTOR, Nancy
PULLEN, Henry
PULLIAM, William
    William Jr.

RAMSEY, William
    William Jr.
RAY, Wilkins*
RAYBURN, Adam C.
READY, James
REAVIS, Anderson*
    Edvins
    James
    Jones
REDWINE, James C.

REEDER, Isaac
RENTFRO, Absalom
    James
RICE, David
    James
    John
    Samuel*
    William
    William J.
RICHARDS, James
    Werry (or
    Warial)
RICHARDSON, Jesse
    Larkin
    Silas
RIDDLE, James
    Joel
    Thomas
RIGGS, Redin
    Reubin
    Samuel
    Silas
    Zadock Sr.
    Zadock Jr.
RISK, William
ROBARDS, James
    John
    Nathan
    William*
ROBERTS, Nathan
ROBISON, Henry
ROGERS, Kirtly
ROLAND, Gasper*
ROSS, James
    William
ROWLAND, John
    Thomas
    William
RUSSELL, David
    Joseph
    Nathan Sr.
    Nathan Jr.
    Patterson
    William
RUTHERFORD, Aaron W.
RYAN, William

SAMS, William
SAMUEL, Edgecomb
    Jesse
    Richard
SANDERSON, Benjamin
SAPPINGTON, Foster*
    Green
    John
    Nancy

SAPPINGTON, Sq--? B.*
SCOTT, William
SCRIVENER, Benjamin
  James
SEARCY, Lemuel
SENIOR, Samuel
SEWELL, James
SEXTON, George
  Isham B.
  William
SHARP, Nancy
SHEETS, Jacob
SHELTON, James*
SHIELDS, William
SHINNER, John
SHOCK, David
  Henry
  John
SHORT, Cornelius
  Glover
  John
  Josiah
SILVERS, Hugh
  John
  William
SILVIN, Hugh
SIMMONDS, Will
SIMPSON, Joseph*
SIMS, Elias
  James
  Tarlton
  William
SINMAN, William
SINN, Elias
  William
SIVIER, Samuel
SLACK, John
SLOAN, David
SLOCUM, Riley
SMALL, Mary
SMITH, Henry
  James
  John
  Lewis
  Mishae
  Parson
  Peter*
  Susanna
  William (two)
  William J. (or G.)
SNEDECOR, Samuel
SNELL, Cumberland
  John
SOAPER, William

6

SPENCE, Andrew
SPENCER, Jeremiah
  Perry
SPRINCLE, Charles
STADLER, Jacob
STEEL, Samuel
STEMMONS, John
  John Jr.
STENE, John
  William
STEPHENS, Elijah
  Milford
STEPHENSON, John
  Newkham
  Wilford
STICE, Charles
  Moses
  Peter
STOGDEN, Newberry
(STOCKTON)
STOKES, John D.
STONE, Asa
  Hardyman
STRONG, Jeremiah
STRODE, Jacob
  Mary
  Stephen
STUCKLIN, William
STURGEON, Hume
SUGART, Samuel
SULLENGER, James
SULLINS, Edward A.
  James A.
  John
 Micajah, estate
SWINNEY, Shepheard

TALBERT, Richard
TALLEY, John*
  William
TALLY, George
TAYLOR, Enoch
  James
  Joseph
TEAGUE, Nathaniel
TEATER, Garrard
  George
TECKHAM, Isaac
TETERS, John
  Lewis
  Robert
THOMPSON, Thomas
THORNTON, John
THRALL, Augustus

TIFFEE, John
TILFORD, Elizabeth
  Samuel*
TILLEY, Bennett
TIMBERLICK, William
TIPTON, Ezrum (Ezrus)
  Thomas
TITUS, George
  Leander
TODD, Roger
  Thomas
TOLSON, Benjamin
  Daniel
TOLSTON, Elijah
  Fountain
  William
TOMLIN, Jeremiah
TRIBBLE, Peter M.
TUCKER, Edward
TURLEY, James
TURNER, Benjamin
  Enoch
  James
  James Jr.
  Jesse
  John Sr.
  John
  John D.
  Nathan
  Smith
  Thomas
TUTTLE, Bilson
  John
  Thomas S.

VANHORN, John
VAN AUSTEN, Charles*
VARBLE, Isaac
VINCENT, Jesse

WADE, John
  Pierce
WAINE, Ellenor
WALKER, John
WALKUP, John (two)
  Rebecca
  Robert S.
  Robert Jr.
WARD, John Jr.
  Joseph J.
  William*
WARNER, James
WATERS, Isaac*
WATSON, Benjamin

WAYNE, William L.
WEATHERS, James
WEST, Jane
    James
    Willis
WESTERFIELD, Dave
      Milly
WESTMAN, John
WHARTON, George
WHITE, Benjamin
    Jesse
    John
    William
WHITLEY, Hopson
    Thomas
WILBORN, Bird
    Edward
    John
WILCOX, Daniel P.
    George B.
    Israel
    Lazarus
    Noah
WILCOXSEN, Isaac
    Samuel
WILHITE, Fielding
    Sampson
    Stephen
    William
WILL, John
    Littlebury

WILLIAMS, Abraham B.
    Benjamin
    George
    John (two)
    Thomas
WILLINGHAM, Isam
    Major John
WILLS, Derril
WILSON, David
WIMMINGHAM, Gabriel
    Isham
    Susannah
WINAGIM, John Jr.
    William
WINDSOR, Alfred*
WINKFIELD, Henry*
WINN, Alfred
    Elizabeth
    James
    John
    William
WINSCOTT, Abraham
    Richard
WINTERBOWERS, George
    Jacob
WIRT, Adam
WISDOM, John
    Pollard
    Thomas
WISEMAN, James
WITT, John

WOOD, Anderson
    Ann
    James
    Jesse
    John (two)
    Michael
WOODRUFF, William B.
WOODSON, Warren
WOODWARD, Gabriel
WREN, Berryman
    Charles
    James
    Shadrick
    Fletcher
WRIGHT, Peter Sr.
    Peter
    Sampson
    Westley
    Will
    Will Jr.
    William
YATES, John
YOUNG, Benjamin
    John
    William D.

....

Boone County was formed from Howard County in November, 1820.
No other counties were taken from it.

....

SECONDARY LIST FROM THE MISSOURI INTELLIGENCER, 1819-1826

CARY, John   stray
COPHER, Elizabeth   estate
    Thomas   "
CORNET, Edley runaway apprentice

DENSMAN, Thomas Rocky ForkTwp. stray

EVANS, John T. Columbia Twp. stray

GENTRY, David M. Perce Twp. stray
GREEN, George   estate

HICKS, Ammon Rocky Fork Twp. stray
HINSTON, Robert Columbia Twp. stray
HOPE, Adam   estate

JONES, Josiah Cedar Twp.   stray

LOWTHEN, Isaac   notice

PATTON, Martha   notice
PACE, Twitty   notice
PULLIAM, Boswell   notice

ADAMS, William
AGEE, Matthew
AHERN, Rebecca
(AKENS?)
ALEXANDER, Benjamin
ALLEN, Archibald
Bethel
Charles
Sampson
ALVIS, Shadrach
ANDERSON, David
William
ASHERN, Dennis
(ARSKREN?)
AUD, Joseph

BABER, Hiram H.
BACON, Benjamin
Martin
William M.
BAKER, Benjamin
Esau
Henry
Jacob
James
Martin
Morris
Robert
Samuel
Sylvester
Thomas H.
William M.
Zebediah
BARNES, Azle
Isabelle
Leal
BARNETT, Joseph
BARTLEY, George
BEADLES, Berryman
(BEEDLES, BEAGLES)
BEAVEN, Charles
Zadock
William
BELL, Mordecai
BENNETT, Anson G.*
John
Moses
BERRY, John H.
Richard
BETHEL, Samuel
BIGGS, Lawrence
(BOGGS?)
BLACK, Isaac
Joseph

BLADENBURG, Jacob
BLITHE, John
BOARD, John
BOONE, Garland
John L.
Joshua M.
Morris
Samuel
BOOTHE, George W.
BRADFORD, George
BRAGG, John B.
BRANHAM, Isaac
BRATTAIN, William
BRITE, Henry
BROOKS, James
Thomas
BROWN, Daniel
Felix
James T.
BRYANT, Henry
William
BURKET, David
John Sr.
John Jr.
BURNETT, Amer
Aquilla
Samuel
BURT, George
Henry
John

CALBREATH, John
CALLAWAY, Joseph P.
Joseph Sr.
Joseph Jr.
Thomas
CANNADY, David
CAPTAIN, Baptiste
CARRUTH, Albert
CASE, Emmanuel
CHANDLER, Isaac
CHAPMAN, Stephen
CHARLTON, John
CLEVELAND, Milton
CLIFTON, Bosman
CLINDENNIN, Daniel
CLENDENNIN William
CLINTON (CLIFTON), Bosman
COATS, James' heirs
John
William Sr.
William Jr.
William
Wilson

COLGAN, Daniel
Robert B.
COLLINS, Lafayette
COMPTON, Richard
CONGER, Dr. John
CONGO Thomas D.
COONS, John
COUNTS, John
COWHERD, William
CRAG, David
CRAGHEAD, Robert
Solomon
William
CRISWELL, Robert
William
CROCKET, Samuel
CROW, Jonathan
CRUMP, Richard Sr.
Richard Jr.
Turner
CUNNINGHAM, Mark
CURPENTER, see
CARPENTER
CURRUTH, see
CARRUTH

DARLING, Mary
DAVIS, Abner
Gabriel*
Jonathan
Robert
DENTON, Thomas
DILLON, Daniel
George
Hugh
Patrick M.
DIRTING, Mary
DOMEAN, John
DOOLEY, Nathaniel
(DULY)
DORRISS, Stephen C.
DOUGHERTY, Charles
Charles*
Hugh
DOUGLAS, Isham
DOYLE, Charles
(DOYAIL) Edward
James
John
DUNAHOE, Martin
DUNCAN, John
DUNHAM, Joseph P.
DUNLAP, David M.
James

8

DUNLAP, Robert
DUNNICA, James
    John
DYER, John
    Samuel

EASTIS, James
ESTES John Sr.
    John Jr.
    John
EDWARDS, Matthew
    William
ELLIS, Abraham
    Edward
ESTIL, James
EWING, James P.
    Patrick
    Robert R.
EVANS, George
    Jesse
    John

FANIER, Iant
FARMER, Jane
FARREE, Thomas
FARRIER, Nathaniel G.
    Thomas Sr.
    Thomas Jr.
FERGUSON, Buonaparte
    John Sr.
    John Jr.
    John S.
    Joshua
    Levan
    Moses
    Napoleon B.
    Rebecca
FERRIER, see
 FARRIER
FIKES, Adam
FISHER, Thomas
FORREST, William
FOSTER, Elijah
    John
    Mark
FOX, Levi
FOY, Antoine
    Charles
    Nicholas
FRAIN, John
FRANKLIN, Thomas
FRENCH, Lewis
    John
FRUIT, Alexander
    Enoch

FRY, Jacob
    John
FUDGE, Alexander

GARDNER, Samuel
GALBREATH, Angus
    Zarkle or
    Torkle
GARMOND, Leonard
GEARHART, Isaac
GEE, John S.
GIBSON, John
GOLDEN, Daniel
GOODRICH, Benjamin
    James
GORDEN, James
    Joseph
GRAZON, Baptiste
  (GREAZER)
GRANT, Israel B.
    James
    William
GRAY, George
    Henry T.
    John
    John B.
GREEN, John
GRIFFIN, William
GRISHAM, William
GRISSMER, William
GUTHRIE, Samuel T.

HALL, Abner
    Henry
    Hiram
    John
HAM, John C.
HAMILTON, John
HAMLIN, John
HAPE (?), John
 (HASSE?)
HARPER, Thomas
    Henry
    Nicholas
HARRIS, James
    Peter
    Thomas
HARRISON, Thomas Sr.
    Thomas Jr.
HART, John Jacob
HATTON, Thomas
HAYNES, Collett
HAYS, John
    John Jr.
    Boone

HELM, Charles
HENDERSON, Daniel
    David Sr.
    David Jr.
    James
    Jesse
    William P.
HERRALDSON, Benjamin
HERRIFORD, John
    Paul
HICKISON, Thomas
HICKS, HIX, William
HINES, William
HIRSH, George
HOCKADAY, Irvine O.
HOLLIWAY, Absalom*
    Jacob
    Jonathan
HOLT, Abner
    Hiram
    Timothy
HOPE, Adam
HORNBUCKLE, Jane
    Rufus
    Thomas
    William
HOUSE, Hardin
HUDDLESTON, James M.
HUDSON, James M. C.
HUFF, Peter
HUGGARD, HUGHART, John
HUME, Reuben
HUMPHREYS, James
    Richard Sr.
    Richard Jr.
    Robert
    Samuel

JAMES, Levi
    William
JEFFERSON, Isaac
JIMMISON, Alexander
    John Sr.
    John Jr.
    Thomas
JOHNSON, John W.
JOINER, Moses
JONES, John
    Richard
    Stephen
    William
JUKS, Joseph

KENNEDY, David
KENT, Andrew

KILBREATH, John H. (?)
KING, George
    Isaac
    Josiah
    Thomas
KITCHEN, Thomas
KOUNS, Nathan

LAMPKIN, George
    William
LANGLEY, Collett
    Isaac
    James
    John Sr.
    John Jr.
    Moses Sr.
    Moses Jr.
LAPLANT, Louis
LARK, Joseph
LAWLER, Patrick
LEBRA, Lewis
LEE, John
    Thomas G.
LENOX, David
    William
LOCKHART, Andrew
LOMAX, Asahel
LUCAS, William

McCAMPBELL, James Sr.
    Jesse E.
McCONNELL, Catherine
McCORMACK, James
    William
McCUTCHEON, James C.
McDANIEL, Francis
    John
McDONALD, Francis
McDANIEL, Peter
McKINNEY, James
McLAUGHLIN, Daniel
    William
McQUEEN, Thomas

MAHONEY, John
MANNING, Stephen B.
MARTIN, John
    William
MAUPIN, George
MAY, Gabriel
    Henry
    Richard
MILLER, Abraham
    John

MILLER, Samuel
    William
MILTON, Silas
MINIX, Hugh
MONSELLE, Stephen*
MOORE, Arthur
    Robert
    Samuel T.
    Wharton R.
MURRY, Enoch

NANCE, Nancy
NASH, Ira
    William
NEILL, Arthur
    Henry
NESBIT, John
    Robert
NEVINS, James
    John
    Joseph
NEWCOMB, Anderson G.
NEWSOM, John
    Robert
NICHOLS, Garrett
    George Sr.
    George Jr.
    James *
    William
NICHOLSON, George
NIX, Caleb

O'NEAL, Oliver
OWENS, William

PARE, Hiram
PARKER, Polly
PATTON, Haris
PEVELER, David
PHILLIPS, Andrew
    Daniel
    James
    Jesse
    John
POWELL, Charles L.
PRATT, John
    William
PRINCE, Albertis
    Orestes
PRINE, Daniel
    William
PUGH, Silas B.*
    Willoughby
PULLEN, James

QUICK, Aaron
    Thomas

RAGSDALE, Thomas *
RAMSEY, Allen
    Beverly A.
    Jonathan
    Josiah Sr.
RANKIN, Thomas
READ, John
    Robert
REYNOLDS, Richard
RIDGWAY, Ninian
RIGGINS, James
    Powell
RIGGS, Simon
RIPPER, James
RIVAR, Joseph
ROACH, Bryant
ROBERTSON, John A.
(ROBINSON) Noah
RHODES,
RODES   George
    Henry
    Rosannah
    Samuel
ROSE, Bazil Sr.
    Bazil Jr.
    James *
ROUNCEVILLE, Josiah
ROY, Francois
    John B.
    Joseph
    Louis
ROYER, Nicholas
RUTHERFORD, Mary
    William

SALISBERRY, John
SCHOLL, Jesse
SCOTT, William B.
SELBY, William
SHANNON, James
SHEARER, Hiram
SHAW, Samuel
SHOBE, John
SITTON, Ezra B.
    Franklin
    Jeffrey
    John
    Joseph T.
SIMMONS, Dudley
SIMPSON, Foster B.
    Selby
SLOAN, John

SLOAN, Margaret
SMITH, Enoch
    Hiram
    John M. (two)
    Rezin
    Thomas
    William
SNELL, Willis W.
STEPHENS, Elijah
    Peyton T.
    Thomas P.
STERIGERE, David *
STEWART, Benjamin
    John
STILES, John
STITES, Samuel
    William T.
STILL, Samuel
STOKES, John D.

TATE, Elijah
    James
TAYLOR, John
    Robert
TEBO, TEBEAU, Joseph
THOMAS, Elisha
    Granville
    Ira
    Lewis B.
    Price
    Solomon

THOMPSON, Jesse
    John H.
    Malinda
    William
THORNTON, William
THURMAN, William
TIPTON, Joel
TOLESON, Daniel
TOULSON, George B.
TRAVILLIAN, John
TUCKER, Thomas
TUMBLINSON, William *
TURNER, Martin G.
TYON, Francis
    Lewis

VAN BIBBER, James
    Joseph
    Erwin or Irvine
VAN CLEAVE, Jesse
VINCENNES, Betsy
    Louis
VINCENT, Daniel

WADLEY, Francis
    John
WAINE, John M.
WALKER, David
WALLACE, William
WARD, Charles *
    John
    Patrick

WARNER, Wynkoop
WILFREY, James
WILLIAMS, Asa
    Benjamin
    Joseph
    Peyton
    Robert
    Samuel T.
    William
WILLIAMSON, Samuel
WILSON, James
WOOD, Martha
    Samuel
    William Jr.
    Zachariah

YOUNG, Benjamin
    William
YOUNGER, Charles

ZEVELY, James
ZUMWALT, Abraham
    Christopher Sr.
    Christopher Jr.
    David
    Isaac
    Jacob Sr.
    Jacob Jr.
Heirs of Jacob decd.
    Francis
    Peter

. . . .

Callaway County was formed in 1820 from Montgomery County, which had
been created only a year before from the original district of St.
Charles. A few identical names will be found in listings from these
two counties.

Most of the county records are intact, starting in 1821. There is also
a state census available for this county in 1844 and another in 1876.

. . . .

SECONDARY LIST FROM THE MO. INTELLIGENCER AND THE MO. REPUBLICAN, 1819-26

BYLE, Henry   Elizabeth Twp.   stray

CUNNINGHAM, Smith   stray
    Round Prairie Twp.

DAVIS, Dr. Stephen C.   stray
    Cote sans Dessein Twp.
DIRTING, Philip   estate
DUNNICA, William H.   stray
    Cote sans Dessein Twp.

FERGUSON, William   AS

KING, Jeremiah   stray
    Cote sans Dessein Twp.

= = = = = = = = = = = = = = =

ABERNATHY, Batty Sr.
           Batty Jr.
           Daniel
           Harley D.
           Jeremiah
           Joab
           John
   John for heirs of
             Lewis Tash
           Joseph
           Larkin
           Lott
           Susannah
           Wash G.
ABLE, Jeremiah
     Margaret
ADAMS, Thomas
AKEN,
AKIN James
      John
AKER, Christian Sr.
     Christian Jr.
     Christopher
     Frederick
     Henry (estate)
     James
     John (two)
John adm. of S.(?) P.
     John P. (estate)
     Sally (Sarah)
AKLEY, Nimrod
ALBRIGHT, Christian
      John
        William I.
ALLEN, Barnabash W.
     Francis
     John B.
ANDREWS, Jonathan
ARCHER, Edward
ARMOUR, David
     Solomon H.
ARMSTRONG, John
ASHBRAN,
ASHBRANER Catherine
        Daniel
      Henry
ATKINS, James A.
ATWELL, Thomas
AUSTIN, Joseph
AXLEY, Frederick
     James
     Nimrod
AYASES, Elisha

BAKER, George
     Henry
     John
     Joseph
     Mary
     Peter
     Thomas
BALDWIN, John
      William W.
BALLAND, James
BARBER, Barbour, Elias
BARKS, Hartley
     Huntell
     Jacob
     John
     William
BARRINGER, John
BARTON, Thomas
BATES, Robert
BENNETT, Benson
     James
     John K.
     Levi
BERRY, George
     Hiram
     Jacob
BESS, Christian
     Frederick
     Henry
     Jacob
     John
     Joseph
     Martin
     Michael
     Peter
     William
BICKUM, Catherine
BIRD, Jonathan
BISHOP, Rezin L.
BIVENS, John
BLAIR, Francis
     John*
     James
     Thomas
     William
BLOCK, James
     Simon Jr.
BLOCKER, George (W.)
     James
BLUNT, James
     Joel
BOHANNON, George (W.)

BOLIN, Samuel
     William
BOLLINGER, Aaron
      Andrew
     Andrew son of Matthias
     Andrew son of David
      David
     David son of Matthew
     David son of Philip
      Daniel Sr.
     Daniel son of Philip
      Elizabeth
    (widow of Philip)
Frederick son of Philip
      George F. Sr.
      George Jr.*
      Henry
   Henry son of Matthew
   Henry son of Philip
      Jacob
      John
      Matthias
      Moses
      William
BONER, William
BOREN
(BOWN?) Matthew
       Riley
BOROND, Richmond
BOWLIN, William
BOYCE, Benjamin
BOYD, Clarissa
 (by gdn Wm. Patterson)
BOYER, Peter D.
BRADY, Thomas
BRANTS, Daniel W.
BRAVAIS, Antoine
BRAWLEY, BRALEY, James
BREWER, Isaac
     Nathan
BRIDGES, Joseph
BROCK, Armstrong
     Uriah
BROOKS, Hardy
     James
     Robert Sr.
     Robert Jr.
BROOM, William
BROWN, Adam
     Benjamin
     John (two)
 (one of Apple Creek)
     Joseph

BRYAN(T), David
BUCKNER, Alexander
    Nicholas
    Robert
BUGG, Henry
BUIS, Jonathan
BULL, Anderson
    Thomas
    William A.
BULLARD, Nathaniel
BULLITT, George
BURNS, Andrew
    James
    John
BURROWS, John
BUST, John
BUTLER, Elijah
BYRD, Abraham
    John son of Amos
    John exr Abraham decd
    John exr John decd
    Moses
    Stephen
    Stephen Jr.
    Thompson
    William G.
    John guardian of Nancy
    A. by adm. Philip Young
BYERS, Wesley
BYRNE, John
    Morgan
    Moses
    Thomas

CAMPBELL, Cyrus ++
    David
    Elizabeth (Betsy)
    Jacob
    Samuel
CALDWELL, David G.L. ++
    John
CANNON, Franklin
CARLOCK, William V. (or G.)
CARPENTER, Benjamin
    Christopher
CARTMILL, John
CASTNER,
  COSTNER Andrew
CAVENDER, George
CEALY, Ezekiel
CENTER, John
CHANDLER, Acy
    James
    Jonathan
CHEEK, Randolph
CHRONISTER, Abraham
    Daniel

CHRONISTER, Martin
    Matthias
    James
++ CLIPPARD, Daniel
CLARK, John R.
CLINARD, Henry
++ CLINGINGSMITH, Adam
    Daniel
    Henry
    Jacob
CLODFELLOW,
  CLODFELTER Jacob
    John
    Philip
CLOOP, Daniel
COATES, Meritime
COBORN, Ephabit*
COBWEN, Phineas
CONNER, Killam
CONROD, Ephraim R.
    John L.
    Peter
COOK, David Jr.
    Devault
    George
    Jacob Sr.
    Jacob Jr.
    John D.
COON (S), Jacob
    John
COSNER, Peter
COTNER, Conrad
    George
    Jacob
    John
    Martin
    Mary
    John by adm. Philip
        Young
COUNCE, Jacob
COUSIN, Bartholomew
COWEN, Robert
COWHAND, Giles S.*
COX, James Sr.
    James Jr.
    John
    William
CRACROFT, William
CRADER,
  CRATER Abraham
    Daniel
    Jacob
    Samuel (two)
CRANDER, Giles
CRAWFORD, James
CREATH, Albert G.
    Nathaniel
    William

CRIDDLE, Edward
CRISWELL, Alexander
    David
    Hugh
CRITES, Philip
CRITZ, Abraham
    Daniel
    David
    Devault
    Ephraim
    Henry
    Jacob Sr.
    Jacob Jr.
    Joel
    John
    Moses
    Peter
    Peter son of Peter
    Peter son of Abraham
    Peter Daniel
    Solomon son of Daniel
CROPPS, James M.
CROSS, Abraham
    John (two)
    Maria J.
CROWDER, William
CROWLEY, John
    Samuel
CUPPLES, Samuel
CURTIS, Ransom H.

DACK, John
DANIEL, John Long
    John M.
DARE, Philip
DAUGHERTY, Abraham
    Elijah
    John
    Ralph
    William
DAVENPORT, John
DAVIDSON, George
    John
DAVIS, Alexander
    Daniel
    David
    Elias
    Green W.
    Hiram
    J. B.
    James
    John
    Joseph
    Warren
DECK, Isaac
    John

13

DECK, Mary
    Thomas
DELAP, John
D'LASHMUTT, Elias N.
  (Elias est. 1822)
        John J.
        Linsey J.
        Van B.
DELF, DELPH, Jacob
DEMPSEY, Rhoda
DESHAY, Robert
DEVAULT, Andrew
    Daniel
    David
    Jacob
DEVORE, Henry
    Isaac
DIAL, John
DILWOOD, John
DOREMUS, Peter
DOUGLAS, Henry
  Henry, estate
    James
DOWTY, James
    John
DROOM, William
DRUM, David
    Joseph
    Susan
    William
  (Wm. estate 1822)
DUNCAN, James
DUNKIN Tavener
DUNHAM, Mary (Polly)
DUNLOP, Andrew
    John
DUNN, Elizabeth
    John
    Ruth
    Samuel G.
DUNNING, Edward

EAKER, Christian
    Christopher Jr.
    Henry
    James
    John
    John Jr.
  John adm. for J.P.
    Joseph
    Sarah
EAKING, James
EDENOR,
EDINGER Christopher
EDMOND(S), James
EDWARDS, James
    John

EIGERT, Philip
(IKERD)
ELLIS, Charles G.
    Erasmus
    James
ELLISON, James
ENGLISH, Joel R.
    Joseph
    Robert
  Robt. exr Thos. Jr.
    decd. (1821)
    Simeon
    Thomas
  Thos. gdn heirs Thos.
    Jr. decd (1821)
    William
ERVIN,
ERWIN James
    John
    Lewis
ESTES, Hiram
    Joseph
EVANS, David
    James
    John
    William
EVERETT, William

FARMER, Betsy
FERGUSON, James
FIELDS, Ambrose
FIKE, James
FINCH, William
FISHBACK, William
FLEMING, George
    Mitchell
FLIN,
FLINN Ebenezer
    James
FLINT, Timothy
FORTS, Job
FOSTER, Asa
    Edmond
    Ezekiel
    Martin
FRANKS, Joseph
FRAZIEUR, James estate
  (Eri McDermith adm)
    William
FRICKE, FRIKEY, George
FRIZEL, Joseph
FUGATE, William
FULENWIDER, Caleb P.
FULBRIGHT, Jacob

GAKS, Christian

GANTT, Edward S.
    William S.
GARNER, William (T.)
GARRETT, Peter R.
GARY, James
GATES, Christian
GIBBS, Jonathan H.
    Lewis
GIBLER, George
GIBONEY, Andrew
    John
    Robert
GIBSON, Titman
GILDER, John
GILES, John
GILLELAND, Hiram
    John
GLASSCOCK, Charnel
    Fielding*
    John
    Scarlet
    Spencer*
GOCHOM, Allen
GOLLIHER, Andrew
    Matthew
    William
GOSA, GOZA, James
GRAHAM, Robert
GRAVES, Thomas W.
GRAY, John
GREEN, David
    Parish
    Peter
    Robert
    Thomas P.*
GREER, Vincent
GREGORY, Isaac
GRIFFITH, Thomas D.
GRIFFY, Joseph
GROSS, Christopher (esta
    Jacob*
    Peter
    Susannah
GROUNDS, David
    Peter
GUIN, E. W. deceased
  by Wm. McGuire
GURTNER, John
    Martin

HAGER, Frederick
HAGERTY, Francis
HAHN, Daniel (two)
    David
    George
    Henry

HAHN, John
    Peter
    Philip
HAIL,
HALE Edward
    Jesse Sr.
    Jesse Jr.
    Joshua
    Thomas
HALL, Benjamin
HAMON, Jonas
HAMMOND, Benjamin
HAMPTON, Thomas*
HAND, Henry
HANDLIN, Matthew*
HANDLEY, John
HARBERSON, George C.
      John C.
      Rebecca
HARBERT, Joseph
HARMAN, John
HARRIS, Elijah
    John
    Milton
    Oliver B.
    Richard P.
    Robert W.
    Samuel
    (decd. 1822)
HART, John
    Robert S.
HARTH, Elizabeth
HARTLE, Daniel
    John
    Joseph
    Simon
  P. decd by Simon
HARTY, Daniel
    Jacob
HATTEN, Henry
HAYDEN, Hiram
    Solomon
    Webb.(B.)
    William
HAYS, Christopher estate
    John
    Sarah
  George decd. by Sarah
HECTOR, Gilbert
    Samuel
    William
HEDERMAN, Conrad
    Jacob
    John
HELM, Hay
HELTERBRAND, Daniel

HELTERBRAND, Jacob
HENDERSON, Carnese
    Cyrus
    George
  Matthew or Mathias
    Robert H.
HENDRICKS, Abraham
    Fanny
    James
    John
    William
HENRY or HENLY, Moore
HEWES, James
HICKLIN, George
    John
HICKMAN, Austin
    Daniel
    Robert
    William
HICKS, Hilyard
HIGGENS, John
HIGNIGH, Nathan
HILDERMAN, John
    Jacob Sr.
    Jacob Jr.
HILER, David
    Nicholas
HILL, Ezekiel
HINKLE, Charles
    Jesse
    Peter
HINMAN, Jonas
HITT, Benjamin
    Ezekiel
    John Sr.
    John Jr.
    John D.
    William
HOFFMAN, John
HOFSTOTLER,
HOSTOTLER Henry
    John
HOGAN, Michael
HOGLAND, James*
    John
HOHOM, Louis
HOLCOM, James
HOLLEY, David
HOOSER, Daniel
HOPE, Lewis
HOPE or HOSSE, James
HORNER, Martin
HORRELL, Benjamin M.
    John
    Thomas
HORSE,
HOSS Adam

HORSE,
HOSS Elizabeth
    Francis
    Jacob
    John
HOSSE or HOPE, James
HOUCK,
HOUK John
    Peter
HOUTS, John C.
HOWARD, Aaron
    Henry Sr.
    Henry Jr.
    Henry P.
    James
    John
    Thomas
  Zakiah or Zadok
HOWELL, John
    Maximilian
HUBBLE, Ebenezer
    Daniel
  Ithamah or Thomer
    Peter
    Widow
HUDSON, Enoch
    Hall
    William
HUGHS,
HUGHES Abraham
    James
    Samuel
    Terrell
HUNCLE, Peter
HUNT, Ephraim
    Wolman
HUNTER, Josiah
HUSTON, Samuel D.
HUTCHINS, William
HUTSON, Haul
    William

IKIRD, IKERE, Philip
  (EIGERT)
IRWIN, James
    Louis
ISABELL, Joseph
ISENHOWER, Daniel
    John

JACOBS, Jacob
JAMES, Adam
    Jacob
JATON,
JETTON Asaph
    Isaac

15

JOHNSON, Constance
    David
    (dec. 1822, by Jonathan)
    Davis
    Edward
    Elizabeth
    Isaac
    James
James decd. by
    Benjamin Shell
    John
    Jonathan
    Noble
    Priscilla
    Ransom
    William
JONES, Benjamin A.
    Silas
    Theodore
    Widow
    William
JUDEN, John Sr.
    John Jr.
    Thomas
JUNY, Robert

KELSO, William
KIBLER, George decd.
    by adm. Benjamin Shell
    Rebecca
KINDER, Adam
    Conrod
    Conrod Jr.
    Daniel
    David
    Elizabeth
    Henry Sr.
    Henry
    Jacob
    Jacob Jr.
    John
    Michael
KINEON, James
    Simon
KING, William
KINNISON, Abner
    Hiram
KINOSE, John (?)
KINYON see KINEON
KIRKPATRICK, Joseph
KIRON, Michael
KLINGLESMITH, see
    CLINGINGSMITH
KNOWLTON, William
KUNCE, Jacob
16

LACY, William P.
LAFERTY, Rachel
    (decd 1823; by
        Nicholas Whitelaw)
    LAUGHERTY in 1822
LAMASTER, Michael
LAMBERT, George
    Polly
LANGDON, John
LARABY, Enoch
LASTLEY,
LESLEY   Samuel
         Samuel
    son of George
LAWRENCE, Franklin
    by gdn. Wm. Kelso
        Martin R.
        William
LEE, Josiah
LEGATE, Margaret
LEMONS, William
LESLEY see LASTLEY
LEWIS, Joseph
    Simon
LIGHTNER, Levi L.
LIKE, Jacob
    Joseph
LIMBAUGH, Daniel R.
    Frederick
    George F.
    Henry
    Jacob
LINCECUM, Asa B.
    D.B.
LINCOLN, Joseph
LUCY, Isham
LUNEY, Robert

McBRIDE, Robert A.
McCAIN, Alexander
    David D.
    Edwin A.
    John Esq.
    Joseph
McCALL, James
McCALLY, William
McCARD, Daniel
McCARTY, James*
    Nathan
    Richard*
    Wm. Nathan
McCLAIN,
McCLANE   David E.
          Edwin A.
          John
          Joseph
          Moses
          William

McCLASKY, Henry
McCLINTIC, William
McCOMBS, John
McDERMITH, Edward
    Eri
McDONALD, Alexander
    James B.
    Joshua*
McFARLAND, Jacob
    John
    Lindley John
    Robert
    R.S.
    Samuel
    Simon
McFERRON, Eve
    Joseph decd by Eve
McGUIRE, William
    Edward decd. by William
McILVAINE, David*
McINTIRE, John
McKELBY,
McKELVEY   Thomas P.
McKINNY, Matthew
McKINZIE, Aaron
    David
    John
McKNIGHT, Samuel B.
McLARD, Daniel
    Joshua
McMELLIN, Elizabeth
McMINN, Samuel

MAIZE, George
MALOAN,
MALONE   John
         Jonathan
         Obadiah
         Stephen
         Thomas
MANNERY, Akins
MANNING,
MANNON   Ezekiel
         Mark
MANSEL, John
MANSKER, Lewis
    Mary
MARTIN, Andrew
    John
    William S.
    Elizabeth gdn of Allen
        and Jared, 1821
MASSEY, Drury
    Drury Jr.
    James
    John

MASTERS, Daniel
  David
  John
  Michael
  Moses*
MASTERSON, Anna
  David
  James
  Jeremiah
MATHEWS, William
MAY, John
MAYFIELD, John
  Stephen
MEDLEY, James
  Joseph
MENEFEE, Josias N.
MIDDLETON, Richard
MILLENY, Daniel
MILER, John C.
MILLER, Alexander
  Fergus
  Henry
  Isaac
  John Sr.
  John Jr.
  John C.
  John
  Joseph
  Nicholas
  Thomas
  Valentine
MINTON, Isaac
  Jesse
  William H.
  Willis
MITCHELL, Sam W.
  Wright
MOORE, Samuel
MORGAN, Thomas
MORRISON, James O.
  John
  Robert
MORROW, George
MOTHERSHEAD, Charles*
  Clifton
MURPHY, Bartholomew
  John
  William
MURRY, Ezekiel
MYERS, MIRES, John

NANCE, Francis
NATIONS, Isaac
  Isaiah
  John

NATIONS, Nathan
NEAL, Thomas
NEELY, Alexander
  Jacob H.
NEWELL, NOWELL, Thomas
NEWFIELD, Abram
NEWKIRK, Richard B.
NICHOLAS, Thomas
NICHOLS, Townsend
NISWANGER, Joseph Sr.
  Joseph Jr.
NOBLE, Henry
NORMAN, Levi
  Moses
  Reuben

OAKS, OKES, John
O'BANNON, Joseph
  Welton
O'GELSBY, ?
O'HOGAN, Michael
OLD, Joshua J.
OLIVER, John
O'SULLIVAN, Jeremiah

PACE, Richard R.
PACKEY, John
  Robert
PARISH, James*
  Price
PARK, William
PARKER, Jesse
  John L.
  Samuel K.
PARKS, Jacob
PARMER, Joseph
  Solomon*
PARR, Samuel
PATTERSON, David decd.
  (by Robert adm.)
  John Sr.
  John Jr.
  Robert
  Samuel
  Walter
  William
  Wm. gdn of Clarissa Boyd
PAULEY, William
PAW, John
  Richard R.
PAYNE, John
  John Jr.
PENICK, Jeremiah
PENNY, PENNEY, William
PERKINS, John

PERRINGER, John
PEW, Andrew
  David
  Nelly
  Samuel
  Robert
PIBOURN, PYBOURN, Richard
PINIC see PENICK
POE, Henry Sr.
  Henry
  Isaiah
  James
  Simon Sr.
  Simon Jr.
  Terry
  Terry Jr.
POLK, John
  William
POSTON, Jonathan
POWELL, Rebecca
PRIEST, Zenas
PRIM, PRUM, John
  (also John for
   Abraham Prum)
PROPST, Daniel
  Henry
  Jacob
  John
PROWFER, Daniel
  George
  Peter
  John

QUEEN, John

RALEY, Joseph
RAMSEY, Andrew
  John
  Samuel
  William
  (1822) Samuel decd.
   by John Stephens
RANNEY, Johnson
  (also J. Ranney adm
   Jason Chamberlain)
RANDAL, RANDOL, Abraham
  Anthony
  Elijah
  Enis
  James
  Jeremiah
  John Jr.
  Lewis
  Medad
  Rebecca

17

RANDAL,
RANDOL William
John
(adm for Isaac Stout)
RAVENSCROFT, James
Samuel
REAVES, William
REED, Samuel H.
William
REEL, Daniel
REEP, Frederick
REMINGTON, Stephen
RENFROW, Joel
REVELL, Aaron
Burrell or Burrew
David W.
Davis
Ethedred
Henry D.
Isaac
John
Micajah
RHINES,
RINES Eli
Henry
John
Martin
Thomas
RHODES, Bennett
Christian
Christopher
Daniel
Frederick Sr.
Frederick Jr.
George
Henry
Jacob
John
Samuel
RICE, Thomas
RICHARDS, Whiting
RICHER, RISHAR, John
RIGBY, George
RINGER, M.P.
ROBERTS, Burwell or
Burwirth
George W.
William
RODNEY, John
(also gdn T.J. & Polly)
Michael
Thomas S.
(also trustee for Lewis,
Martin, Polly, T.J.)
ROE, Berryndn

18

ROE, Dinah
John
ROGERS, Hugh P.*
Joseph
RONNEAU, William
ROSS, Enoch
John
ROW, ROWS, John
Daniel
ROY, George
Russell
RUSSELL, James Es.
Lewis*
William
RUTAN, John
RUTLER, Edmond
RUTOR, Charles

SANDERS, Samuel*
(or SANDERSON)
SCAY, James G.
SCHRUM, Jacob Sr.
Jacob
Joseph
SCRIPPS, George H.
SEABACH,
SEABAUGH Adam
Christopher
Christian Sr.
Christian Jr.
Jacob
Joseph
Manuel
Peter
SEAFORD, Caleb
Henry
Jacob
Lewis
Samuel
William
SEAVERS, Charles
Nicholas
Chas. adm. Nich. decd,
SEAWELL, Jesse
Joseph decd.
(by J. Frizel)
SEELY, SEALY, Ezekiel
SELF, Carlock
David
David C.*
SENTOR, John
SEXTON, Charles
Jacob
Joseph

SEWELL, I. (decd)
by Johnson Ranney
Polly
SHANER, Henry
SHAVER, Levi*
SHAW, Timothy
SHEETS, William
SHELBY, Eli
SHELL, Avy
Benjamin
David
Gasper
George
Benjamin adm. George
Kibler and James
Johnson
SHEPPARD, Elisha
Isaac
Jacob
John Sr.
John Jr.
William
SHRUM, Andrew
Frederick
Henry
Jacob
Nicholas
SHOLTS,
SCHULTS David
Joseph
Mark
SHURLDS, Edward
SHURRELL, Jesse
SHUTS, Jesse
SIDES, Levi
SIFFORD, Caleb
Henry
Jacob
Lewis
Samuel
William
SIMMONS, Casper
SIMPKINS, John
SLATEN, James
SLAGLE, Henry
SLINKARD, Daniel
Frederick
David
SLOAN, Thomas
SMITH, Daniel
David
George
Henry
James
John and Dr. John

SMITH, Joseph*
 Matthew
 Michael
 Peter
 Philip
 Robert Sr.
 Robert Jr.
 Nicholas
 Thomas J.N.
 William
SNIDER, Barnett (Bernard?)
 George
 Isaac
 John
 George adm. for John
  Snider decd.
SPEAR, Thomas
 William
 Wm. adm. Sarah Thompson
STABLER, Christopher
STANFORD, James
STANHOPE, William
STAR, James
STARLING, Lyne
STARN, Peter
STATELIER, Mary
 Peter
 Mary adm. Peter decd.
STATES, Jacob
STEARMAN, Thomas
STEAVERS, Nicholas
STEEL, Henry
 Robert
 Henry adm Robt decd.
STEINBECK, Daniel F.
 William
STEP, Gollon
 James
 Mary
STEPHENS, Benjamin
 David
 John
 John adm. Sam'l Ramsey
STERRETT, Washington
STEVENSON, James
STEWART, Charles
 Robert
STOE, Roberson
STORY, Jesse
 Thomas
STOUT, Isaac (1821)
 Isaac decd by J. Ranney
STOTLER, Adam
 Andrew

STOTLER, Catherine
 Christopher
 Conrod
 Jonas
 Mary
 Peter
 Christopher adm. Peter
STRICKLIN, James
STRODE, Alexander
STRONG, Johnson
 Sarah
STROTHER, Alexander
STROUP, Andrew
 George
SUBLETT, Lineas B.
 Samuel
 Thomas
SULLINGER, Thomas (1821)
 Rutha
SUMMERS, Alexander
SURRELL, William

TANEY, Michael
TANKERSLEY, Charles
 George
 John
 William
TARLTON, Azion
 James
TASH, Lewis decd.
 (heirs of)
TAYLOR, David P.
 George W.
 Margaret
 William
THOM, Michael
THOMAS, Baker
 Claiborne S.
 Gabriel
 Isaac
 Martin
 Richard S.
THOMPSON, Benjamin
 Isaac
 James
 John (S.)
 Joseph
 Royal
 Sarah decd by Wm. Spear
THORN, Joseph
TINKER, Jacob
TINNEN, Azariah
 William
TIRER, Asa
TRICKEY, John

TROTTER, Robert
TUCKER, Milton

UMBERFIELD, Eli
UNDERWOOD, Thomas*
 Valentine

VANANBURG,
VANDERBURG   Joseph
VANCE, John G.
VAN HORN, Nathan
VAN GILDER, John
VANN, Gabriel
VEST, Thomas
VILEY, Thomas
VINCENT, Josiah
VIRGIN, Samuel

WACKER, John
WAGGENER, David
WAITWORTH, Winston
WALKER, Henry
 John
WALL, Charles
WALLACE,
WALLIS   Beard
 James
 John
 William Sr.
 William Jr.
 William B.
WALLER, Henry
 John
 Leonard
 Susanna
 Richard
WALLIN, Nelson D.
 William
WALLS, Charles
 Thomas
WARD, Ezekiel
WARFIELD, Stephen
WATKINS, Levin
 Nathaniel W.
WATSON, John C.
WATT, James
WEAVER, John
WELCH, Eve
 Samuel
 Ann
 Thomas
 William
WELKER, Daniel
 Sarah
WELL, Abraham
 Daniel

19

WELTY, Abraham
    Daniel
    Jacob
    John
WEST, Thomas
WESTLEY, John
WHEELER, John B.
WHIPPLE, D.H.
WHITE, Samuel
WHITELAW, Nicholas
  (also adm. for
    Rachel Laugherty)
WHITLEDGE, John F.
WHITNEY, Joseph
    Minor M.
WHITTENBURGH, Henry
    John
    Rachel
    William
    ?. T.
WHITWORTH, Winston
  (WAITWORTH)
WIDENER, Abraham
WIKER, Henry
WILEY, James
    John
    Matthew
WILFONG, Martin
  (also adm. for
    Christian Gross)

WILKERSON, James
WILKINSON
    William
WILLIAMS, Charles
    Isaac (S.)
    James
    John C.
    Smith
    William
WILSON, Benjamin
    Fincas
    James B.
    James C.
    John
    John C.
    John G.
    William
WINFIELD, Joel
WINSETT, James
    Joseph (two)
WIRE, Levi
    Philip and mother
WISE, David
    Mary
WOLF, Elizabeth
WOOD,
WOODS Hugh
    John
    Samuel L.
WOODALL, Elijah*
WRIGHT, Alexander

WRIGHT, B. D.
    John (P.)
    Richard
    Susannah

YANCY, Sanford
YODER, YOWDER, Adolph
YOUNCE, Lorance*
YOUNG, Austin
    Elizabeth
    Morris
    Philip
    William
  Philip adm. for John
  Cotner & for A. Byrd
YOUNT, David
    Elizabeth
    Henry
    Isaac
    Jesse
    John
    Maria
    Philip
    William
  John exr. of Jacob
    decd 1821

ZILIFROW, John

· · · · · · · · · · · · · · · · · ·

Cape Girardeau was one of the five original districts of the
Missouri Territory. In 1818, Wayne County and part of Madison
County were formed from Cape Girardeau. It is also the parent
county of Ripley (1823), Stoddard (1835), Dunklin (1845) and
Bollinger (1851).

CAPE GIRARDEAU, SECONDARY LIST: FROM THE HERALD AND THE INDEPENDENT PATRIOT

Both published in Jackson, Cape G. Co.

BARBERSON, Rev. John C.	notice	
BERRY, Alias Pew	notice	
Andarena	"	
Elvy	"	
Robert P.	"	
BROOKS, Nancy	notice	
BLUNT, Malinda	notice	
BRADY, David	estate	
Esther Dixon	"	
BURNS, Arthur	estate	
Mary Dixon		
BYRES, Margaret	notice	
CHAMBERLAIN, Eliza	notice	
CHANDLER, Elizabeth	estate	
CLARK, Jacob Lorance Twp.	stray	
CROPPER, J. M. land	sale	
CROSS, Sally	notice	
DIXON, Frederick	estate	
Hezekiah	"	
Nathan	"	
Zilla	"	
DOWTY, Julia Ann	notice	
ENGLISH, John P.	estate	
Matthews	"	
HAND, William	bankrupt	
HAHN, Abraham	estate	
Eave		
Joshua		
HAYDEN, John	notice	
Louisa	"	
HECTOR, Ann Dixon	estate	
HEWS, Polly	notice	
JUDEN, George W.		
LIGGITT, Henry	stray	
LINCECUM, Harmon	stray	
Byrd Twp.		
McFARLAND, Mary	notice	
McLANE, Elizabeth Cochran	estate	
MASTERSON, Samuel	notice	
MALONE, Eliza	estate	
MATHEWS, Sally	notice	
MEDAD, Randal land	sale	
MOSELEY, Thomas Jr. land	sale	
MOTHERSHEAD, Elizabeth	notice	

O'BANNON, John	estate	
Martha	"	
Polly	"	
William	"	
PEW, Polly	notice	
John	"	
PURDY, Jonathan	estate	
Unice Dixon	"	
RENNICK, Polly O'BANNON	estate	
ROSS, Mary	estate	
RUNYEANS, Benjamin	stray	
SINKLIER, Liddy	estate	
Presley	"	
SMITH, Archibald R.	notice	
SNIDER, Catherine	"	
SPRIGG, J. T.	land sale	
STAHL, Jacob	bankrupt	
STEINBECK, Agatha	estate	
STUMP, John RandolTwp.	stray	
SUBLETT, Boling Randol Twp.	stray	
TINNIN, John	stray	
WATERS, Emily	notice	
Fanny	"	
WHITTRIDGE, Elizabeth	notice	
YOUNG, Sally	notice	

To the Public.

THE undersigned proprietors of the Northern enlargement of the Town of Cape Girardeau, offer for sale at Public Auction, thirty two lots containing one fourth of an acre of ground each. These lots are handsomely situated (immediately on the bank of the Mississippi river) above the point of rocks which project out from the shore at the Old-Town; this scite is admirably calculated for public business of every description; there are two never failing springs breaking out within a few rods of the place, meandering through the lots make a handsome little brook, from which the water can be carried to every man's door; in front of the lots, on the bank of the river, the proprietors have left a large space for a boat yard and landing, it being the best situated for that purpose; the bank gradually descends to the waters edge. The proprietors think it entirely unnecessary to give any further description of this enlargement, as almost every person in the country has seen it, particularly those who have either ascended or descended the river—The conditions of the sale are—The proprietors will give a general warrantee Deed to the purchaser, be giving bond with approved security for the purchase money; one third payable in six months, one third in eighteen months, and the other third in twenty four months. The sale to commence on the first Monday in January next, and to continue until all the lots are sold.

Charles G. Ellis.
Jenifer T. Sprigg.

Cape Girardeau Dec. 2d, 1819—16

21

CHARITON COUNTY: COMBINED LAND AND PROPERTY 1821; DELINQUENTS 1825

ADAMS, Thomas
ANDERSON, Thomas
ASHBY, Benjamin*
       Daniel
       Henry*

BAILIE, David
BAINBUCK, Frederick W.
BAKER, Charles Sr.
       Charles Jr.
       Joseph M.
       William*
BANKS, Baylor
BARNES, James
       Philip
BARNETT, John
(BARRETT?)
BATY, James
BEATY, David
       Elizabeth
BELL, John M.
BENSON, James H.
BERRY, Taylor
BINNS, Thomas
BISHOP, Elias
BOLLS, Benjamin
       William
BOSWELL, Greenberry
BOTTS, Joshua
       Seth
       Thomas
BRADFORD, F. A.
       Frederick*
       Henry H.
BRADLEY, Thomas
BRASEFIELD, Leonard
BREWER, Joseph
BROOKS, Thomas
BROWDER, Pleasant
BROWN, Jesse
       Josiah
BULL, John
BURCKHARTT, George
       Nicholas L. (T?)
BURTON, May
BUTLER, Nathaniel

CABEEN, William
CABELL, Edward B.
CAMPBELL, David H.*
       Isaac
       Samuel
CAP, William ***
CARPENTER, Samuel

22 *** possibly CASS

CARTER, Charles W.
CATES, Jesse
       John
CLARK, Andrew
       Henry
       Jesse
       Reuben
CLAYBROOKS, William
COATS, Alfred A.
COCHRAN, James
COCKRELL, Joseph
COGDALE, Frederick
COLLENS, James
COX, William
CRAIG, Hiram
CRAWFORD, William
CROSS, Benjamin
       Houston
CURNUTT, William

DANIEL, Robertson
DAVIS, James
       Samuel
       Wilson
DENNY, David R.
DINSMORE, Samuel
DINWIDDY, James
DONOHOE, Stephen
       William
DOXEY, John
DRAKE, Jesse
DRINKARD, William
DRUMMOND, James
       John
DUNLOP, James*
       John
       Robert
DUNN, Henry
       James
DUNNINGTON, Lawson
DUSTIN, Wilman*
DYSART,
DYSERT James
       John*
       Nicholas

EARICKSON, James
       Perrigrine
EARL, Isaac
EDWARDS, Benjamin F.
       Cyrus
ELLIOTT, William
ELLIS, Lewis
ERWIN,
ERVINE John
       Robert

EWING, Finis

FARR, Edward
FARRAR, Anthona
       John
FIELD,
FIELDS John
       William
FINDLAY, Dabney
       John P.
       William
FLEETWOOD, Edward*
       William and
       Edmond
FLOID, Davise
       Gentry
FOOT, Simeon
FORREST, James
       Samuel
FORT, William
FOSTER, Anderson*
       George F.
       James L.
       Josiah
FOWLER, James*
       James R.
       John*
FOX, Benjamin L.
FURGERSON, James*

GAGE, Thomas P.
GAITHER, John
       Mary
GILLETT, John
GORHAM, Thomas
GRAVES, John*
GREEN, Duff
       Willis M.*
GRIFFIN, Thomas
GROSS, Abram

HALLETT, Moses
HARDWIN, Thomas
HARRIS, Andrew
       Benjamin
       Jesse
       Moses
HASKINS, Allen
HEAD, Anthony
       James
       Joseph
HEDDEN, Ira (?)*
HERRIFORD, James

HERRINGTON, Thomas
        William
HICKMAN, Edwin T.
        Henry L.
        William
HILL, Wright
HIRONEMUS, William
HIX, Archibald
     Richard*
HOID, Jacob
HOLEMAN, John*
      Joseph (two)
      William
HOOZER, Christian
HOSKINS, Allen*
HOWEL, John
  (HOUSE?)
HUGHS, Joseph
     Roland
HUMPHREYS, John*
      Josiah
      Samuel
HUNT, Daniel
    Nathan

JACKMAN, Thomas*
JOHNSON, Sabret
JOICE, Thomas
JONES, William

KELLY, Thomas
KENDRICK, Walter
KING, Andrew
    Joel
    Moses*
KIRBY, Asa*
    David
    Francis
    John
KNOX, Susan

LAMMER, William
LATHEM, William
LEAPER, James
LEE, Abel
LEWIS, Henry
LOCK, Abram
    Thomas*
LONEY, Thomas D.
LOVE, David
LYON, Peter

McCALISTER, Clark
McCLAIN, Charles
McCOLLUM, David
      William

McCOWN, James
McDANIEL, Bernard
     John
McGEE, James
McKILLAR, Daniel

MAGGARD, Jacob
MARSH, Nathan
MARTIEN, William
MASON, Jacob Sr.
     James Jr.*
MATTOX, Ignatius*
MAYO, Thomas
    Valentine*
    William
MEDLEY, Jacob
MILLER, Isaac
MLOAN, Daniel*
MOBLEY, Richard
MONROE, Joseph Jones
     William
MOON, MOOR John*
MOORE, Ephraim
    John
MORGAN, David
    Martin
    Russell
    Sterling
MORRISON, Col. James
MORROW, John
MORSE, John
MOSSE, James W.
MOTT, William
MUNN, Stephen B.

NOBLE, Mark

OWENS, Jesse
OWNBY, Joseph
    Powel

PARKS, James
    Peterson
PATTERSON, Thomas
PEACOCK, Edward
PEDCOCK, William
POTTER, John*
    Joshua
PULSE, Frederick

RAGAN, William
RAY, Perry B.
REDMAN, Daniel
RIGGS, Samuel
    William

ROGERS, Josiah
ROOKER, Capt. John
ROSS, James
ROWLAND, Jesse*

SALE, Elias
SAMPLE, James
SEARS, Hardy
    Iveson(?)
    John
    Joseph
SIMMONS, Charles
SLAYTER, William*
SMITH, Blandy
SOMERS, Jeremiah
SPLAWN, John
SPORTSMAN, Abram
STANFIELD, Samuel
STONE, Jerriba
STONEMAN, Collen C.
SWINNY, Edmund

TAGGART, Archibald
TAYLOR, Isaac
    James
    Levi*
TEMPLE, James
TERRILL, Richardson*
THORNTON, John
     Richard B.*
TIFFANY, C.*
TILMAN, Daniel
TOOLEY, James
    John
TRENT, Alexander
TURNER, John J.
    Talton
TRENT, Alexander
TURPIN, Champion

VANCE, Joseph
VANDUSEN, Jacob*

WALWOOD, Silas*
WATSON, Josiah
    Thomas
WEBSTER, Addison
WELDON, Phoebe (Philip?)
    John
WELLS, James
WHEAT, Martain*
WHITE, Lewis*
WIGGINTON, Henry*
    John*
WILKERSON, Henry

23

WILLIAMS, John
     Samuel
WILSON, Adam
     John

WOODFOLK, Joseph
WOODS, David

WOODSON, James
     Richard
WRIGHT, Hill

=+=+=+=+=+=+=+=+=+=+=+

Chariton County was formed from Howard in 1820. It is the parent county of Linn and Randolph, and by extension of Macon, Putnam, Sullivan, Adair, and Schuyler.

. . . .

SECONDARY LIST FROM THE MISSOURI INTELLIGENCER, 1820-1826

BESORE, John	stray	MANSON, Thomas	stray
		MONTGOMERY, John	estate
CASTLER, Robert		MORGAN, Asa	estate
COSTLER	stray		
CHAPPELL, Abner	stray	ROBERTSON, John	stray
Chappell Twp.		RYAN, James	estate
CLARK, Robert P.	estate		
COLLINS, John	estate	SANFORD, John Jr.	estate
CUNNINGHAM, Theodotia	stray	John	notice
CRUSON, William	stray	Nancy	notice
FINDLEY, Jonathan S.	stray	TANNER, James	stray
FRISTOE, Mariann	notice	VANKIRK, John	estate
GENTRY, Richard	notice	WALDEN, WALTEN, Austin F.	notice
		WHELDON, John	stray
IRVIN, John	stray	Salt Springs Twp.	
40 mi. n. of Grand River		WRIGHT, Thomas	stray
		Salt Springs Twp.	

. . . .

$ 50 Reward.

RANAWAY from the subscriber a negro man named JIM, formerly the property of Joseph Beatty of Chariton; about 5 feet nine inches high; has a side look when spoken to; speaks hastily, and is rather impertinent. Had with him a new pair of coarse cloth pantaloons, a new pair of coarse shoes, a blue cloth soldier's coat. He took with him a rifle gun, and it is expected will make for St. Charles county or state of Illinois. The above reward will be given for him if apprehended out of the territory, twenty-five dollars if out of the county or ten dollars if apprehended in the county and all reasonable charges paid if secured so that I get him, or delivered to me at Chariton, Howard county, Missouri territory.

               Charles Simmons.

april 5—78

ADAMS, Joshua
    Pleasant
    Richard
    Thomas
ADKINS, James
    Owen
    Mrs. Sally
    William
    Wyatt Sr.
    Wyatt Jr.
AKERS, Joseph
ALLEN, James
    John
    Shubael
    Whitley *
    William
ALLEY, William *
ANNOOD, Joseph *
AVERITT, Howard
AVERETT, Martha
    Matthew
    Western
    William *
    Zachariah

BAILEY, George
BAKER, Mrs. Elizabeth
    Morris
BALDWIN, Andrew
BANCROFT, Timothy
BARBER, Jesse
    Robert
BARCROFT, Elias
BARTER, Stephen
BARTLESAN, Andrew *
    John
BATLOFF, Lewy
BAXTER, Stephen
BENTON, Mrs. Elizabeth
BESS, BEST, Humphrey
BICKERSTAFF, Richard
BIVENS, Freeman
BOGGS, David P.
BRADHURST, John
BRAWLEY, Hugh *
    John
BRADBURY, George *
BROWN, Cicero
    Hugh
    Jesse
    John
    Joseph
    Josiah

BROWN, Townsend F.
    William
BUCKBRIDGE, James
BUCKRIDGE, Joseph *
BUNDS, John L.
BURNETT, George
BURNS, Jeremiah
    Luman
BUSTER, James

CAIN, CANE, Robert
CAMMON, Elisha
CAMRON, Jonathan
CAMPBELL, James
    Thomas
    William
CAREY, Daniel
CARPENTER, Jonathan
CARRELL, James
    John
CASTEEL, Joseph
CASTINE
CATES, John
CHANEY, Lydia
    Nathan
    Richard *
    William
CHAPMAN, John
CHILDERS, William *
CLARK, Phineas
    Tilman *
CLAYTON, Walker
CLEMENS, Henry
CLOSE, Frederick *
COCKRELL, Simon
COGDELL, William *
COLEY, James
COLLIER, John
    Monterge
COLLINS, James *
CONNELLY, Henry
COOLEY, Joseph
COOTS, Abraham
COPELAND, Andrew
CORNELIUS, Absalom *
    Benjamin
    John
CORUM, Mrs. Nancy
COURTNEY, John
    Thomas
CRAVENS, Joshua *

CRAWLEY, James *
CROWLEY, John Sr.
    John Jr.
    Samuel
CREASON, Elijah
CREEK, Abraham
CROCKETT, David
    Joseph
CULP, Jonathan

DAGLEY, James
DARRIS, Harman
    William
DAVIS, Harman
    John *
    Lacket *
    William
DEAN, John
DENTON, Jonathan *
DERBIN, Daniel
DOTSON, George *
DUNLAP, James

++ ELY, Michael ++
ENGLISH, Charles
    Jonathan
    Mrs. Rebecca
ENO, Lue
ESTES, Henry
    Joel
    Joel Jr.
    Estate of Joel
    John
    Littleberry
    Peter
    Thomas
    William Sr.
    William Jr.
++ ELLIS, John ++
EVANS, John
EWING, John D.

FADDIS, John
FERRENS, John
FINLEY, T.? H.?
    Travis
FLETCHER, Jesse *
FOWLER, Joseph
    Robert Y.
FOX, William
FROST, Thomas
FRY, Isaac *
(cont)

25

FRY, Solomon
    Thomas
FUGATE, Sarchael C.

GAGE, Abner
    Joseph
GEORGE, Baley
GESS, Henry
GILLIAM, Cornelius
       Epaphroditus
       Jesse
       John
       Robert*
GILMOR, James
    Joseph
    Robert
    Samuel*
GLADDIN, Elisha*
     James
     Jared
     Joseph*
     Mrs. Mary
GRAGG,
GREGG Benjamin
     David
     Samuel
GRAND, Lue Corresbentte
GRAND SUE, Barthelette
GREEN, Garrett
    Henry Sr.
    Henry Jr.
    Joseph*
    Leven
    Samuel
GRIFFY, James
GROMER, Jacob
GROOM, Abraham
    Francis
    Isaac
    John
    Mrs. Sarah
    William
GUINN, Benjamin
    Elizabeth
    Thornton
GUM, John

HAINES, Collet
HALE, Edward B.
HALL Elisha
    James E.
    Jeremiah
    John D.
    Samuel
    William

HAMILTON, David
    Jesse
    Mentt (?)
HAMLETE, William
HAMLIN
HAMMOND, John B.
HARDWICK, Alexander
    John
    Louis Sr.
HARRINGTON, Charles
    Jacob
    Thomas
    William
HARRIS, John
HARNS William
HART, John*
HENDERSON, David*
    William P.*
HENRY, James*
HENSLEY, Benjamin
    John
    Samuel
    William
HIGHTOWER, John
HINKSTON, Harlow*
HILE, HILL, Richard
** HIRTT, James
   HIRTE John *
     Samuel*
HIXON, Andrew
HICKSON Thomas
HOLMES, David
HUFFAKER, George L.
HUFFMAN, Ezekiel
    Uriah
HUGGINS, Fielding*
HUGHES, Thomas
HUNT, Daniel
HUTCHENS, John
HUTCHINGS Joseph
    Moses *
    Robert *
    Smith
    William

INMAN, Michael *
IRE, Thomas
IRONS, Peter
IRVIN, Robert

JACKS, Thomas
JAMERSON, John *
JAMMISON
** possibly HIETE

JAMES, David
    James
JEFFERS, George
JENT, Henry
JONES, John (two)

KING, John
KINZEY, Solomon
KIMZEY

LAKEY, John
LANCE, Isaac *
LANEHART, William
LANEY, Patrick
LEDGWOOD, John
LEDGERWOOD
LIGGETT, Jonathan
LIGGON, Leonard
LINCOLN, Abraham
    David
    George
    John *
LINVILLE, John *
    Richard
LIVINGSTON, John
    Samuel
    William
LOGAN, Philip
    William
LONCAS, John
LUEL, James
LUTHER, Eliphalet
LYON, LYONS, James *
LYNCH, Isaac

McAFEE, Robert
McCLELLAND, James W.
McCROSKIE, Isaac
McDANIEL, James
McELROE, David
McELWEE
McFEE, Wallace
McGEE, Charles
    Zachariah
McKAY, Jacob
    Robert*
McKINNEY, John
McKISSICK, John
McKOUN, James
  (see also MACCOUN)
McQUIDDY, Benjamin
McWINANT, James

MACCOUN, James Sr.
    James Jr.
    Thomas

26   **two in 1824,
     one John B.

MAGEE, Charles
   Zachariah
MAGILL,
MAGILE Caleb
   David Sr.
   David Jr.
   John
   Samuel
MAIL, MAILES, Henry*
MALLOTT,
MALLOT John
   John L.
   William
MANCHESTER, David
MARTIGEE, Calles
MARTIN, William
   Zadock Sr.
   Zadock Jr.
MAY, Ware L.
MEAD, Stephen C.
MEANS, Abijah
   Adam
   Adam Jr.
   Andrew*
   Clemon
MILLER, Mrs. Constantia
   David N.*
   William
MONROE, Daniel
   Thomas
   William
MONTGOMERY, David
MOORE, David D.
   James K.
   John Sr.
   John Jr.
MORRIS, Edward
   Richard*
MUNDAY, Edmund
MUNKERS, Benjamin
   James
   Redman
   William Jr.
MURRAY, Robert

NEELY, Clement
NEWMAN, Alexander
NICHOLS,
NICKLES Benjamin
   James

ODELE,
ODLE Abigail
   Mrs. Malinda
   Nehemiah
OFFICER, James*
   Thomas
ONAN, Thomas

OSBURN, William
OWEN,
OWENS Mrs. Elizabeth
   Jesse*
   John
   Nicholas
   William Jr.

PALMOUR,
PARMER Benjamin
   Martin
   William*
PEARCE,
PIERCE Robert
PEEBLY. Mrs. Hannah
   Thomas
PENCE, John Sr.
   John Jr.*
   Richard*
PIBOURN,
PYBOURN Edward
POAGUE, Andrew
   Andrew M.
   Robert
PORSELL, Nathaniel
POTEET, Mrs. Mary
   Samuel
POTTER, Eldridge
   Wilson
POWE, William
POWELL, Nathaniel
PRICE, Richard
   William
PRINE, Francis*
   William
PULKET, Paul*
PURTH, William

REED, Jonathan*
REYNOLDS, James
   Reuben B.
   Russell R.
RICE, Claiborne*
RICHARDS, Jesse
   Louis
   Nicholas
   Noah*
   Samuel
   Mrs. Susannah
   William*
RIGGS, Samuel
RILEY, Amos
RINGO, Samuel Jr.
RITCHIE, John
ROBERTS, Aaron
   Edmund
   John

ROBERTS, Jonathan*
   Jonas
   Moses
ROBERTSON,
ROBINSON Andrew Sr.
   Andrew Jr.
ROGERS, Edward A.
ROLLINS, William
ROSE, Jeremiah
RUSSELL, Andrew

SAMPSON, Benjamin
SHAW, Hugh*
   William*
SHELTON, Lewis
   William H.
SIDDEN, John
SIMMS, Benjamin A.
SLAUGHTER, Francis
SMITH, Abner*
   Ahi
   Elijah
   Elijah W.
   Humphrey
   James
   John*
   Mrs. Polly
   Terah
   William
   William L.
SNEED, Lebron G.
SOLLERS, Elijah
   John B.*
   Sabret
   Thomas*
SPERGER, John
SPICER, William
STALLINGS, Jesse
STANLEY, Page*
   William
STEPHENS, Clark
STOUT, Daniel
STROTHER, Thornton
SUEL, Alexander
SULLIVAN, Robert
SUTTON, Jonas
SWEET, Samuel

TAGGARD, Archibald
TAYLOR, George
   Shadrack*
TENNILE, George
TETHERON, Solomon
THOMAS, Silas
THOMPSON, John
THORNTON, John

THORP, Christopher
    John
    Joseph
    Owen
    Squire B.
    William Sr.
    William Jr.
TILFORD, Samuel
TILLERY, Clayton
    Esse
    James
    Jesse
    Reuben
TITHEN, Solomon
TODD, Elisha
    Joseph
    William *
TOFFELMIER, John *

VAUGHN, Enos
    Thomas

VESSER, Jenks
    (Jenkinson ?)
    John
    Peter
    Samuel

WALLIS, George
WATERS, James
WEATHERS, Bush rod*
WELDON, Benedict *
WENDEN
WHAN, George *
WHITE, William
WHITLEY, James
WHITLOCK, Tarlton
WHITSON, Abraham
WIANT, Jacob *
WIGGINS, Zebulon *
WILHART, James
WILHORT

WILLIAMS, James
    George
    Master *
    Shrewsberry
    William
WILLS, Archibald
    David
    James
WILSON, Mrs. Elizabeth
    John
    Thomas
    William
WINNINGHAM, Littleberry
WOODWARD, Blumen E. *
    (Elumen?)
    Chesley
WRIGHTMAN,
WRIGHTSMAN Francis *
    John
    Peter Sr.
    Peter Jr. *

YOUNG, Chesney
    William
YOUNGER, Charles

= = = = = = = = = = = = = = =

Clay County was taken from Ray in 1822. It is the parent county of
Clinton (1833) and by extension DeKalb, Gentry, and Worth.

= = = = = = = = = = = =

ADDENDA TO TAX LIST:
(Archives)

HOLMAN, Hugh
MORRIS, J.P.

RILEY, B.W.
RUKEY, John

VAUGHN, David
    Singleton

. . . .

SECONDARY LIST FROM THE MISSOURI INTELLIGENCER, 1822-26

HILL, Richard   estate

LEVINGSTON, Sarah   estate
    Thomas
    William

RICHARDS, Jane   notice
    Lewis   "
ROLLINS, William   estate

WIRT, Elizabeth   notice

x xxxxxxxxxxxxxxxxxxxxxxxxxx

COLE COUNTY: DELINQUENTS 1821 FROM THE MISSOURI <u>INTELLIGENCER</u> AND MISCELLANEOUS LEGAL TAXES FROM THE STATE ARCHIVES

ALLEN, Hiram
    Solomon
ANDERSON, David
ANTEBUS, James

BASS, P.
BERRY, Taylor
BIGERSTAFF, John
BROWN, John
BYRNS, Samuel

CHACE, John
CHISM, Jacob
COLVIN, Jacob
COURTNEY, Samuel

DILLON, George

EADS, Moses

FULKINSON, J.

GARNETT, R.
GILES, Roland

HARRIMAN, Jason
HERRYMAN, Edward

INGLISH, Joseph

JACKSON, Joseph
JAMISON, Samuel
JOHNSON, C.
    Samuel
JONES, Robert H.
    William

LANGHAM, A.L.

McKINZIE, Daniel

MERRAY, James
MILLER, John
    Richard
    Thomas
MOON, H.
MOORE, Robert & wife

MULKY, John
MYERS, John

NEDEVER, Isaac
NIDEREK, Jacob
NORMAN, Gideon P.

PETTIGREW, George A.
    and wife

ROYSTON, Jesse F.
RUNNELS, Michael

SCRUGGS, John
SMITH, R.
STUART, John

THOMAS, J.P.
TOOMS, J.
    William

WALKER, Andrew J.
WOODWARD, George

....

Cole County was taken from Cooper in November, 1820.
It is the parent county of Miller and part of Moniteau.

....

SECONDARY LIST FROM THE MISSOURI <u>INTELLIGENCER</u>, 1821-1826

CARTER, Edward Moreau Twp. stray
CASEY, Christoper stray
    Hardin "
    Jefferson Twp.
CHARLTON, Silas Moreau Twp. stray
CLARK, John J. " "
CLAYBROOK, James " "
COLGAN, Daniel stray
    Jefferson Twp.
COTTEE, Susannah notice

DAVIS, Drury Moreau Twp. J.P.

EADS, Jesse Moniteau Twp. stray

GARTIN, Hugh " J.P.
GORDON, John C. stray
    Jefferson Twp.

HARRIS, Christopher estate
    Nancy "
HARRISON, Jason Moreau Twp. clerk
    Samuel Moniteau " clerk
HENSLEY, John notice

INGLISH, James Marion Tp. stray
    John " "

KENNY, Abraham Moniteau Twp. stray
McKENNY, James Marion Twp. stray

MARTIN, Jonathan P. notice
MAUPIN, James Moreau Twp. stray
MILLER, James estate
    John Moniteau Twp. stray
    Thomas estate
MURRAY, Thomas Moniteau Twp. stray

NEWMAN, William Moreau Twp. stray
NORWOOD, Charles Jefferson Twp. stray

PETTIGREW, Matthew L. estate

RAMSEY, Jonathan Jefferson Twp. stray

SAILING, Henry Moniteau Twp. stray
STEWARD, James Jefferson Twp. stray

TODD, David notice
VIVION, Isaiah notice
    John estate

WADE, William Marian Twp. J.P.
WILLIAMS, John D. Moniteau Tp. stray

ADAMS, David
    William M.
AERHART, Peter
ALLEN, Alexander
ALEXANDER, James
ALLEY, David
ALLISON, Robert
    William
AMOS, Benjamin
    John
ANDERSON, James
    John
    William
    William H.
APPERSON, Alexander
    Francis
    John
ARMSTRONG, William

BALEY, Reuben
    Rial
BANKSON,
BANKSTON Aquilla
    Sarah
BARTON, David
    Jobe
BARTLETT, William*
BATEY,
BATY Samuel
BELL, Zephaniah
BERRY, James
    R. C.
    Taylor
  (R.C. also paid 50¢
   for Wm. Netherton)
BEST, Thomas
BIGHAM, John
BILER,
BYLER Joseph
BILLINGSLEY, Jephtha
BIRDSONG, James
BLASINGIN, Turner
BOLES, Sarah
BOLIN, Delaney) same land
    William)
BOUSFIELD, Henry
    Richard
BOWDEN, Uriah
BOWLES, Benjamin*
    John
    Peter*
    Sabella
BOYD, Matthew
    Robert

BOYD, Robert guardian
  of heirs of Linsey
    William Minor
BRADLEY, Edward
BRETTON, Hugh
BRISCOE, Andrew
    John
BROILES, Louis
BROCK, Perry
BROWN, Alexander
    John R.
    Oliver
    Sloman
BRUFFEE, James
BRYANT, William (two)
BUCKNER, Henry
BURGAN, Thomas
BURKE, Linsey
    William
BURNARD, Joseph M.
BURNES, Lard
    John
BURNETT, Cooper
BURNEY, James C.
BURRIS, David Sr.
    David Jr.
    Henry
BUTCHER, Joshua W.
    Thomas

CAIRY, Evans
CAMPBELL, James D.
    Joseph
    Russell
    William Sr.
CALVERT,
COLVERT John
    William Sr.
    William
CANNER,
CONNER Frederick
CARPENTER, Peter
    Samuel
CARSON, Charles R.
CARTER, Freeman
CARTNER, William
CASSEDY, Jesse
CASTEEL, Jacob
    Shedrick
CASTELLOE, Joseph*
CATHEY, George
    George Jr.*
    James
    John

CATHEY, Joseph
CATLETT, Abraham
CATRON, Christopher
CAULK, George
CAYTON, William
CHAMBERS, Benjamin
    James
    Thomas
    William
CHANEY,
CHAYNEY John
    Richard
CHEEK, William
CHISM, Jacob
CHITCOAT, John
CLARK, Benjamin L.
    John B.*
    John J.
    Michael
    Patience
CLARKE, Robert P.
CLAY, Jeremiah
CLEMMONS, James
COFFEY, Benjamin
COLDWELL, Elverton
COLE, Hannah
    Hobert
    Rodden
    Samuel
    Stephen Sr.
    William
COLLINS, James L.
    Thomas
COMBS, Stephen
CONERLY, Daniel
CONNEHAM, Benjamin
CONNER, John
    John W.
    Frederick
COOPER, David
    William
COTTEN, Benjamin
    John
COX, Matthew
CRAWFORD, George
CREAMOR,
CREMOR John
CROPPER, Levin
CUMMINGS, Richard W.
CURTIS, Williamson

DAVIS, Charles
    Isaac

DAVIS, James
    John
    Joseph L.
    Samuel B.
    Wilson
DAWSON, D. Robert
DELLIS, Joshua
DE WITT, Larkin*
DICKARD, James
DICKSON, Alexander
    John
    Josiah Sr.
    Josiah*
    Robert*
DICONS, William
DILLAR (D), James
    Joseph
    William
DONELSON, James
DRINKWATER, Manuel
    Robert
DUGAN, Daniel
DUNAWAY, James
DUNN, Byron
    Michael

EASTUS, John
EDGAR, George
    James*
    Lewis
    Russell
EDWARDS, Daniel
    William
ELLER, Jacob
ELLIS, Isaac
ELLISON, Ephraim
    Thomas
EMMANS, Julius
ERVINE, Anne
ESTIS, Henry
    Joel
    Littlebury
    Peter
    Thomas
EVANS, Elisha
    John
EWIN, Finas
EWING, Irbin
    Reuben (?) A.

FARRIS, James
FINDLAY, Asa
FINE, David
FISHER, Anthony
    Caleb
    Jacob
    John
    Joseph
    Peter Sr.

FISHER, Peter*
    Trussey
FITZHUGH, John
    Thomas
FLACK, James
FORCE, Charles
FORT, Spear
FRAZIER, William
FURGASON, Jesse
    William
    (together, no land)
FULKERSON, James

GABRIEL, Abraham
    Jacob
    John
GEORGE, Reuben
    William
    Lewis) together
    Jesse
    William
GIBSON, Abraham
    William) together
    George
    Humphrey
    William
GIST, Benjamin
GIVINS, Alexander
    Robert
GLASS, Samuel
GREEN, Duff
    George
    Henry Sr.
    Henry
    John
    William
GUIN, Henry
GUYER, Henry

HALFORD, Jesse
HALL, Benjamin
    Lawrence
    Joseph
    Sylvester
HAMMAR(S), George
HAMBRICK, Enoch
HAMMOND, Eli E.
    John
    Samuel
HANNAH, Benjamin
HANNEIGH, Tarlton
HARPER, James
HARRIS, Hezekiah
    John
    Peter
    Reuben B.
    Thomas
    William

HASSELL, John
HART,
HARTT George C.
HATFIELD, Mansfield
HAYDEN, P. R.
HAYS, William
HEATH, John
    Robert) together
HELM, Allen
    William
HENRY, Eli N.
    John
HEPBOURN, John*
HICKCOX, Benjamin
HICKON
HICKMAN, Benjamin*
    Hope H.
    James
    John
HICKS, John Sr.
    John Jr.
HILL, James (two)
    John A.
HINDRICK, Littleberry
HOBOUGH, Peter*
HOLT, James
HON, William
HOOK, Elijah
HOP, Rudol ***
HORNBACK, Michael
HOUX, Frederick
    Jacob
    John
    Matthias
HOUSE, George
HOWARD, Edward
    Hiram
    Joseph
    Lott
    Seth
    Waid
HOWE, John
HUFF, Abraham
    Absalom
    John
    Nathan
    Peter
HUGHES, Polley
    Rolinder
HUNT, Clayton
HUNTER, Elisha
    John
HURLEY, Jonathan
HUTCHISON, James

INGLISH, Charles
    John   31
***possibly HOSS

ISH, Jacob
   William

JACK, William
JENNINGS, William
JOBE, Enoch
   Reuben
   William
JOHNSON, Alexander
   David
   David Jr.
   James
   Jesse
   Robert (two)
   Vincent
   William
JOLLEY, John
   Joseph
   William
JONES, Abraham
   David
   Jabez (two)
   James
   John
   Lewis (H.)

KAVANAUGH, Archibald
KELLEY, James
KELLY, John
   William
KETCHUM, James
KILBREATH, Alexander
KINCHELOE, J.
   William
KIRKPATRICK, Robert
   Robert Jr.

LAME, James
LAMM William
LANCE, Edward
LANE, Absalom
   Thomas
LANGLEY, John
   Moses
LAPSLEY, Samuel
LAWLESS, Burton
   Clabourn
LEE, Juel
LEONARD, Abiel*
LETCHWORTH, Thomas
LEVEN, Bazaleel W. (H?)
LEWIS, Joshua
   William
LILLARD, John
   William
LINVILLE, Thomas
LOCKHARTT, Byrd

LONG, James
   Willey
LONGAN, Augustin B.
   John B.
LOWREY, William
LUCAS, John B.
LUTCHWORTH, Benjamin

McARTHUR, Charles
McCARLEY, James Sr.
McCARTY, Nicholas
McCLAIN, Andrew
   Charles
McCLANAHAN, Absalom
   Joshua
McCLENCHAN, Absalom
   Adam
   Job
   Joshua
   Lacy
McCLURE, John
   Joseph
McCORKLE, Archibald
McCOY, Robert
McDONALD, William
McFALL, Alexander
McFARLAND, Alexander
   David
   Elijah
   George (two)
   Jacob
   James Sr.
   James Jr.
   Jesse
   John*
   Samuel
   William (two)
McGEE, David
McHENRY, James B.
McKENZIE, Kennith
McMAHAN, James
   Thomas
McPHARTRAND, David

Mahan, David P.
   James
MANION, Edward
MARLY, Eri
   (MORLEY, Eli)
MARSH, Ephraim
MARTIN, Baker
   James
   Jesse
   Job
   Moses

MASSEY, James W.
MAYSBACK, Charles
MELTON, Joel
MILLER, James
   John (two)
   Joseph*
   Samuel
   William (two)
MILLSAPS, Jonathan
MINES, John
MITCHELL, Charles B.
   Fleming
   Henry*
   Thomas
   William
MOON, George
   Jesse
   Joseph
   Nathaniel
   William
MOORE, John H.
   Thomas
   William
MORGAN, Asa
   Stanley G.
MORLEY, Eli
   (MARLY, Eri)
MORRISON, Nathaniel
MORROW, James
   Robert
MULENS, Abner
MULLINS, Ahab
MURPHY, Davis
   Joseph

NAVE, Jacob
NEWMAN, Jacob
NOWLIN, Bryant
   Peyton

OBANION, William
OBRYAN, Jordon O.
ODAIR, Francis
OWNBY, Nicholas

PARHAM, Wyatt
PARSONS, Jesse
PATE, George
   Thomas
PATRICK, John
   Robert
PETERS, Samuel
PHILIPS, Thomas
POER, William
POGUE, Robert

32

PONTON, William
PORTER, Allen
      William C.
POTTER, George
      John
      Samuel
      William
POWERS, William*
PRIGMORE, Benjamin
PROCTOR, John
PUCKETT, Elijah
PURSLEY,
  PUSLEY John

RAIN, Thomas
RANDOLPH, Elijah
REAM, A.
REAVIS, Andrew A.
      David
      Edwin
      James
      Samuel D.
  (also Sam'l D. for
    Corben West)
REED, William
REID, John*
      Solomon
      William
RENFRO, Isaac
REVICE, David
RICE, John
RICHARDSON, Shelton
RIDDLE, John
      Widow
  (probably of Stephen)
RIED, William
RIGGS, Thomas
ROBERTS, Edward
      Eli (two)
      John
ROBERTSON, Charles
      James (two)
      William
ROBINSON, Andrew
      Edward
      Jane
      John
      Joseph
ROCHESTER, John C.
ROGERS, Thomas
ROSS, C.B.
      John
      William Sr.
      William Jr.
ROUSE, Polser

RUBEY,
  RUBY Thomas
      William
RUBLE, Owen

SAPPINGTON, Sebastian
SAVAGE, Hiram
      William
SCOTT, Adam
      Hiram
      John L.
      Joseph
      Kemp
      Robert
      William C.
SCRITCHFIELD, James
SEAT, Green
      John B.
      Littleton
SEEGRAVES, John
SELF, Job Sr.
      Joshua
SHACKELFORD, Nancy
      Richard
SHIPLEY, Robert
SHIRLEY, Frederick
SHOCKLEY, Isham (?)
SHOEMAKER, Charles
      George
      John
      Philip
      Rufus
      William
SIBLEY, George C.
SIMONDS, Jacob
SIMS, James
SLOAN, Alexander
      Robert
      William
SMALL, George
      Henry
SMALLWOOD, Russell
SMELSER, David
      Harmon
SMILA,
  SMILEY Thomas
SMITH, Daniel
      Isaac
      Jacob
      James D.
      Jesse
      John
      Joseph
      Nathan
      Samuel (G.)
      Thomas

SNODGRASS, James
      Joseph
      Samuel
      William
SON(S), James
      John
      William
      Michael Sr.
SPITHA, Elisha
SPOONAMORE, William
STEPHENS, Andrew
      Jacob B.
      Joseph Sr.
      Joseph Jr.
      Lawrence C.
      Peter
      Thomas
      William (two)
STANLEY, Jonathan
STEELE, Joseph B.
      Ninian
      Robert
      William
STEWARD, Richard
STINSON, James
STONE, John
      Robert
      William
STORY, Cornelius
      James
STRAIN, James
      Thomas
SWEARENGEN, John
      Nicholas
      William
SWITLER, Lewis

TAYLOR, Elijah
      Hiram
      James Sr.
      James Jr.
      William M.
TENNEL,
  (TERVEL?) George
THOMAS, Anthony
      Frederick
      Isaac (two)
      Jacob Sr.
      Jacob Jr.
      Jesse
      Notley
      Peyton
      Silas
THOMPSON, Gideon
      John F.

THOMPSON, Robert C.
TOMPKINS, George
TOWNSEND, Sanders
TRAMMEL, Philip
TRAVIS, William
TROTTER, David
TUCKER, Alexander
TURLEY, Jesse
        Stephen
    Jesse for heirs of
    Stephen Riddle
TURNER, Ephraim
        James
        John
        Lydia
        Moses (two)
TWENTYMAN, Thomas

VAUN,
VAUGHN   Benjamin
         Elisha
         Obadiah
         Thomas
VAUGHT, John
VIVIAN, Isaiah
        John

WADLEY, David
WALKER, Anthony
        Henry R.
        John
        Robert
        Samuel
        Winston

WALLACE, Andrew
         Drury
         John
         Joseph
         Robert
WALLER, Zachariah
WARD, David
WARDEN, Hezekiah
WASHINGTON, J. B. C.
WEIGHT, George W.
WEIR, George
      Hugh
      James H.
      James L.
      John
      Samuel
      William B.
WELLS, Dolphin
WESTBROOK, Joseph
          Joseph Jr.
          Richard
          William
WHITE, Andrew
       Hartley
       William
WHITLEY, Paul
WIGGIN, Zebulon
WILKINSON, James G.
           John
WILLIAMS, Ezekiel
          Giles L.
          James
          Joel
          Justinian

WILLIAMS, Marcus
          Polly
          Richard
          William
WILSON, James
WINDERS, Edward
WOLF, John
WOLFSCALE, William
WOOD, Alexander
      Archibald
      Charles
      Green
      Jesse
      Joel
      John
      Joseph
      Levi
      Nancy
      Ruth
      Sarah
WOOLERY,
WOLLERY   Abraham
          George
          Henry
          Joseph
          Lawrence
          Stephen
WYAN, Jacob

YARNAL, John
        Joseph
        William

....

Cooper County was formed in 1818 from Howard County,
which had been taken from the original districts of St.
Charles and St. Louis two years earlier (1816). Cole
County was formed from Cooper in 1820; so was the county
originally called Lillard, later Lafayette. Saline County,
also formed in 1820, was taken partly from Cooper and
partly from Howard.

ALLISON, Hugh	stray
Clear Creek Twp.	
ASHLEY, William H.	estate
CALDWELL, Elverton	stray
Boonville Twp.	
CARROLL, Henry	notice
CHAMBERS, David Moreau Twp.	stray
DAVIS, A.	deponent
DIXON, John Jr.	notice
Joseph	notice
EADS, Moses Moreau Twp.	stray
FORBES, J. Lamine Twp.	stray
GIBBS, Samuel adv for runaway	slave
GOUGE, Martin Moreau Twp.	stray
GREEN, Leven Lamine Twp.	stray
HENSLEY, John Moreau Twp.	stray
HICKCOX, Charles	stray
Lamine Twp.	
HOUX, Nicholas Lamine Twp.	stray
HOWARD, William Moreau Twp.	stray
LAWLESS, Bradford	estate
Elizabeth	"
near Arrow Rock	

MAHAN, William	stray
Arrow Rock Twp.	
MISCAL, Charles Y.	deponent
MORELAND, John	notice
NOWLIN, Patrick	stray
Arrow Rock Twp.	
RECTOR, Elias	estate
William	"
RICE, Jeremiah	notice
ROSS, Elizabeth	estate
RYAN, James Moreau Twp.	stray
SAVAGE, John Boonville Twp.	stray
SHACKLEFORD, William	stray

=+=+=+=+=+=+=

ABBOTT, Samuel
ADAMS, Burrell B.
 John
 Joseph *
 Mary
 Phineas
ALDER, John
ALLEN, Gideon R.
 James
ANDERSON, Clairy
 David
 Edmund
 James (two) (1*)
 James' heirs
 Joshua
 William R. (H?)
ANTROBUS, Thomas
ARBUCKLE, Hugh
ARMSTRONG, Jane
 John
ARTHUR, William

BACON, John
BAILEY, Caleb
BAKER, Mathias *
 William *
BALL, John
BARCLAY, Hugh
BARNS, Brackett
 George (two)
 John Jr.
BASCUS, John
BAY, Robert
BEGLOW, Louis
BELL, Daniel
 John
 Philip
 William
BENTON, Abraham
 Susanna
BERRY, William
BIDDIX, John
BIRD, James
BLACKWELL, Matthew
BLAIR, James C.
 Thomas
 William
BLANKENSHIP, Mathias
BOSWELL, Henry
BOWLES,
  Ambrose
 BOLES

BOYD, Mary
 Thomas
BRADY, William
BRAMMEL, Richard
BRAY, William
BREEDING, Elijah
 John Sr.
 John Jr.*
 John's heirs
 Mary
BROCK,
BROOK Elisha
  Joshua
  Robert
  Tarlton F.
  Tubal
BROWN, Asa
 Benjamin
 Cain *
 Clement
 Edmund*
 Elizabeth
 George*
 Henry
 James Sr.
 James Jr.*
 Jesse *
 John B.
 Joseph (C.)
 Nicholas
 Russell
 Thomas
 Walker P.*
 William
BUCKNER, John W.
 Thomas
BURCH, John M.
BURLESON, Jonathan
BURNS, Uriah
BURROWS, Edward
 George
 Thomas *
BUTLER, John
BUTTES, John
BYRNSIDE, Elizabeth
 John's heirs

CALDWELL, Andrew (Hoppy)
 David
 James
 John Sr.

CALDWELL, John Jr.
 Kinkead
 Mary
 Matthew
 Micajah *
 Robert
 Samuel
CALL, Elizabeth
CALVIN,
COLVIN John
  Mary
CAMPBELL, James S.
 William
CANTLEY, John Sr.
 John Jr.
 Samuel
CARMAN, Andrew *
CARR, Samuel
CARROLL, Jackson
CAULK, Thomas
CAVANAUGH, Joseph
CHAPMAN, Absalom
CHEEK, James
CHEVONING, Richard
 (CHEWNING?)
CHILDERS, Thomas G.
CHITWOOD, John
 Seth
CLARK, Austin
 Jacob
 John *
COBB, Daniel
COLE, Elizabeth
 Jacob
 Matthew
 Plato
COLEMAN, Anderson
 Sarah S.
COLLARD, Charles
COLLINS, Jacob *
 Joseph
COMPTON, John
CONN, Edmund
 Samuel *
CONWAY, Walter
COOPER, Francis
COULTER, Hiram
CRAFT, Moses
CRAIG, James
CRAWFORD, Bratton

DANTEN,
  DARTEN   Nicholas *
DAUGHERTY, William
DAVIS, John Sr.
       John Jr.
       Richard
       William
DECKER, Enoch
       John *
DENT, Bailey
      Henry *
      Josiah *
      Samuel
DODSON, James
- DORRISS, James
DOUGLASS, Sarah
DOYLE, John
DUFF, Ebenezer
DUNCAN, Bowles W.
       David *
       John *
       Robert
ENLOW, Anthony
      Benjamin
      Felix
      Jesse
ESTES, Elisha *
      Hiram
EVANS, Benjamin

FARRAR, John F.
       Leonard
       Richard
FISHER, George
       Jacob
FITZGERALD, ?
FOWLER, Robert
FRAZIER, John
       Robert
FRYER, George
FULLERTON, William
FUNK, Joseph

GALL, David
     John Sr.
     John Jr.*
GARVIN, John H.
GIBSON, Elias
      Samuel
      William
GLASCOCK, Stephen
GRAFF, Andrew
      Henry
      Margaret
GREENSTREET, Absalom
       Ellen

GREENSTREET, Enoch
       James Sr.
       James Jr.
       James' heirs
       Robert
       William
GRISWOLD, Frederick

HAINS, Benjamin *
HALE, Sarah
HALL, Drury *
      Lewis
      Zachariah
HAMILTON, Andrew
       Jeremiah
       Ninian B.
HAMMOCK, William
HARDIN, Garland *
       Isaac
HARGROVE, Joel
HARRISON, John B.
       Reuben
       Samuel
       William
HART, Armstrong *
HAWK, George *
HAWKINS, William
HEARST, George's heirs
       William
HEATHERLY, Benjamin
       Leonard *
       Osias
HEDSPETH, Jacob
HENRY, Thomas
HENSLY, Lasine
      Lenna *
      William
      Willis Sr.
      Willis Jr.
HERRINGTON, Samuel
HILTON, James
HINES, Richard
HINTON, Clayton
       Jacob
       John Sr.
       John Jr.
       Mary
HITZ, John
HODGES, Benjamin
       Gilbert
HOLLAND, Samuel W.*
HORINE, John
       John's heirs
HORNSINGER, John Sr.
       John Jr.

HOWARD, Edward
       John
       William
HUFF, Alpheus
HUGHES, John
HUSKY, William
HULSY, Eli
      Elijah
HURT, Littlebury Sr.
      Littlebury Jr.
      Wilson D.
HUSKY, William
HUTTON, Samuel
       William
HYDE, Elizabeth
      John

IVOIRS, Charles *

JAMISON, Ephraim
       Hugh M.
JARVIS, William
JEFFRIES, Achilles
JENNINGS, Clement *
JOHNS, Henry *
      John *
      Thomas
      Timothy
JOHNSON, James
       Nathan
JOHNSTON, Abraham

KAVANAUGH, Joseph*
KEATLY,
KEATHY   William
KIDD, William
KIMBERLING, James Sr.
       James Jr.*
KING, Andrew
      Samuel
KINKEAD, Ann
       Archibald*
       James
LANGHAM, John
LANHAM, Sylvester
LARRIMORE,
LAREMORE   James *
           Levi
           Philip
LA RUE, Anthony
       Robert
       Richard Sr.
       Richard Jr.
       Samuel
LASLEY, Alexander
LAUGHAM, Elias L.

37

LEONARD, Hugh*
LEWIS, Charles*
    John
LOFTON, James
LOLLER, Margaret
LONG, Thomas

McCOURTNEY, James
    John
McCULLY, William
McDONALD, Benjamin
    James
    Jesse B.
    William
McINTIRE, John
    Lucy
McKINNY, Charles W.
    William
McKINSEY, Daniel
    William
McLIN, John D.
McMANUS, Charles
    John

MADDOX, Francis (Frank)
MALONE, William
MARQUIS, James
MARTEN, Bartlett
MAUPIN, Daniel
    David
    George
    John
    John's heirs
    Leah
    Lewis
    Sear
    Thomas
    Widow
    William
MEDLOCK, William
    Thomas
MILLER, David
    Francis
    John
    Philip
MITCHELL, John
    William Sr.
    William Jr.
MOORE, Daniel B.*
    Perry
MORRIS, John
MORRISON, John
MUIR, Levian
    (Severn?)
MULLANPHY, John

MURPHY, Nancy
MURRY, William

NANCE, John
NANN, Lewis
NIGHT, Aaron
NORTH, James
NOWLES, John M.

OBANION, John
OSBURN, William
OWENS, Dexter
    Samuel C.
    William G.

PALMER, Thomas
PARK, I. (?)
    Jesse
PARTNER, Amiable *
PATTON, John
PEPPER, James
    Mary
    Paris
    Robert
    Samuel
    William
PERKINS, Ephraim
    John
    Scina
    William
PERRY, John
PHILLIPS. Charles
PINSON, Joseph
POTTS, Jonathan
POUNDS, Newman
PRATHER, John
PRIOR, William
PRITCHETT, Jesse
    Scions
PURSLEY, George

QUICK, Jacob

RAMSEY, DeLafayette
RANSOM,
    RANSON Ambrose
REED, Edward
    George
    Henry
    John Sr.
    John Jr.
    Leonard
REEDER, Augustin
REEVES, Josiah
    Thomas

RENFRO, James
REYNOLDS, William
RICE, Andrew V.
RICHARDSON, Aaron
    Abraham *
    Absalom
    Amos Sr.
    Amos Jr.
    Benjamin
    George *
    Gideon
    James
    Larkin P.
    Nancy
    Nathan
    Richard
    Susanna
RIDENHOUR,   Barnett
    RIDENOUR   Henry
    Jacob
    John
ROARK, James
    Michael
    Thomas *
    William
ROBINETT, James
    Nathan
    (Nathanelly)
    Sarah
ROBINSON, David *
    James
    John R.
    John
ROGERS, Lewis
    Williamson
RULE, Presley
RUSSELL, William
RYAN, James

SAPPINGTON, Benoni
    Fielding
    Hartley
    John
SHELTON, James
    John
    Miller
    Samuel
SHOBE, Abraham
SHOOKMAN, William
SHORT, Aaron
    Eli
    Samuel
SICKLES, John
SIMPSON, John

SKAGGS, David Sr.
     David Jr.
SMITH,
SMYTH Baxter
     Hamilton
     James
     Scudder
     Thomas Sr.
     Thomas Jr.
     Zemro *
SNELSON, James
SONE, Michael
SPENCE, Patrick
SPENCER, William
STANTON, John
STEEL, Elizabeth
     Henry
     John
     Samuel
STEPHENSON, Edward
     John's heirs
STEWART, Riley
     William
STILES, David
STITES Firman
     John Sr.
     John Jr.
     William
STRICKLAND, Barnabas
     Ephraim
SULLINS, Peter *
     John Sr.
     John Jr.
     Reuben
     Richard
     Zachariah

SULLIVANT, John B.
     Mark M.
SUMMERS, William

TANSEY,
TANZY Joshua
     William
TAYLOR, John
THOMPSON, George
     John B.
     John W.
     Samuel*
THURMAN, John
     Samuel
TODD, Isaiah
     William
TURNER, James
     Thomas
TWITTY, Albert* (***)
     John Sr.
     John Jr. *
     Russell

VALENTINE, Agnes
     Eli
     Ira
VANN,
VAUGHN Harrison
     James
     William
VEATCH, Thomas L.
VINYARD, Jonathan

WAIN, Thomas
WALL, David's heirs
     John
     Peggy
     Robert
     Simon
     Thompson

WALTON, Taylor
WELCH, Charles
     Joseph
WEST, Hulda
     John
WHEELER, Malcolm *
WHITE, William
WHITMIRE, Henry
     Moses
     Thomas
WHITTLESEY, Charles
WHITWORTH, Samuel
WILCOX, Preston B.
WILLIAMS, Benjamin F.
     John L.
     Rev. Lewis
WILLIAMSON, Charles
     Elizabeth
WILLSON, Ephraim
     Jacob
WOODLAND, James
WORTHINGTON, John
     Thomas
WYNN, Thomas *

YOUNG, John Mc.
     Lewis *
     Robert
     Thomas *

....

Franklin County was formed from St. Louis in 1818. Two years
later part of the area was cut off to form Gasconade County.

*** also shown as Allen

Taken up,

BY Leonard Reed, living on the Gasconade in
Franklin county, one sorrel mare, fifteen hands and
one inch high; with two white feet, five years old, appraised to sixty dollars—One bay mare, six years old,
thirteen hands, three inches high; one small white spot
on her off flank; appraised to thirty-six dollars—and
one bay Horse, fourteen hands high, gray on his shoul-
ders, small white spots over his rump and body, with
a small bell put on with a leather collar, and nineteen
years old; appraised to thirteen dollars by William
Clark and Bartlet Woollans. Sworn to and subscribed
before me this twenty-ninth of November 1819.
     John Woollans, J. P.
Recorded the 4th Dec. 1819.
     Isaac Murphy, Clk,
march 26—75

BARTON, Patsy Bonhomme   stray
BROCK, Winifred   legal notice

CALDWELL, Jesse   stray
    "Calvy," Merrimac Twp.
CLARK, Thomas Calvy Twp.   stray
    William   stray
    "on the Gasconade"
CLEMENT, Andrew   AS
COLVINS, William Bowls Twp.   stray
COTES, William   Beauff Twp.   stray

EDWARDS, David St. Joachim Twp. J.P.

GREENSTREET, Allen Boeuff Twp. stray

HAMILTON, Levy   stray
HARTY, John   Merrimac Twp.   stray

JOHNSTON, Hannah   legal notice

KEEGAN, James   stray
    N. Gasconade Twp.

McDONALD, Susanna   legal notice
McDOWELL, David   stray

MANSKER, Lewis M. St. John's Twp. stray
MURPHY, Isaac   clerk

NEWPORT, Sarah   adv.

PARKENS, John   Beaoff Twp.   stray
PEPPER, John "on the Calvy"   stray
PINNELL, Wiley Merimac Twp.   stray
PRYOR, Robert   stray
    N. Gasconade Twp.
PURKINS, Isaac Gasconade Twp.   stray
    James   "   "

RANDOLPH, E. H. Boeuff Twp.   stray
REAVIS, James   "   J. P.
REAVES Joseph   AS
ROBERTSON, John   stray
    N. Gasconade Twp.
ROBNETT, Joseph Calvy Twp.   stray

SHELTON, David   AS
SON, Garret   stray
STARKY, Joel Gasconade Twp.   stray

TULERTON, William St. John's Twp.
                                    stray

VALANTINE, George   estate
    Ichabod

WARE, Henry St. John's Twp.   stray
WOOD, William   adv
WOOLAMS, Bartle H.   stray
    "on the Gasconade"
    John   J.
WOOLERY, John Beaoff Twp.   stray
WYATT, Thomas   estate

ADDENDA FROM THE INTELLIGENCER
        (Howard County)

CARROLL, Charles   estate
    Henry   "
DODD, Margaret   notice
KNOX, Col. George   notice
RAY, James S.   estate
    John   "
    Varlender   "
PAYNE, John attorney   notice

--:-:-:-:-:-:--

ANDERSON, James
ABLY, Gabriel

BALES (BATES?), Thomas
BARBARICH, Frederick
BAYER, James
BEARD, Samuel
BIGGS, Jesse
    Samuel
BRISTO, Francis
BROWN, William
BUCKHART, Joshua H.
BUTTER, Margaret

CASON, Pemberton
CLEMENS, Abon
COATS, Andrew
COBB, Eli
    Jeremiah
COIL, Benjamin
COMPTON, Thomas
CRANDOL, John H.
CRAWFORD, Robert
CROW, Henry
CULLENS, Mayo
CUNNINGHAM, Charles
    John

DAY, John
DEHATER, Lewis
DEWEY, Abel
DICOSY, John

EDMONSON, Thomas

FIELDS, Jonathan
FRENCH, Nathan

GARVIS, William
GLOVER, Samuel
GREEN, James
    Squire

HALL, Henry
HARRIS, John
HARTSHORN, David
HAWKINS, Carter
HIGGINS, Julius
HINCHY, Ezekiel
    John
    Uriah
HUGHS, Joseph
HUMPHRIES, John
    Jonathan
HUTTON, George Sr.
    George Jr.

IVORS, Charles

LANE, Henry H.
    Martin
LAY, Willis
LOGAN, Ephraim

McCALL, Caurill (?)
McDONALD, Archibald
McKEE, Eleazer
    Seth
McPHERSON, John

MASSAY, Charles
MARTIN, John
MOORE, Thomas

NIGHT, James
NOWLON, Daniel

ORMSLEY, John

PECA, PICA, Baptiste
    Polette
PERKINS, Levi

RAPIEN, Joseph
READ, Leonard
REAVIS, Washington
RICHARDSON, Gideon
ROBERTSON, Samuel

SHRUM, William
SKAGGS, John
STEPHENS, William
STITES, William

THOOKMAN, William
THROCKMORTON, Jacob
TICKNELL, John
TRIBBE, Absalom

VEST, John
VAN BIBBER, Mathias

WALTON, George
WARDEN, Polly
WITCH, Greg (?)
WOOD, David
WOODLAND, John

YOUNG, Henry

....

SECONDARY LIST FROM THE ENQUIRER AND THE REPUBLICAN, ST. LOUIS

ABBOLTS, Samuel		notice
BAULDRIDGE, John		notice
BELTICK, Thomas Gray Twp.		stray
BOULWARE, Philip		stray
Boulware Twp.		
DUNCAN, John		notice
HOOPS, David Gray Twp.		J.P.
LEIF, Fontaine Gray Twp.		stray
RACINE, Joseph Gray Twp.		stray
REED, Henry "		"
RENFRO, Bartlett "		"
SKAGGS, Andrew		estate
Benjamin		"

STARKY, Joel		notice
TRIBBLE, Absalom		notice
WALDO, David Boulware Twp.		clerk
WALTER, Peter "		stray
WOOLOMS, John		estate

....

Gasconade County was formed from
Franklin in 1820. It is the parent
county of Crawford and Osage and by
extension of Maries, Phelps, and
Pulaski.

....

41

HOWARD COUNTY: COMBINED LAND AND PROPERTY, 1822-23-24

ADAMS, George
    John (two)
    Robert
    Thomas
    Walter
    (Walton?)
    William M.
ADKINS, James
AINSWORTH,
AYNESWORTH William Sr.
    William Jr.*
ALCORN, George T.
    James
ALEXANDER, Reuben
ALLEN, James
ALSOP, Thomas
AMEND, Mathias
AMICK, David
    George
    Nicholas
ANDERSON, Andrew
    Caleb G.
    James
    Middleton
    William
ANDREW, William
ANDREWS, Aaron
    David
    John*
    Moses
    Richard
    William
ANESWORTH see
 AINSWORTH
APPLEGAET, Joseph
ARNOLD, John
    Price
    Price Jr.
ARTMAN, John
ASH, Robert
ASHCRAFT,
ASHCROFT Amos
    Jesse
    Middleton
    Otho
ASHLOCK, William
ATTEBURY,
ATTEBERRY Ashford*
    Edward
    Greenberry
    Israel
    James Sr.
    James
    John
    Simon

ATTEBURY
cont. William
    William Jr.
    Zaccheus
AVERILL,
AVERITT James
    James J.

BAKER, Isaac
    Joseph
    Richard
BAILEY, David
    Urial
    Jesse
BALLARD,
BULLARD Jesse
BALLEW, Barnabas*
    Hiram
BARBA, Thomas
BARBEE,
BARBEY William
BARCLAY, Robert
BARNES, Abraham
    James
    James' heirs
    Philip
   2) Shadrach
    Shadrach*
BARNETT, David
    Samuel
    Solomon
    Zachariah
    (Zaccheus)
BARR, Robert S. & Co.
    Robert heirs 1823
BARRON, Mathias M.
BARTON, Elizabeth
BATES, Moses D.
BAXTER, Hugh
    James, under age
    Mary
    William
    William Jr.
BAYER, Alfred
BAYSE, Alfred,
BEAL, BELL John B.
BEALMARE, William
BEAN, Samuel
BEATY, Andrew
BECKETT, John
    Sally or Sarah
    William
BECKNELL, William
BEDFORD, Stephen

BELEW, see BALLEW
BELL, John B.
    William*
BELLMEAR, Samuel
    (see also BEALMARE)
BELLOW, George
BENNETT, Zachariah
BENSON, James H.
    Mathias
    Zachariah
BERNARD, Isaac N.
BERRY, Taylor
    also for Madrid grants
    to Steward and Welen ?
    Cummings, Thos. W Cook
    Jr., Firmin Deshaun,
    Peter Dumay, Francis
    Lashear, and Peter
    Westbrook, and B.F.
    Ernard or Conard
BINGHAM, Henry V.
    Wiatt
BIRD, John
    Richard
BLAKELEY, John
    Thomas
BLANSET, Peter
BLEVINS, Matthew
BLOY, John
BLYTHE, John
BOGGS, David P.*
    Joseph
    Thomas J.
BOLES, Benjamin*
    Thomas*
BOOMER, BOWMER,
BOUMER, Priscilla
BOONE, Elijah*
    Lemuel
BOOZER, Henry
BOTTS, Joshua
    Seth
BOUCHER, Robert
BOWINE (?), Richard
BOWYER, Henry
    William
BOZ (?), Mike ?
BOYWELL,
BOZWELL William
BOZARTH, Andrew
    David
    Hiram
    Jonathan

42

BOZARTH,
cont   Joseph
           Joseph S.
BRADFORD, Henry H.
BRADLEY, Alexander
           Edward K.
           Joel
           John Sr.
           John Jr.
           Joseph
           Nathan
           (under age 1823,1824)
           Richard
           Sion
           Squire
           Thomas Sr.
           Thomas Jr.
           William *
           William M.
BRAGG, Joseph
BRALEY, John Jr.
           Josiah
BRAMLY, Jonah
BRANAN, James W.
           Richard
BRASFIELD, Leonard
BRASHEAR, Asa L.
           Cyrus
           Gideon M.
           Jonathan C.
           John C.
           Joseph
           Judson M.
           Neri
           Waymack
BRAWLEY, Hugh
           John Sr.
           John
also see BRALEY
BRETT, Berry
under age in 1823,
taxed on a horse
BRIDGES, Pemberton L. (S?)
BRIGGS, Robert*
BROADDUS, Andrew
           Jeremiah
BROADHURST, John
           Joseph
BROWN, Benjamin
           Francis
           (under age 1823-24)
           Henry L. (S?)
           James
           James W.
           Joseph
           Josiah

BROWN   Nancy
CONT.   Robert
            Samuel
            Townsend
            Thomas G.
            William
William: Madrid grant
    to Thos. Harris
Robert for heirs of
    Braxton Cooper
    and gdn heirs of
    Frances Cooper decd
BRUNDAGE, Bartlett
           Joel
           John
           Solomon
BRUMMITT, William
BRUNTS, John
BUDGES, Pemberton F.
    (BRIDGES?)
BULLARD, Jesse
BULLER, William
BUNCHE (?), H. Peter
BURCH, John
           Thomas C.
           William
    (under age 1823-4)
BURCKHARTT, Christopher
BURCHARTT)   James B.
             Mary Ann
             Nicholas S.
BURKE, James
           Joseph
           William*
BURGE, James
           Bennett*
BURLESON, Edward
           James
           Joseph
BURNES, Benjamin
           Isaac
           Jeremiah
BURNETT, Aaron
           Cornelius
           George
           James
           Samuel*
BURNHAM, Elijah
           Foster
           Henry
           Hickason
           Isam
           Joel
           Squire

BURRIS,   George
BURROUGHS   Thomas
    Thos. also Madrid
    claim ___ Benson
BURTON, Hutchings
           William
BUSTARD,   James
BUSTER   Mary
           William Jr or J
    (no property, marked
     "Madrid")
BUTLER, James
           William
BYBEE, John
BYNUM, Gray
    "Madrid" entered in
    name Gerrard Dorlac
BYRNE, James T. (?)

CAIN, George*
           James
           John
CALLAWAY,   Ambrose
CALLOWAY   Charles
              James
              John
CAMPBELL, Allener
           Jeremiah
           John
           Joseph
           Reubin*
           R.L.
           Samuel
           Thomas
CANNON, Simon or Simeon
CANOLE, Charles
    also adm Thos. Miller
CARNEE, James W.
CARNES (?), Amos N.*
CARROLL, Daniel D.
           William
CARSON, Linsey's heirs
           William
CARTER, Christopher*
           Stanton
CASEY, Eli*
CASH, Benjamin*
CASON,   Andrew
CASSON   George
CASTEE, Joseph
CATES, Jesse
           John
CATON, Benjamin

43

CAVE, John
CHAMPION, Dury (?)
CHANEY, William
CHAPMAN, John
CHAPPAL, Abner
CHERRY, John
CHRISTIAN, William
CHRISTMAN, George
CIRKENDOLL, Peter
(see also KUYKENDOLL)
CLARK, Bennett
Bennett H.
John B.
Robert
Robert P.
Tilman
William T.
Bennett adm of JonesIrwin
or Irvine
CLARKSON,
CLARKSTON John
William
CLEMENS, Anthony C.
CLETON,
CLEYTON James
(under age 1823)
John
William
CLEVELAND, John T.
CLOUD,
CLOYD Gilbert M.
Joseph
COALTER, John
COATS, COTES, Alfred
COCKRAN, William (?)
COGDELL, Frederick
William
COLIER,
COLLIER Aaron
John*
Michael
COLLEM, Nancy
COLLET, William
COLLINS, Garland
Thomas
William Jr.
William L.
COMBS, John
COMPTON, Thomas
CONNELL, George T.
CONWAY, A.W.
Thomas
COOK, Benjamin
Stephen
COOLEY, Edward
James
John and
John*

COOLEY
cont. Joseph
Marcus D.
(under age 1823)
Perrin
Rebecca
COOPER, Benjamin
Benjamin Jr.
David
Henley
John (two)
Joseph
Robert
Ruth
Stephen
Tobias (?)
COPELAND, Joel
William
COPHER,
COFER Samuel
CORNELIUS, Benjamin
James
Jesse
Levi
CORUM, John
also as adm Herod
decd 1822
CORNETT, William
COSTY, John
COTENEY, Lewis
CRAIG, George
also agt for Emily
CRAMPTON, Thomas
CRAVIN,
CRAVINS Emsley
Charles M.
Thomas*
CRAWFORD, David
(not subject to poll tax)
John
CRAWLEY,
CROWLEY Jonathan
William Sr.
Jonathan gdn heirs of
S. Cooper
CREWS, David D.
Enoch
Thomas
William Jr.
CRIGLER, Christopher
CRITCHFIELD, Henry
CROCHAN, William
CROCKETT, William
CROGIN, Isaac*
CROSE, John
William

CROUDER, John B.
Nelson
CULLAY, John
CULP, Agness
Jonathan
Nathan
CUNNINGHAM, William
CURNETT, William
CURRIN, Wady T.
CURTIS, Enoch
Samuel

DADES, John
DAILEY,
DALY James
James Jr.
Lawrence J. (t
Thomas
DALE, Abram Jr.
Adam
Jonathan
DALES, Henry
DAVIDSON, John
John*
Nathaniel*
Samuel*
DAVIS, Augustus
Edward
Robert
DAY, Job
DEARBORN, Daniel
DEATHERAGE, Amos
DELANEY,
DULANY George
Joseph S.
DEMPSEY, James
DENNY, Alexander
Charles
James
DICKEY, Thomas E.
DILL, Philamon
DINWIDDIE, John
DODSON, John
Joseph
William
DONALDSON,
DONELSON James
John
William
DORRELL, James
John
William
DOUGLASS, George
James
DOW, James

44

DOWLAN, James
DOWNING, David R.
DOWSON, Robert
DOZIER, William
DRAKE, David R.
    Isaac
    Jesse
    John
    David R. as: gdn for
    Christopher Hough, exr.
    for Roger Barton, gdn.
    and exr. for James
    Richardson and Christ-
    opher Richeson
DRINKARD, Francis
DULEY,
DOOLEY Henry
DUNCAN, David
    John
    Nimrod
    Sarah
    Thomas*
DUNNEY, see DENNY
DUNN, James
DURAN, John
    Marian
DUSAN, John

EARICKSON, James
EARTHMAN, Henry
    John
EAST, Daniel
    Urban
EATON, George
ELKINS, James
ELIOT,
ELLIOTT David
    John
    Josiah
ELLIS, Elijah
    Walter
    William
ELLISON, Robert   ++
EMBREE, Demarcus D.
    Isom (Isham)
    Mathias
    Martitus
    Thomas
ELMORE, Christopher ++
EMSHELL, Lewis
ENYART, David
    Silas
ERELSON (?), Bennett
ESTEES,
ESTUS   John
    William

EVANS, Andrew
EVINS Augustus H.
    Lawrence
EWIN, Watts D.
EWING, Trammell

FARRER, Anthony
FARRIS, Jonathan
    Kimsey
FELAND, Andrew
    David R.*
    John
    William D.
FENALL, John
FERRELL, John
FIELDING, Andrew
FINDLEY,
FINELY Alexander
    Jonathan L. (S?)
    John Sr.
    John
    Samuel
FINNELL, John
    Jonathan
    Stephen
FINNEY, James
FISHER, Charles*
    William
FLEMING, John Sr.
    John Jr.
    Robert
FLY, Enoch
    John*
FOLEY, Henry
FOOT, Simon
FORD, Daniel
    Laban
    Nathaniel
    Peter
    Samuel*
FOSTER, George S.
    James*
    James S.*
    Jonah
    Josiah
FRAKES, George
   (under age 1824)
FREEMAN, Foster
FRENCH, Charles*
FRISTOE, Robert
    Thomas
FROST, Porter*
FRYER, Alexander
FUGATE,
FUGETT Braxton C.
    Hiram
    Jonathan*

FUGATE, Malinda
FUGETT Sarchel*
(cont)
FURGASON,
FERGUSON Nancy
    also as
    gdn heirs Peter decd
FURNISH, William

GAGE, David
    Richmond
GAMBLE, Hamilton R.
GARCEY (?), Gideon
GARETT, Isaac
GARNER, Jesse W.
GARRETT, Abel
GARY,
GERRY James
GASH, Samuel
GAW, John
GEIM, Joseph
GENNINGS, Eli
    James
    Josiah
GENTRY, Reuben E.
GEORGE, William
GIBBS, Frederick*
    John
    Samuel
    Thomas
    Samuel alt.for
    Richmond
GIBSON, Isaac
    John
    Martin
GILL, Joseph
GILLET, John S.
GILVIN, Malinda
GIVENS, Alexander
    Benjamin
    James
    Samuel
    William
GLENN, Spencer
GOFF, David*
    Daniel
GOIN, John
GOOD, Edward
GOODWIN, Abraham*
    Joseph
GORDIN, Jonathan C.
GORHAM, Thomas
GOWEN, John
    Judith or Jude
GRAGG, Hiram
    (cont)

GRAGG,
cont.   Malcolm
         Robert
GRAY, James
GREEN, John
        Samuel H.
        Stephen
        Westly S.
        Willis E.
        William
GREGG, Harmon
        John
(see also GRAGG)
GRIFFIN, Henry*
        James
GRIGGS, John
GRIMES, John
        William
GROGEN, Spencer*
GROSS, David
        Nancy
GRUBBS, William
GRUNDY, Armistead L.
GULLY, George
GUM, Jonathan
GUNN, Spencer

HALE, Benjamin
HALL, James
      John
HALLET, Moses*
HAM, Jacob
HAMM, Tice*
HAMMETT, Reuben H.
HAMMON, Eson
HAMSON, John*
HANCOCK, Abbott
        John
        Nancy
        Robert
HANDY, Robert C.
HANKS, Zachariah (two)
HARCH, William
HARCIEN, James
HARDIMAN, John and Thomas
   (together 1822)
        Thomas*
   John: Spanish grant
   claimed by J.P. Nash;
   claim granted to
   P. Bearleceam
HARDIN, George W.
        James
        Samuel Sr.
        Samuel Jr.
   Madrid located by
   Taylor Berry (?)

46

HARDWICK, Philip A.
         Thomas
         William
HAREMAN, John
HARGIS, Hardin
   (under age 1823-24)
         Isaac D.
         Isaac
         William
HARLE, William
HARMON, John
HARNER,
HORNER   Major
HARRIMAN,
HERRIMAN Charles
          John
HARRINGTON,
HERRINGTON Jacob
            Thomas
HARRIS, Andrew
        Benjamin
        David*
        Hezekiah (two)
        Isaac
        John
        Joshua
        Peter B.
        Western
        William
HARRISON, Charles
         John
         Samuel
         Thomas
HART, William
HARTLEY, Elisha*
HARTWIG, Jesse
HARVEY, Charles
   (under age 1824)
        John (two)
        William
HASTINGS, Jesse
HATTON, James
HAUGH, Christopher
HAWKINS, James*
         William
HAWLEY, Presley
HAY,
HAYES Benjamin
       Charles*
HAYTER, James H.
HEAD, Alfred
      Gavin
      William
HEADRICK, Jacob*
         Joseph Sr.
         Joseph Jr.*

HENDERSON, James A.
HERD, HURD, Jane
HERRALL, John*
HERRILSON, Bennett
HERRINGTON, see
   HARRINGTON
HERRIMAN, see
   HARRIMAN
HIATT, Moses
HICKMAN, James
   James and Thomas,
   together 1822
   Madrid entered by
   P. Laforge
   Hickman & Lamme:
   Madrid entered by
   Rachel Lasceur
   Thomas (1823)
HICKS, Ammon
       Henry
HIGGINS, Josiah
HILL, Charles D.
      Davis*
      John
      John W.
HILTON,
HITTON   William
HINCH, Michael
       Uriah H.
HINES, Anthony
       Charles K.
       David*
       Jonathan
       Westley
HIRONYMUS, John
HIX, Philip
   under age 1824
HOLER, James
HOLLAND, James
HOLLIDAY, Benjamin
          Elizabeth
HOLLOWAY, James
          Samuel
HOLT,
HOTT (?) Henry
          William
HOLTSCLAW, James*
HOOD, Allen
      Robert
HOOK, Henry
      William
HOOTEN, William
HORNER,
HARNER   Major
HOUCE, James Sr.
       James Jr.

HOUGH, Christopher*
    under age 1823; by
    D.R. Drake, agent
HOUX, George
HOWARD, Ephraim
    David
    Joseph B.
    Matthew
HOWELL, James Sr.
    James Jr.
HOY, James
HUBBARD, Asa K.
    Asaph E.
    Thomas
  Asaph & Agnes Stephenson
  adms Thomas Stephenson
  Asaph adm Marcus Stephens
HUFFMAN, Isaac
    John
HUGHES, George
    Joseph S.
    (Joseph Sr.?)
    Rollin or Roland
    Samuel M.
    William Sr.
    William
  John's heirs; Wm. Sr., agt
HUNGERFORD, Levi
HUNT, Allen
    David
    William
HURD, HERD, Jane
HURT, Allen
    Joshua
    Peyton
    William
HUTCHINSON, Andrew*
    John
    Nathaniel
HYTOWER, John

IRVIN, Benjamin
ISAACS, David
    John
    Nancy S.
    Robert
ISBELL, Jason

JACKMAN, Porter
JACKS, Elias
    Richard
    Thomas
JACKSON, George
    Hancock
    James

JACKSON cont.
    John
    Stephen
    Thomas
    Ulrich
    William
  George exr. John Morin
JAMES, Robert
    Thomas
    William
JENERETT, Charles C.
JENKINSON, George
JENNINGS, Alexander
    Sarah
  see also GENNINGS
JEWELL, see JUEL
JIBSON, Isaac
JILSON, John
JIMMERSON, Jonathan
JOHNSON, Alfred W.
JOHNSTON
    Andrew
    Dabney
    Daniel*
    David*
    John C.
    John Jr.
    John
    John*
    Richard
    Robert
    Robert*
    William
JONES, Aquilla
    Daniel
    David and Elijah
    together 1822
    separate 1823
    James
    Joel
    Levi
    Phoebe
    Robert
    Thomas
    Wiley
    William
JORDIN, James
JOURDAN
JOURNAGIN, Becton*
JONAGIN (Beckman?)
JUEL, William

KAVANAUGH, Francis
    William

KELLEY, John
KELLY
    Thomas
KEMPER, Elijah
    Enoch
KERN (?), John
KERR, Augustus
    John C.
KEYKINDOLL, Peter
KIMBROUGH, Moses
KIMSEY, Benjamin Sr.
    Benjamin Jr.
    James
    Littleberry
    Solomon
    Thomas
KINCHELOE, Joseph
KING, Aaron
    James
    John
    Samuel
KINGSBURY, Jeremiah
KINGSBERRY
KINNEY, Thomas
KIRKPATRICK, Thomas
KIVITT, John
KNOUSE, Catherine
    Henry Sr.
    Henry Jr.
KUYKENDOLL, see
  KEYKINDOLL

LACEY, Stephen
LAKEY, Jeremiah
    Joshua
LAMBERT, William
LAMME, Joshua
    Thomas
    William*
LAND Joskun
(LAUD?)
LANE, Hardage
    Joshua
    Mordecai
LANTER, Asa*
    Richard W.
    Thomas
LAUD Joskun
(LAND?)
LAWLESS, Benjamin
    Byrd
    Maston
LAWREY, John J. (Jr.?)
LAWSON, James

47

LAY, Daniel
    James H.
LEACH, John
LEE, Joel
    Jonathan
    Richard
    William
    William Sr.* (sic)
LEGETT,
  LIGGET   James
          Joseph
          Thomas
          William
LEONARD, Abiel
LEWIS, Henry
LIGGET, see LEGETT
LIGHTFOOT, Henry
       Henry T.
LIKLETTER, Henry
 LICHLETER
LILES, John M
LINVILLE, James*
      William
LISLE, John*
LITERAL, Charles
      John
      Joseph
LIVELY, Benjamin
LOCKE, John
LOE, James
   John
   Thomas
LOGAN, William
LOGSTON, John
     Joseph
LONG, Daniel
   Gabriel
   Reuben
   William
LOVE, David
   John
LOWREY, see LAWREY
LYNCH, Isaac
    Solomon
    William

McBRIDE, Allen
    James
    Thomas
McCAFFERTY, Catherine
  Hugh (taxed double)
     Thomas*
McCLURE see McLURE
McCORD, Adam T.
McCORKLE, Alexander
    (cont.)

48

McCORKLE, John*
 cont.   Lydia
      Robert
      Samuel
McCORMACK, James
McCOUN, John
McCRARY, Benjamin
 McCRAIRY Elijah
       Elisha
McCULLEY, John
 McCULLOH William
McDANIEL, Elisha
     Isaac
     Peter
McDONALD, Isaac
     Peter
McDOWELL, John
McGAVOCK, Robert
McGEE, John
   Robert
McGIRK, Andrew S.
   George
   John W.
McGRUE, Charles
McKINNEY, Abraham
McKINZIE, Daniel)
    William ⌋
 together 1822,
 separate 1823
McLAIN, Ephraim
 McCLAIN, Ewing
 McLEAN Jonathan
 Ephraim adm David 1822
 Ewin adm David 1823
McLURE, Samuel
 McCLURE
McMILLAN, Alexander
 McMILLAN William
McMUN, James
McNEES, Samuel C.
 Madrid in name of Boles
McPRICE, Samuel C.
McQUEEN, Edward
McSPADE, Moses

MADDOX, Joseph
 MADOX Samuel
MAGNER, Jeremiah
MAHAN, James
   Peyton M.
MANCHESTER, David
MANNIS, Thomas
MANSFIELD, Nicholas

MARCH, Roudolph
MARKLAND, Levi
MARLEY, Abel*
  (Abbott?)
MARR, John
MARSHALL, Bailey
 also agt for Lindsey
    John
    John T.
    Lindsey P.
    Richard
MARTIN, David G.
   John
   Joseph (two)
   Neeley
   Orsin*
MASON, James Sr.
   James Jr.
   Thomas
   William
MASTERS, James
MATHEWS, John
 also Madrid loc. by
  Theo. Hunt
   Lazarus
MATNEY, Broadwaters
MAUPIN, Cornelius
 MOPPIN Dabney
   William
MAXEY, Boaz
MAYBERRY, John

MEAD, Davis
MEALS, John
MEANS, James
   John
   Robert
   William B.
MERRIT, Samuel*
MILLER, Catherine
   Henry
   John
   Richard
   Thomas
   William
MIMCUS, John
MINNIS, John
   Thomas
MINOR, George H.
MITCHELL, James
    Richard
MIZE, Thomas
MIZEL, James
MOBLEY, James
   John
   William (two)

MONROE, Joseph J.
    William W.
MONTGOMERY, David
      James (W.)
      John (two)
      Joseph
      William
MOORE, Elisha
    John (two)
    Levi
    Robert
MORGAN, John
    Joseph
    Joseph Jr.
MORIN, James
    Jane
    John
    Sarah
James adm John 1822
MORLER, Joseph
MORRIS, Hammond
    Harmon
    Jane
    John P.
    Nathaniel
    Robert W.
    Shadrach
    Thomas
    Wildon
MORRISON, James H.
Jesse taxed double 1822
James & Jessee together '23
MORROW, William
MOSS, James T.
    John T. (?)
MOWREL, Daniel
MULHALL, John
MULLINS, David
    Joshua
    Susannah
    William
MUNROE, Daniel Sr.
    Daniel Jr.*
MUNSEL, Chauncey*
    William M.
MURPHY, Jeremiah
    Jesse W.
    Neil
MURRY, Adam
    William H.
MUSICK, Josiah
MYERS,
MYRES James
    John
    William

MYRTLE, Johnson W.
    Reuben*

NANSON, John
NASH, Ira P.
NELSON, Drury
NEWCOMB, Charles
    Lance
    William
NEWTON, Lewis
    Joseph
    William
NICHOLS,
NICKOLS Jesse
    John
NOBBS, James
NOBLE, James
NOX, George Jr.
NULEY, Clemens

ODELL,
ODLE James
    Jeremiah
    John
O'NEIL,
O'NEAL Thomas
ORR, Patrick
OVERTON, Aaron
    Jesse
OWENBY, Powell S.
OWENS,
OWEN Glen }two
    Glenn
    Isaac
    Ignatius
    Nicholas
    Owen
    Thomas
OWINGS, Nathaniel

PADGET,
PAGET William
PAGE, James
    John Sr.
    John Jr.
PALMETARY, Daniel
  under 21 in 1824
      James Sr.
      James Jr.
PARKER, Thomas B.*
PARKES, Hutchings
PARKS, Johiel
    Willis
PARRISH, John G.
PARTIN, James
    Martin
    Thomas
  under age 1823-24

PARTIN,
PARTON William
cont.
PATTERSON, Archibald
    Jesse
    John
    Joseph
    Thomas
PATTON, John S.
    Nathaniel
    Robert
    Thomas W.
    Wilson
Thomas and Joseph
  together 1823
Estate of John G.'24
PATRICK, Garrison
    Luke
    William
PAYNE, Robert
  also Madrid loc. to
  Duppron and to
  Godair
PEARSON, Alonzo
PEAVLY,
PEEBLY James
PEEBLES, James
    Samuel
PEELER, David
    John
PENDLETON, James
    Mace
    William
PEOPLES, Robert
PEPPER,
PEPPERS Amelia
    Nelson*
    Samuel
    William
PERRY, James
    Thomas*
    William*
PERSEVILLE, Robert
      William*
PEYTON, John C.
PHARIS, James
    Kesiah
    Lewis
    William
also see FARRIS
PHILIPS, James
PIPES, George
    James Sr.
    James Jr.
    Pleasant*
    Silvalus*

49

POLKE, POKE, Andrew
  POAKE
POOL, Samuel
PORTER, Hezekiah*
POTTER, Wilson
POWELL, Grief
PREBLER, Samuel
PREWITT, David
     Joel
     John
     Moss
     Price
  also Price as adm of
    John Thomson
  also Prewitt & Foley
PRICE, Richard
PRINCE, John
PROPHET, David
     James
PURSINGER, Adam
  PERSINGER Rachel

RAGIN, William
RAINEY, James
RAINS, Henry
RAMEY, James
  RAMSEY
RATLIFF, James
RATHBONE, Edmund B.
RAWLINS, Jane
     John
  Jane adm John decd
     Owen
RAY, Benjamin B.
    James (two)
READ, William J.
  REDD
RECTOR, Daniel*
     Enoch*
     Nimrod
     Thomas
REDDICK, Anne
     James
     James K.
  "says he is under 21"
REDMAN, William
REED, Andrew
     Hiram
     James
     John
     William J.
     William
REILY, Henry
REEVES, Benjamin H.
REMLEY, Adam
     John

RENISON, John (two)
RENSHAW, Absolem
REYNOLD, George
  REYNOLDS Robert
     William
RICE, Jeremiah
     Oliver
RICHARDSON, James
     William
RICHISON, James
  refused to give in his
  list, double taxed
RIDGEWAY, Elijah
     Thomas
RIGGS, Daniel
RIGHT, John*
     Townsend
RINGO, Cornelius
     John *
     Peter
     Robert
     Samuel Sr.
RITCHIE, William
ROBB, Michael
ROBERT, Aaron
ROBERTS Isham
     James
     James W.
     Joel*
     Michael
     Michael*
     Nicholas
     Westly
     William
ROBERTSON, Garrard
  ROBINSON James
ROGERS, Ebenezer

ROLLINS, Boswell
    James D.
    John
    John D.
    Owen
    Thomas
  John gdn heirs of
  John Rawlings decd.
ROLLS, Hardy D.
ROOKER, John
ROPER, Jesse*
ROSE, Cary H.*
    Thoret
  "came in since Jan. 1st
       1824"
ROSS, George P.
(cont.)

ROSS, John Sr.
  cont. John Jr.
     John
ROSSON, Jeremiah*
ROUSHENBERGER, Jose
RUCKER, Henry T.
     Thornton
     William E.
RUNION, Isaac
RYLAND, John F.
  also agt S. Grund

SAILES, Elias
  SALE
SAILING, George
  SALING Henry
     John
     Peter
SAMUEL(S), Giles M.
     Presley*
SANDFORD, John D.
SAVAGE, Daniel
SCOGGINS, Isaac*
SCONCE, Robert
SCOTT, Davis
     James*
     Lewis
     Richard
     Wilcome
     William
SCOTTEN, Peter
SCURLOCK, Terry (?)
SCUTCHFIELD or
  SCRUTCHFIELD, Henry
  "of Huricane"
SEARS, Daniel
     John
     Joseph
SEBREE, Uriah
SETTLE, Martin
SEVIER, Henry C.
SEXTON, Thomas
     William
SEYBERT, John
  SIBERT William
SHADEN, James
SHANKS, Robert*
SHARROW, Joseph
SHATTUCK, Hiram
SHAW, John
  also adm Joel Shaw
SHEPHERD, Beverly
     Humphrey
     James
     Jonah
     Samuel

SHIELDS, Hugh
    Francis
    James
    Thomas
SHIFLET, Hasting
SHIPP, Fielding
    John
SHIVERS, Stephen
    Thomas
SHOCKLEY, Isam
    Josiah*
SHOEMAKER, George
    John* 1823
      Joseph
      Philip
      Rufus
      William
SHORN, Joseph
SHORT, John
    William O.*
    Zachariah M.*
SIBERT, John*
    William
see also SEYBERT
SIDEBOTTOM, Joseph
SIGHTS, Isaac
SILVEY,
SYLVA Alexander
    Gabriel
    John
SIMES, Nicholas
SIMMONS, Charles
    David M.S.
    Thomas
SIMONS, David
    Edward
    Matthew F.
    Thomas
SIMPSON, James
    Joseph
    Thomas
    William
SIMS, Mary (Polly)
    Nathaniel
    James
SINTON, Thomas
    William
SKELTON, Isaac
SKIDMORE, Joseph
    Samuel
SLITAM, John
SMART, Denton
    James D.
    John
SMITH, Andrew
    (cont.)

SMITH, Dennison (?)
cont.   Derrison (?)
    Dickerson*
    Henry (two)
    Hopey (widow)
    Ira
    James H.
    John
    Joseph (D.)
    Mashack
    Samuel
    Spencer
    Thomas (A.)
    William
    William (S) (H*) (L)
SMOOT, John
SNEED, John
SNELL, William
SNODDY, James
    John
    Joseph W.
SOJOURNER, Lewis
SPENCE, Anne
SPENCER, James
    Nancy
SPURGIN, John
STANDEFORD, Ruth
STANFORD   Shelton
    (or Skelton)
STANLEY, Harris
    Robert
    Thomas
  Minard or Winard
STEELE, David
STEEPLETON, George
    Harrison
STEMMON, Stephen
STEP, Abijah
STEPP Benjamin
    James
    John
STEPHENS, John*
STEVENS Joseph
STEPHENSON, Agnes
  (not assessed in 1822)
    Elizabeth
    Hugh
    Joseph
STERNS, Elam
STEWART, John
STONE, David
    Hardeman*
    Jereby
STORRS, Augustus
STORY, Thomas

STOUGHTON,
STAUNTON John
(STANTON?) John*
STREET, Samuel
    William
STUART, James D.
  also see STEWART
SUART, John
    William
SULLENS, William*
SUTTON, Rowland
SWAEZER, Daniel
    David*
SWANSON, Francis
  taxed double
SWAT (SMAT?), James D.
SWEARINGEN, John R.*
    Joseph
    Martha
    Nicholas
    Obed
    Samuel
    William
SWITZLER, John
    Lewis
    Michael
SWOPE, Charles

TATE, Allen
    Stephen
TAYLOR, Levi
    William
TEETER, George P.
    Samuel
TEMPLE, George
    Margaret
TEVIS, Snowden
THEVEAT, Thomas
THOMAS, Fleming
    John M.
THOMPSON, Ann
    Asa
    Elmore
    Ephraim
    Henry
    John
    John decd 1824
    Joseph*
    Nero M.
    Philip W.
    Wallace
THORNTON, John
    Peter
THORP, Dodson*
    Dodson H.*
    (both same year)

THORP,
cont.
    Jackson
    Josiah
    Owen*
    Squire
    Thomas
    William
THRASHER, Robert
THWEATT, John
TILTON, John J.*
TINDELL, Obediah Sr.
        Obediah Jr.
TITUS, John
TODD, Asa
     Coy
     Davis
  Davis agt for Levi
     David
     Elisha (two)
     Griffin
     Jesse
     Joseph
     Thomas
     William
TOMPKINS, George ++
TOOLEY, Charles P.
TOULSON,
 TOLSON John
         Thomas
         William
TOMLIN, John   ++
TRAMEL,
TRAMMELL Fields
          Jarrett
          Philip
TRIGG, Christopher*
      Stephen
      Stephen Jr.*
TURNER, Anne
       David
       Edward
       Ephraim
       James
       James Jr.
       Lynch
       Philip
       Talton
       Thomas
     Philip adm. P. Owens
TUTTLE, Miller
TYRE, Frederick
      Thomas*

VANHORN, John
        Simeon*
VAUGHN, Thomas
52

VICKRY, Abner
VILEY, John

WAID, John
WALDEN, Austin F.
 WELDON
WALKER, Ellis
        Federal
John* (two, same year)
        John
        Johnson
 heirs of Jonathan C.
WALLACE, John B.*
         John S.
         Samuel
WAMACK, William
WANTON, James
WARBOURN, Henry
WARD, John
      William
  Ward & Parker
WARDEN, Elijah
        Elisha
        John
        Peggy
   Sinclair, under 21
WARE, Elias N.
WARMATT,
          John
 WARMOUTH
WARREN, David
        Edward V.
    Umphrey and
        Humphrey
         William (B.)
WASH, Carr
      Z. ?
WASSERMAN, Jacob
WASSON, John
        Joseph
        Reuben
        Thomas
WATKINS, Elisha
WAYSMAN, Jacob
WEATHERFORD, Benjamin H.
            David
WEATHERS, James
WEBB, Joseph (S.)
      Thomas
WEEDEN, Benjamin Sr.
        Benjamin Sr.
   Caleb and Henry, joint
      taxed double
WELCH,
 WELSH James
        John*

WELDON, see WALDON
WEST, Samuel
WETMORE, Alphonso
WHARTON,
 WHORTON Samuel
WHITE, David (two)
       Crenshaw
       John (R.)
       Randolph
       Richard
       Robert
       Thomas K.
       William
WHITING, Jason
    joint with
        Benoni Wills
WHITLOCK, Francis
          Frances
WHITNEY, Aaron
         Joseph
         Wade H.
         Waid
WHITTON, Elijag
WIGGINS, William
WIGINTON, Henry*
          John
WILCOXSON, David
           Isaac (two)
           John*
    William W. under 21
WILDS, John
       Robert
WILHITE, John
        William
WILKERSON,
 WILKINSON Antony P.
            Charles S.
            John
WILLIAMS, Alfred
          Benjamin
   Buel* or Ruel* (L.)
          Colden
          Edward
          Hiram
          James (two)
          John
          John*
          Otho R.
          Parks
          Thomas
          Uriah
          William
WILLIS, Anderson
WILLOUGHBY,
 WILIBY   James
           Solomon
           Vincent

WILLS, Benoni C.
  (with Jason Whiting)
  John
WILODY, Solomon
  Vincent
WILSON, Bluford*
  Edward
  Elizabeth
  Ezekiel
  George
  John
  John* and John* same year
  Pleasant
  Robert*
  William
  Ezekiel for James Jones
  Pleasant adm. J. Cooley
WINBURN, Henry
  Jesse
WINN, George J.
  James
  John
  Thomas
  William

WISDOM, Elijah
  Joseph
  Lewis
  Nancy
WISE, Henry
WITT, Elisha B.
  Littleberry
  Nelson
  William
WOLFSCALE, John
WOLKSKILL, Joseph
WOOD,
WOODS Aaron
  Adam C. (two)
  Archibald
  Benjamin F.
  David
  Henry M.
  John K.
  Michael
  Patrick
  Peter
  Nancy
  Stephen
  William (two)

WOODARD, James
WOODRUFF, William B.
WORKMAN, David*
WOUTE(?), Joseph*
WREN, Shadrach
WRIGHT, David
  Derrell
  (Durlan?)
  Joseph (A.)
  Townsen F.
  also see RIGHT

YANCY, Laten
  Phebe
  Stephen
YATES, George
  James
  John
  Samuel
YORK, James
YOUNT, David
  George

....

Howard, one of the oldest counties, was formed from the original districts of St. Charles and St. Louis in 1816. It is the parent county of Randolph, Cass, Boone, Cooper, Macon, Chariton, Saline, Pettis, Adair, Ray, Linn, Clay, DeKalb, Daviess, Gentry, Livingston, Carroll, Grundy, Harrison, Lafayette, Johnson, Mercer, Cole, Moniteau, Morgan, Putnam, Henry, Schuyler, Jackson, Bates, and Worth counties; in other words, at the early period it covered an enormous area of central Missouri, north to the present Iowa line in some cases, west to the present limit of the state.

Many of the names which appeared in the first year of the Howard County lists (1822) are not found there the succeeding year. It seems likely that these names represent early residents of counties formed from Howard, possibly Lafayette and Saline, for whom no early tax lists are known to exist.

The Howard County courthouse burned in the late 1880's but there is no known loss of records. There is also an excellent early newspaper for this area, the Missouri Intelligencer, which began publication in 1819.

AILEBURY, Manons	stray
Moniteau Twp.	
AIMWORTH, John	stray
Boone's Lick Twp.	
ALEXANDER, John	estate
AMICK, Philip	stray
ARNOLD, Grace	estate
ATTEBURY, Mrs. Mary	notice
AUSTIN, Joseph	stray
Moniteau Twp.	
AVERETT, Howard	notice
William sale of a horse	
BABBITT, Obadiah	estate
BAKER, James	stray
BARNES, Amos	stray
Moniteau Twp.	
Daniel	stray
Bonne Femme Twp.	
Elisha	estate
Mary	"
Tarlton	"
BASS, Lawrence	notice
BAUM, Jacob	notice
BEATTY, James	stray
Chariton Twp.	
Joseph	notice
BEST, Humphrey	stray
Chariton Twp.	
BIRD, Kitty	estate
BLASENGAM, Turner	stray
Franklin Twp.	
BLUBOUGH, Benjamin	stray
Franklin Twp.	
BROWN, Hudson	estate
John R.	notice
BROWNING, Elijah G.	notice
BUCHANAN, James F.	stray
Bonne Femme Twp.	
BUIE, Daniel	notice
BURKELOW, Samuel V.	stray
BURLET, John Cedar Twp.	stray
BYRNE, Morgan	notice
CAMPBELL, Robert Clark	notice
CARROLL, Charles	stray
CARSON, Mrs. Rebecca	notice
CHAPMAN, George	J.P.
Franklin Twp.	
CHRISTY, Edmund T.	estate
CLARK, Isaac	stray
Reuben	"
Grand River Twp.	

COLIER, David runaway apprentice	
COLLEN, John	notice
COLTRELL, Gilbert	stray
CORUM, Nancy	estate
COURTI, John	stray
COTE, Henry B. Jr.	notice
COX, Write	notice
CRISSWELL, William	stray
Moniteau Twp.	
CROWLEY, William	stray
Boone's Lick Twp.	
CUNNINGHAM, James	J. P.
DALE, John	estate
DALES Robert Moniteau Twp.	stray
DONALDSON, Robert "	"
DOOLEN, James Franklin Twp	stray
DUNN, Henry	stray
Samuel	"
ELLINGTON, Alexander M.	notice
EWING, Finis	notice
FERGUSON, Nancy	estate
FOSTER, John T.	clerk
FONTAINE, Peter	stray
Bonne Femme Twp.	
FORBES, Samuel	stray
FOWLER, Robert Y.	notice
FOX, Ezra	stray
Prairie Twp. near the headwaters	
of the Salt River	
FREEMAN, Burrell B.	stray
Bonne Femme Twp.	
FRISTOE, Markham	estate
GAGE, Reuben Chariton Twp.	stray
GOFORTH, James	stray
Roche Perce Twp. (?)	
GOOCH, B. lost land certificate	
GORDON, David	notice
Sugar Tree Bottoms	
GRAGG, Benjamin	estate
Henry	"
Samuel	"
GRAYUM, John Moniteau Twp.	stray
GROGEN, John	estate
GROOM, Abraham	notice
HANCOCK, Adam Boone's Lick Twp stray	
HANKS, George	notice
R. C.	"
HARDIN, Charles runaway apprentice	

HARRIS, Higgason	stray	MURRAY, Eleanor	estate
Moniteau Twp.		Urial	"
HARRISON, Peter W.	attorney	Reuben	"
HARRYMAN, Edward Cedar Twp.	stray		
HERN, Clifton Moniteau Twp	stray	NEWBROUGH, Joshua	attorney
HIATT, James	notice	NIELD, Elias	estate
HICKS, Absalom	estate		
Elizabeth	"	OWENS, Philip	estate
Young E.	"		
HILL, Claburn A.	estate	PARKER, Lemnon	lawsuit
HIXON, William	stray	PHILIP, John G.	estate
Boone's Lick Twp.		Thomas	lawsuit
HOLEMAN, Joseph	stray	POTTER, Joshua Chariton Twp.	stray
Bonne Femme Twp.		PRINE, William "	"
HOLLANDSWORTH, Thomas G.	notice	PROCTOR, Micajah	estate
HOLLIDAY, George	estate	PULLIAM, Broadhurst	stray
HOOZER, Christian	stray	Franklin Twp.	
Grand River Twp.			
HUBBARD, Elizabeth	estate	RANDALS, Benjamin	estate
Jabez	"	Dosia	"
		REDDICK, John	estate
JACKSON, Minerva	notice	RIDGEWAY, William	notice
JAMES, Moses	bankrupt	RISK, Charlotte Chambers Ludlow	"
JAMESON, Harrison	stray	ROBERSON, Charley	stray
Bonne Femme Twp.		ROBERTS, Edward	stray
JONES, Christopher	stray	Boone's Lick Twp.	
Cedar Twp.		Thomas	notice
		ROSS, James Boone'sLick Twp.	stray
KEENEY, Thomas	stray	RYAN, James Chariton Twp.	stray
KELLY, Katherine	estate		
KILGORE, Isham	stray	SCUDDER, John W.	notice
Moniteau Twp.		SHAW, Amandian	estate
KINCHELOE, William	notice	Archibald	"
KINKADE, John	notice	Baker U.	"
		David	"
LAUGHLIN, Charles	stray	Delila	"
Roche Perce Twp.		Elizabeth	"
LIENTZ, William	notice	James	"
LUCAS, Alexander	lost steers	Jefferson	"
near Cooper's Fort		Kitty	"
LUDLOW, J. C.	notice	Louisa	"
town of Madison		Lovicy	"
		Maria	"
McPHERSON, Charles	estate	Sadoni B.	"
Polly	"	Samuel	"
McQUITTY, Andrew	stray	William	"
David	"	SHIPMAN, Moses Chariton Twp.	stray
Moniteau Twp.		SISK, Barnett	stray
		William Richmond Twp.	"
MILLER, James D.	estate	SMALL, Katherine	notice
also stray, Roche Perce Twp.		Mary	estate
Samuel	notice	SMITH, Cornelius	stray
MINTER, Joseph	stray	Franklin Twp.	
Moniteau Twp.		SNEDECOR, Isaac C.	stray
MOORE, Nathaniel	stray	Roche Perce Twp.	
MULLINS, Elizabeth	stray	STANHOPE, William	notice

STEPHENSON, Marcus	estate		WARREN, Martin	stray
STICE, Peter Bonne Femme Twp. stray			Boone's Lick Twp.	
STOUT, Daniel M.	banker		WARSON, Rebecca	notice
SULLENS, Edward W.	estate		Reuben	"
			WASHINGTON, Caldwell	notice
TANNER, James	lawsuit		James G.	"
TAYLOR, James	stray		WATKEN, Thomas	estate
Boone's Lick Twp.			WELCH, William	estate
TAYLOR, Jonathan	notice		WESTLAKE, Thomas	estate
TEFFT, John	estate		WHITFIELD, Joseph	stray
TENNILLE, George	stray		Franklin Twp.	
TILLERY, Eppe Moniteau Twp. stray			WHITTENBURG, John	notice
TURNER, Benjamin	notice		WILHITE, James	estate
TUTTLE, Thomas S.	stray		WILHOITE Sampson	"
Cedar Twp.			WISEMAN, James Cedar Twp.	stray
TWIGG, Henry Moniteau Twp. stray			WOODWARD, Chesley	stray
			Moniteau Twp.	
VAUGHN, Enos Moniteau Twp. stray			WRIGHT, Sampson	stray
WARE, John	notice		ZUMWALT, Jacob Cedar Twp.	stray

. . . .

ADDENDA: JEANS, Elizabeth   notice (Mo. Intelligencer)

$200 Reward.

RANAWAY from the subscribers on the night of the 26th instant, a negro man named PETER, (commonly calls himself Peter Johnson,) of black complexion, about thirty years old, about five feet 9 or 10 inches high, stout made and clumsy in his motions; pretends to be religious and can read a little. Has on one of his arms, a deep scar occasioned by a burn; when closely interrogated, stammers very much. His clothing was a dark brown cloth coat and pantaloons with gilt buttons, scarlet cassimere vest; shoes nearly new, the soals of which are fastened on with pegs Also a negro woman named ELLEN, about twenty seven years old, black complexion, of good size and well formed, answers very pleasantly when spoken to. Had a considerable quantity of clothing, particularly of fine articles. Also, a negro woman named SILVIA, of black complexion, about twenty-five years old, of good size, stout made, and pleasant countenance; took with her many articles of clothing, particularly fine articles. Also a negro boy, black complexion, about ten years old, named MARTIN; lisps much when speaking; had on a plain linsey round about and flesh coloured cassimere pantaloons. They will probably direct their course for the state of Illinois.

The above reward will be given for the four if taken any where out of the territory and confined in jail so that we can get them again, or fifty dollars for each. If taken in the territory and confined as aforesaid, one hun'red dollars for the four or twenty-five dollars for each.

Justus Post.
Saml. B. Sydno.

Bonhomme, St. Louis county,
29th march,   77

ALEXANDER, Matthew	estate
William	stray
Plattin Twp.	
ANDREWS, Joseph	stray
Herculaneum Twp.	
BATES, William "	stray
BISSELL, Franklin	stray
Joachim Twp.	
BOND (BOYD?), Austin	stray
Sulphur Springs	
BOYD, L. B.	stray
Big River Twp.	
BORING, J. Joachim Twp.	stray
BRINLEY, Jacob	stray
Little Rock Creek	
Mathias	estate
BURGISS, W. Joachim Twp.	stray
BUTLER, Edward Plattin Twp.	stray
BYRD, Benjamin "	"
BYRNS, Samuel Merrimac Twp.	stray
CLAY, Thomas	stray
Waters of Joachim	
CONNOR, John H. Herculaneum	stray
COUCH, Leonard	stray
DEAN, Thomas Plattin Twp.	stray
DEWITT, James "	"
DONALD, James "	"
DOWLIN, James	estate
FINLEY, John	estate
FOSTER, James	stray
Waters of Joachim	
GAY, Josiah Plattin Twp.	stray
GOOCH, Drewry "	"
GRAHAM, Samuel	stray
HAMMOND, G. Joachim Twp.	J.P.
HANSELL, B.	J.P.
HARTZ, William M.	stray
Big River Twp.	
HELDERBRAND, Jonathan "	"
HENDRICK, H.	notice
HERRINGTON, Joshua	stray
William	"
Joachim Twp	
HOGAN, William Big River Twp.	stray
JOHNSTON, B. Sr.	estate
B. Jr.	stray
Little Rock Creek	
Thomas Merrimac Twp.	stray

KENDALL, Jonathan Sulphur Spgs.	stray
KINDS, Joseph Plattin Twp.	stray
LEWIS, Samuel Woodson	stray
McCORMACK, James	stray
Peter Plattin Twp.	J.P.
McCULLOUGH, James	estate
McDONALD, William Herculaneum	notice
McMILLEN, William	estate
McMULLIN, Samuel Plattin Twp.	stray
MASSEY, John H.	stray
METCALF, Nancy	notice
Washington	"
MOON, Elisha	stray
Joseph Plattin Twp.	"
MOORE, Z. Sulphur Springs	stray
MOTES, Henry Herculaneum	"
MURPHEY, Joseph Merrimac Twp.	"
NASH, John Joachim Twp.	stray
NOWLAND, John	notice
OGLE, Thomas Joachim Twp.	stray
QUICK, Benjamin	estate
RANKIN, James "Big River"	stray
SMITH, James Joachim Twp.	stray
STAPLES, William Plattin Twp.	"
STODDARD, John "Waters of Joachim"	"
STURGIS, John S.	estate
THOMAS, Claiborne	notice
TIMBERLAKE, Samuel Herculaneum	"
VAN SANT, Abner	miller
WARNER, J. Joachim Twp.	stray
WHITEHEAD, Robert Plattin Twp.	stray
WICKERHAM, William "Big River"	"
WILKINS, Timothy N.	estate
WILSON, G. E. Herculaneum Twp.	stray
Jacob	"
John Merrimac Twp.	"
WISE (WIRE?), David	stray
Herculaneum	
WOODSON, Samuel "Big River"	stray

· · · · · · · · · · · · · · · · · · · ·

Jefferson County was formed from
St. Louis and Ste. Genevieve in
December 1818. Part of this county
was taken to form St. Francois in
1821.

LAFAYETTE-LILLARD: 1821 DELINQUENTS AND MISCELLANEOUS LEGAL TAXES
From the State Archives of Missouri

AULL, James

BIRD, John

BOUNDS, James

BRADLEY, Edward

CAMPBELL, H.

CASTLES, Robert

CATRON, Solomon

CHINNETH, Gabriel

COCKRIL, James

COLEMAN, A.

COX, Joseph
     Thomas

DOWNIE, William H.
DOWNEY

DUMASTER, Elijah

DUNBAR, Alexander

ELY, Michael

ERWIN, J.

EWING, Young

FLETCHER, James

FRISTOE, Markham

GRAHAM, Abner

HOPPER, Thomas

HORN, William

INGRAM, John

JONES, John D.

LIGHTNER, Abia L.
     Adam

LILLARD, James

McCAFFERTY, Green

McCLELLAND, Abraham

MILLER, W. A.

NELSON, J.

OWEN, Abel

REES, Amos

RENICK, Henry
     Robert
     R. A.

RICHARD, R.

RIGGS, James
     R.

RILEY, Amos

ROSS, J.

ROTHWELL, James

SALADY, John

SCOTT, Richard

SENSEBOY, Thomas

SIMMONS, William F.

SMITH, James

STOKELEY, Thomas

STOTHART, Scott

THARP, Dodson

THOMAS, John D.
     John M.

WARDER,

WARDEN John
(WARREN?)

WESTON, Samuel

=====

. . . .

SECONDARY LIST FROM THE MISSOURI INTELLIGENCER, 1819-1826

CARY, Armenius	stray		HICKLIN,		
Lexington Twp.			HECKLIN James		estate
CATREN, Christopher	estate		John		"
Jacob	"		Jonathan		"
CLEMENSON, John	notice				
CRISP, Redden	stray		LINCH, Elbert		stray
Sni-a-Bar Twp.			Lexington Twp.		
			LIGHTNER, Lydia		notice
EDMUNDSEN, Leah	estate				
Richard	"		RENICK, Burton L.		stray
EWING, Chatham Sr.	stray		SNOWDEN, Lovel		notice
			WHITE, Benjamin		stray
GALBRAITH, William H.	stray		WHITSETT, James Lexington Twp.		"

. . . .

Lafayette County, formed from Cooper in 1820, was originally
called Lillard. The name was changed late in 1825. It is the
parent county of Henry, Jackson, Johnson, and by extension of
Bates, Cass, St. Clair, as well as parts of Cedar, Benton, and
Vernon.

LINCOLN COUNTY: DELINQUENTS 1819 (from the Missouri Republican),
ASSESSOR's LIST FOR 1821 (from the 1878 Lincoln County Atlas) AND MIS-
CELLANEOUS LEGAL TAXES FROM THE STATE ARCHIVES OF MISSOURI

Note: the Atlas listing gives townships, where known, and these are indicated
by the abbreviations B (Bedford) H (Hurricane) M (Monroe) and U (Union)

ABBOTT, Reuben H
ALLEN, Benjamin H
      Seth   B
ALLISON, Sylvanus
ARMSTRONG, John B
          Thomas B
AVERY, Frederick B

BAILEY, David   M
       Samuel   M
BARKER, John   B
       Wilson   B
BARNETT, Hugh   U
        Joseph
BARTON, Elijah
        Benjamin H
        Thomas   H
BEATTY, William
BECK, Jeremiah   B
BELL, John   B
BLACK, John   B
BLANTON, Benjamin   B
        Thompson   B
BLOCK, Emanuel
BOYD, David   B
BROADWATER
  or BROADMAKER Charles
BROWN, Gabriel   B
       Levi   B
       William Sr. B
       William Jr. B
BRUNK, John   B
BURNES, James   H
        William H

CALLAWAY, Zachariah M
CANNON, James
        John   B
        Samuel   B
        William B
CANTRIEL, James   U
          John   U
CHAMBERS, James   B
CHANDLER, John
CLARK, Christopher B
COLES, Edward
COLLARD, Elijah   B
         James   B
COLLIER, Lambert B

COOSE, Adam   U
COPES, Thomas P.
COTTLE, Almond   M
        Andrew   B
        Benjamin B
        Ira   M
        Isaac   B
        Jonathan H
        Joseph   B
        Lee F.T. B
        Sherman   B
        Stephen   B
COX, John
     John   U
     Meredith U
CROCE, Benjamin   B
CUMMINS, Hugh

DAVIS, Samuel L. B
       Silas
DEVENS, Thomas
DIGGS, David   H
DOWNING, Andrew
         Ezekiel H
         James
         John N.
DRAPER, Daniel   U
DUNCAN, Cary K.   B
        James   B
        John S.   B
        William S. B
DUNNING, Ezekiel M

EARLY, James
EMORY, Walter
ERWIN, David   B
EUTON, Susannah
EZELL, John   H

FARNSWORTH, Terah B. B
FENTON, Richard U
FULLERTON, Rufus B

GALLOWAY, Charles   U
          James Sr. U
          James Jr. U
          John   H
          Peter Sr. H
          Peter Jr. H
          Samuel H
          William H

GALLOWAY, William N. U
GAMMON, Thomas   B
GEIGER, John   B
GIBSON, Guian   U
        James   U
        Samuel   U
GILBERT, Andrew
GILILLAND, John   U
           Matthias U
GLADNEY, Samuel   H
GREEN, E. P.
GRIFFITH, John
GROSHONG, Jacob B
          Jeremiah B
          Samuel   B
GUINN, George   B
        Thomas A. B
        William   B

HAMMOCK, Brice   U
         Martin   U
         William H
HAMMOND, Thomas   U
HARD, John
HARLEY, George
       James
       Martin
       William
HARRIS, William   U
HARRISON, Lovell
HENRY, Malcolm Sr. B
        Malcolm Jr. B
HIGHSMITH, Abijah M. M
           Benjamin
           William
HILL, Alexander
HINES, John
HOWDESHELL, Henry
           John   U
           Joseph U
HUDSON, Isaac   U
        John   U
        Thomas   U
HULL, John
HUNTER, John   B
        Joseph B

59

JAMESON, Allen   B
         George   U
         Robert Sr. U
         Robert Jr. U
JORDEN, J.G.

KELLER, David   B
KENNEDY, Abraham   B
          Armstrong B
KING, Joseph   B
KNOX, James Sr.   B
       James Jr.   B

LARD, David   M
LEWIS, James   U
        Samuel   U
LINDSEY, John   M
LOVE, Andrew
LOW, Jesse

McCORKLE, Lydia
McCOY, David
        Joseph   U
        William
McCRAINEY, Thomas
McFARLAN, David W. B
McLANE, William
McNAIR, Robert U

MANN, Thomas   B
MERIKLE, David   U
         Thomas   U
MILLER, Andrew
MILLSAP, Hiram   B
MORRIS, Jonathan D. B
MOORE, Quinten   U
        Thomas   U
        William   U
MYERS, Elijah   H

NOWELL, Reuben
NULL, John   B

OAKLEY, Cary

PADDOCK, James E.   M
PALMER, Bennett
PARKER, Cyrus
        Francis
PARKINSON, John   B
PATTERSON, Andrew
PECK, Otis   M
PEERS, V. I.
PERKINS, Elisha   B
         Jesse   B
PETTY, Isham
PILES, John   B
PLUMMER, Joseph
PORTER, David   U

POWERS, Philander B
PRESSLEY, David   B

RAINEY, Moses
RAMY, Nathan   B
RIFFLE, Thomas   M
RIGGS, Bethuel   B
        Jonathan   B
ROBBINS, Joshua N.
ROBINSON, Abial
          William H. B
ROSS, Shapley   B
       Mervin   B
       William O.
RUSSELL, Joseph   M

SAPP, John   H
SARGENT, Samuel
SCONCE, James   H
         Samuel   H
SEYMOUR, John M.   B
SHAW, James   U
       Samuel
SHRUM, John   B
        Nicholas   B
SIMONDS, Nathaniel
SIMPKINS, Jeremiah
SITTON, Guian   U
         John L.   H
         Jesse   H
         Joseph Sr U
         Joseph Jr U
         Lawrence B. U
         Philip   U
         William   U
SMILEY, Samuel   U
SMITH, Andrew
        George M.
        Samuel
SPAFFORD, Omri
SPILLMAN, Thomas
STANLEY, James   B
STEWART, Charles
STRONG, Return

TALBERT, William
TALBOT, John   B
TEAGUE, Peter
        Rollin
THORNHILL, Barnabas M
THURMAN, Isaac
         John   B
         Joseph
TRAIL, William   U
TURNBULL, James   M
TURNBAUGH, George H
           John

TURNER, Elias   B
        Miles   B
        Winslow Sr B
        Winslow Jr B

VAN BURKLON, Daniel H
(VAN BURKLEO?)
VESS, Jonathan

WAGGONER, John   B
WALKER, John
WALLACE, Severn
WARD, John   B
WELLS, Nicholas   U
        Stacy   U
        Thomas   U
WIATT, Edward   H
WILLIAMS, Alembe   B
          James   B
          John   B
          Levin   B
          Thomas   B
WILLIAMSON, Jacob
WILSON, David   H
         James
         John
         Josiah   U
WITHINGTON, Francis H
WOODS, James   M
        Kesiah
        Martin   M
        Minerva
        Zadock   B
WOOLFOLK, A. C.   M
           Allen   M
WRIGHT, Morgan   B

YATER, Conrad   B
        Peter   B

ZIMMERMAN, G. M.   B
            J. M. B

. . . .

Lincoln County was formed
from St. Charles in 1818.
No counties were formed
from it. . . . .

LINCOLN COUNTY: SECONDARY LIST

From the Republican and the Enquirer, St. Louis, and the Missourian,
St. Charles

ALLISON, Nancy	estate			
BRICE, D. Burrus	notice	SMEAD, Ezra	notice	
		SMITH, Henry	license	
DRAPER, David	stray	SUTTON, John L.	stray	
Bedford Twp.		Union Twp.		
HEARTNETT, John	stray	TANNER, Jacob	stray	
Union Twp.		Monroe Twp.		
KENRICK, Samuel	stray	TYLER, Nancy	notice	
Union Twp.		Rebecca	"	
McCLURE, Ellen	estate	WALLIN, Severn	stray	
McCOY, John	stray	(Wallace?) Union Twp.		
Bedford Twp.		WATSON, John	stray	
		Union Twp.		
MAYS, Oliver	stray			
Union Twp.		. . . .		
RAIL, William T.	stray			
Union Twp.				
ROBBINS, Pros K.	license			

. . . .

sentatives in Congress. The list contains other names of national reputation.
There were several revolutionary soldiers among the early settlers of this
county. Of these the names of Noah Rector, Isaac Hudson, John Chambers,
John Barco and Alembe Williams are known to the writer. Noah Rector died
near Millwood about 1840 at the age of one hundred and two years. Isaac
Hudson was born in North Carolina, and after the war lived in Washington
county, Georgia, until 1799; he then went to South Carolina, and in 1804 moved
to that part of Logan that is now included in Simpson county, Kentucky; in
June, 1819, he came with his wife and four sons, John, Thomas, William and
Charles, to this county and settled in what is now Nineveh township. He died
many years ago at an advanced age. He was a blacksmith and farmer and was
much respected for his strict honesty. John Chambers was born in 1740. In
1778 he enlisted in Capt. Alexander Cummins's company of the Fourteenth
Virginia regiment, and was in the battle of Monmouth. He died in Clark
township in 1844 or 1845. John Barco was born in 1744; enlisted May 24,
1777, in Camden county, North Carolina, as a drummer in Captain Dempsey

From the Atlas of 1878

Gregory's company of the Tenth North Carolina Infantry, Col. Shepherd com-
manding; was at Valley Forge and West Point; in 1779 was sent to Charles-
ton with his command and assigned to Gen Lincoln; surrendered with the other
forces to the British May 12, 1780, and put on board a prison ship where he
remained five months. A short time after exchange he was mustered out of
service at Richmond, Virginia. Alembe Williams was born in 1757; he enlisted from Guilford county, North Carolina, June 10, 1781, in Capt. Moore's
company of the First North Carolina Infantry, commanded by Major Armstrong.
He was afterwards in Capt. Michael Randolph's company, in Col. Henry Lee's
legion. He was present in several battles and at the storming of several forts.
He received his discharge from Gen. Nathaniel Green.
This county has had two State officers, Nathaniel Simon
. . . monds, of Troy, was State Treasu

ANTHONY, William Castor Twp.   stray

BENNETT, Joseph   Castor Twp.   stray
    Mme.   "   "

BURNES, Peter St. Michael's
               Twp.   stray

CLUBB, Anthony   estate
COOK, Col. Nathaniel   notice

DOLTON, John   Castor Twp.   stray

FARLAND, John M.   notice
FARRAR, John   estate

GARRETT, Westley   J.P.
         Liberty Twp.

GRIGGS, Thomas   stray

HERRICK, Ezekiel B.   notice
HUDDLESTON, Archibald   stray
    St. Michael's Twp.

JOHNSTON, Adam   stray
    St. Michael's Twp.

JONES, George   estate

KIMBREL, John   Castor Twp.   stray

McARTHUR, John   J.P.
    St. Michael's Twp.

McCABE, John   "   stray

MATTHEWS, John Jr. "   stray

MILLER, Jacob W.   notice
    Mary Ann   "
MOSELEY, Thomas Jr.   clerk
    St. Michael's Twp.

NIFONG, Jacob   J.P.
    St. Michael's Twp.

PETTIT, I.L.   "   stray

RINGER, Mathias P.   stray
ROBINSON, Jeremiah   notice

SHARP, Anthony Liberty Twp. stray
SHELL, Benjamin   estate
SIMS, Bardet   notice
SMITH, John   Liberty Twp.   stray
    Lawrence   estate
SOLIBILDES, Joseph   notice
SPIVA, Elisha Castor Twp.   stray
STEPHENSON, Elizabeth   notice
STOUT, Ephraim Liberty Twp. notice
SUTTON, John   "   "

TOMURE, Nicholas   stray
TUCKER, Henry Castor Twp. stray

UNDERWOOD, Henry   estate
      William   stray
    Castor Twp.

VAUGHN, John T.   stray
    St. Michael's Twp.

WILLIAMS, Elizabeth   notice
      William   "
WITENER, Henry   estate

. . . .

Madison County was formed from
Ste. Genevieve and Cape Girardeau
in December, 1818. Part of Madison
was taken to form Iron County in
February, 1857.

. . . .

Sheriff's List of Delinquents

IN Montgomery county, territory of Missouri, for territorial and county Taxes, for the year 1819.

In Cote Sans Dessein Township.

	TER.		CTY.	
	$	Cts.	$	Cts.
Sutton Ezra				25
Vanbibber Joseph				50
Wiggins Joseph	7	20		
Charette & Loutre Townships.				
Anderson Robert				25
Bennifield Samuel				50
Cantley James		7 1-2	1	18 3-4
Casleman John	4	4 1-2		56 1-4
Carver William				50
Griggs Leonard				50
Griggs Wiley				50
Gordon Jonathan		3		31 1-2
Harris William				31 1-4
House John				31 1-4
Holder Francis				50
Hobbs Joseph				31 1-4
Marshall Antoine				56 1-4
Moore Jeremiah				25
Moore Miniman				25
McKinzie John				50
Prichard Drury R.		67 1-2	1	31 1-4
Patton William		3	1	12 1-2
Stotts John	3			
Smith Thomas				87 1-2
Ward Joseph				50
Amounts,	11	5	11	87 1-2

I. S. Pitman, Sheriff.

Montgomery county, }
Nov 30, 1819.   }   46 1t*

AGA, AGEE, Matthew
ALFREY, Isaac
    James
ALLEN, Bethel
    Charles
    David
    Elias
    Leland
    Mary (Polly)
    Robert
    Thomas
ALEXANDER, Charles Lee
    Lee
AMMERMAN, Isaac
AMMONS, John L.
ANDERSON, James
    James D.
    Presley
ANTROBUS, James
APLIN, George
APLING (B'slick Road)
    William
ARMSTRONG, William
ARNOLD, Robert
ASKRIN, Dennis
ATON, Isaac
ATTERBURY, Israel

BABER, James
BACON, Sumner
BAILEY, Abraham*
BAINBRIDGE, Darius
BAKER, Esau
    Henry
    Jacob
    John
    Robert
    Samuel
    Sylvester
    Zebediah
BALDRIDGE, Melchian
BALLARD, Walter
BANE, David
BANO Daniel
BARIBO, Joseph
BARNES, Hosle
    James Sr.
    James Jr.
    John
BARRIAN, Jack
BASH, Ambrose
BAST, George

BATY, James
BEAVEN, Charles (two)
BEVINS Francis
    John
BENEFIELD, Samuel
BENNING, John W.
BEST, Isaac
    John
BETHEL, Alphonso
    Samuel
BLOICE, William*
  BLOYES
BOATRIGHT, Daniel*
BOON, Alfonso
    Chloe
    Daniel M.
    Jesse B.
    Samuel
BOONO, Jack
BONO
BOOTHE, George M.
BOUCHER, Amous
BOWEN, Thomas
BOWER, James*
    Joseph
BOWLER, Thomas
BOWMER, William
BRADFORD, George
BRAWDY, Joseph
BRIGGS, Thomas P.G.
BRIGHT, George
    Henry
BROOKS, Thomas
BROTHER, Benjamin
BROWN, Andrew
    Ezeriah*
    Gabriel
    Joseph
    Joshua G.
    Orus
    Susannah
    William (two)
BROWNING, Nathan
BRYAN, Betsy or
    Elizabeth widow
    David*
    Henry
    James
    John
    Morgan
    Willes
BRYANT, Michael

BURCH, William E.
BURGIT, David
BURGOT John Sr.
BURMAN, Lauck
BURNET, Cornelius
    Dabney
BURNS, Jeremiah
BURT, Henry
BUSH, Ambrose
BUTCHER, Benjamin
BUTLER, John

CAIL, COIL, Jacob
CALBERT, James
CALLAHAN, Beston
CALLAWAY, Flanders
    Joseph
    Joseph Jr.
    Larkin
    Thomas
CAMRON, John*
CANE, James
CAIN Jesse
    John
CANNADY, Guyon
    James
    Thomas
CANTLEY, James
CARLISLE, Israel J.
CARTER, Cyrenus
    John B.
    Larkin G.
CARTNER, John
CARVER, John
    William
CATEN, Jesse
CATON Jonas
    Noah
CATES, William Sr.
    William Jr.
CATTLEMAN, John
CHAMBERS, James
    Thomas
CHANDLER, George
    Isaac
    John
    William
CHAPEL, William
CHINWORTH, Gabriel*
CLANTON, Drury
    Henry

63

CLARK, Harold
    Isaac
CLAY, George
CLENDENNON, George W.
CLIFTON, Rossian
    (Bosman?)
CLOTHIER, Asa*
CLYCE, William
COATS, James
    William
    William Jr.
COBB, Adam
    Philip
    Samuel Sr.
COCHRAN, Andrew (two)
  (one shown as single,
    1824)
      David
    George
COIL, Jacob
COLE, Mark
COLGAN, Daniel
    Robert
COLLINS, Lafayette
    Simon
COMER, John
COOK, Burton
    Grove*
    Joel B.
    John*
COX, Cyrenus
    Jesse
CRAIG, David
    John
    Robert
CRAIGHEAD, Robert
CRAWFORD, John R.
CREECH, Everett
    George*
    John
    Limon
CRISWELL, Robert
    William
CROGHAN, William*
CROW, John
    Jonathan
    Joseph
    William
CULLOM, Tillman
CUNDIFF, James
    John
    Joseph
    Lewis
    Richard
    William

CURTIS, Larkin G.
CUSTNER, John

DANNIEL, Francis
DARNELL, William*
DARST, Jacob C.
DAVIS, James
    John
    John Jr.
    Robert
DAVIDSON, Abraham
      Alexander
DeHAIT, Lewis
DeMOSS, Howell
DeNOYER, Francis
DIGGS, Cole
DILLON, Walter
DOBBIN, James B.
DORRIS, Stephen C.
DOUGHERTY, Charles
      Charles Jr.
      Samuel
DOZIER, Thomas*
DUDEN, Godfrey
DUKE, Hugh
DULEY, Samuel
    Thomas
DUNNICA, John
    William H.
DUTTON, John H.

EASTES, James
EDMONDS, Samuel*
    Joseph
EDMONSON, Joseph
EDWARDS, Lewis
    Moses
ELLIS, Abraham
    Benjamin Sr.
    Benjamin Jr.
    Edward
    Isaac
    Jacob
    James Sr.
    James Jr.
    Moses
ELSTON, Jonathan
    William
ELTON, Thomas F.
EPLIN, George
ERWIN, Janet (?)
    Jared
    James
    John

ESTES, James
    John Sr.
    John Jr.
ESTILL, James
EVANS, George
    James
    Jesse
    John
EVERSMAN, Lewis
EWING, Patrick

FARIS, James
FARRIS John
FARMER, Jane (Jean)
FARRIER, Nathaniel
FARROW, Daniel*
FAULCONER, John M.
FAUNT, Andrew
FAYE, Charles
FERGUSON, James
      John (two)
      Joshua
      William
FINE, Abraham
    Levi
    Mary
    Widow of Levi
FITZHUGH, Richard
FLAUHERTY, Raphael
FOURD, Andrew
FOURT Francis
FORD, Edward
FOREMAN, Benjamin
    James
    William
FOSTER, Mark
FOYE, Antoine
    Nicholas
FRAME, John
FRAZIER, John
    William
FRIER, John
FRYER
FRUIT, Alexander
    Enoch
FULLER, Abner A.

GALASPA, Robert
GALBREATH, Torkle
GAMMON, Benjamin
GARMAN, Leonard
GARNER, Thruston
GAY, Richard
GEE, Albert
    John (cont.)

GEE, Robert
    Thomas
    William
GIBSON, Archibald
    George M.
    John
    Joseph
GILKY, David
GIMMISON, John
GINKENS, Eli
GIPSON, John Sr.
GLASS, Michael
GLOVER, James
    John P. Sr.
    Philip
    John P. Jr.*
GOE, Tarlton
GOODRICH, James
GOPIN, Daniel
GORDON, James
    Jonathan
    Joseph
GOSEN, Daniel
GOUGANE, Capt. Baptiste
GRAHAM, Daniel
    Moses*
    Robert
GRAVES, Thomas A.
GRAY, Isaac
    Joseph
    Robert
GRIFFIN, William
GRIGGS, John
    Leonard
    Samuel
    Wiley
GRIMES, Daniel
    Moses
GRISHAM, Jonathan
    William
GRISWOLD, Frederick
GROOM, Aaron
    Jacob
GUNNINGS, Clem

HACKETT, George
HALL, David
    Henry
    John
    William
HAM, Jabez
    John C.
HAMLIN, John
HANCOCK, Stephen's heirs
    Thomas G.
    William

HARDESTY,
HARDESTER Edward
HARRIMAN, John
HARRIS, William
HARRISON, James
    Thomas
HART, Nathaniel
HAUN,
HAWN Jacob
    John Sr.
    John Jr.
    Mathias
    (Matthew)
    Peter
    Tice
HAVENS, John S.
    Peter
HAW, John
HAWLEY, William L.
HAYNES, Collet
HAYS, Absalom
    Boon
    Daniel
    Greenup
    John
    Joseph
    Samuel
HAYWOOD, Joseph
HEATH, John G.
HENDERSON, James
    David
    William
    William Jr.
HENRYMAN, John
HENSLEY, Samuel B.*
HERLSON, Benjamin
HICKERSON, Thomas
HILL, John
HITTERBURN, David*
HOBBS, Joseph
HOLDER, Francis
HOLLOWAY, Jonathan
HOMESLEY, Barbery
    Joseph
HOPKINS, Isaac
    Walker
    William
HOUSE, George
    John
    Joseph
HOWARD, Andrew*
    Cornelius
    David
    Joseph
HOWEL, Newton
(also as guardian for
John Long heirs 1824)

HOYT, Jonathan
HUBBARD, Charles Sr.
    Charles Jr.
    David
HUGHART, John
HUGHES, James
HUMPHREYS, Richard
HUNTER, Andrew
    James
    Peter
    Robert
    William
HURT, John*
HUTTON, James

JACKSON, James
JAMES, Benjamin
    Jacob
    Joshua
    William
    Walter T.*
JEANS, William
JOB, Robert
JOHNSON, Abner
    John
JOHNSTON, John (two)
    Joseph
    Robert
    Thomas
JOINER, Moses
JONES, Dr. John
    Lewis
    Thomas*
    William
JOURNEY, James

KEELE, Isaac
KELLY, Thomas H.
KENNEDY, Guyon
    James
    Sarah
    Thomas
KENT, Andrew
    Isaac Sr.
    John
    Robert
    Thomas
    William
KERR, William
KETCHING, Thomas
KIBBY,
KIBBLE Amous*
KILE, Jacob
KINCAID, James
KING, Asaph
    David T.M. (cont.)

KING, George
    Isaiah
    John
    Joseph
    Preston
    Thomas
    William
KITCHEN, Thomas
KNOX, William
KOUNS, Nathan

LACRAY, Mary
LAMNILL,
LAMNE 'William T.
LAMPKIN, George
    Rachael
LAND, John
LANGFORD, William
LANGHAM, Alexander
    Angus L.
    Henry
    William
LANGLEY, Collect
    Isaac
    James
    John Sr.
    John Jr.
    Moses
    Moses Jr.
LAPLANT, Louis
LARK, Daniel
LAURARAMIE, Lawry
LAUSHWAY, Joseph
LAWLER, Patrick
LAWRENCE, George
LAWSON, Henry
LEE, John
    Thomas G.
LENOX, John
    William
LEVEL,
LEVEAL Edward
    James
LEVANE, William
LEVI, Daniel
LISLES,
LISLE Ann
    Hugh
    James
    Joseph
    William
LINN, Daniel
LYNN James
LIZENBY, John
LOGAN, Alexander
    Henry
    Hugh

LOGAN, William
LOMAX, Asael
LONG, John C.
    Matthew P.
LOSSON, Henry
LYNCH, David

McCAN, Neal
McCANCE, Margery
McCART, John
    Thomas
McCARTY, Ezekiel
McCLAIN, Charles
McCLENNY, Smith
McCLURE, Benoni
McCONNELL, William
McCUTCHEON, James
    John G.
McDANIEL, Daniel
    (David?)
McDERMID, Hugh Sr.
    Hugh Jr.
McEWEN, Oliver
McFARLANE, Caleb
    William
McGARVIN, Dennis
McGAUGH, Matthew
    Patton
    Robert
    Tristram P.
    William
McGIRK, Isaac C.
    Matthias
McGLOCHLIN, William
McHUIN, Oliver
McKINNEY, Alexander Sr.
    Alexander Jr.
McKINZEY, John
McLAUGHLIN, William
McNIGHT, Thomas
McQUEEN, Thomas
McREYNOLDS, William
McWILLIAMS, Andrew

MACCAN, Neill
MAHANY, Andrew
MALLOW, Jacob
MANIFEE, Campbell
MANN, William
MANNON, Asa
MARTIN, John
    Joseph
    William
MARR, Thomas
MARSHALL, John
MARVIN, Wells E.

MASON, Jesse
    Obediah
MATTOCK, David
MAY, Henry
MERCHANT, John
MERSHALL, Antoine
MILIGAN, John C.
MILLER, Abraham
    George
    Samuel
MILLS, Henry L.
MINET, Hugh
MISSONSMITH, John
MOODY, Isaac
    James
    Judy
    (Audey, widow?)
MOOR, James D.
    Jeremiah
    Levi
    Merriman
    Thomas
    Vincent
MORGAN, Mordecai
MORLEY, Henry
MORRIS,
MORRICE Joshua
    Samuel
    William
MORROW, John
    Richard
MOUSER,
MOUZZER George Sr.
    George Jr.
    John
MURRY, Enoch

NANCE, Hugh
NASH, William
    William Jr.
NAVINS, James
    Joseph
NEILL, Jeremiah H.
NETTLE, Matthew
NEVIT, Hugh
NICHOLS, James L.*
NIVEN, John
NIX, Caleb
NORTHCUTT, John
NOWEL, Isaac

ODEN, Jacob
    Thomas
OUSLEY, Micajah
    (also adm. estate of
    Joseph Stephenson)
OWENS,
OWINGS Henry
    John
    Thomas C.

PACE, Samuel A.
PAGE, William F.
PAIN, PANE, Hiram
PARRISH, Henry
PARSINGER, Alexander
        Joseph
PATTERSON, Schuyler
PATTON, Jacob Sr.
        Jacob Jr.
  (Jacob B. est. 1823)
        James B. (two)
        John
        Mary widow
        Robert
        William
PELTIER, Dabney
PENNINGTON, James
        William
PETTUS, Dabney
PEVELER, David
        Sibby
PEW, Reuben F.
PHILLIPS, Andrew
        James
        Jesse
        John Sr.
        John Jr.
PITMAN, Irvine L.
PORTER, Benjamin
POTES, John
POWEL, James
PRATT, John
        William
PRESTON, John
PRICE, James
        Lemuel Sr.
        Lemuel Jr.
        Param
PRICHARD, Drury B.
PRINCE, Orastes
PRINGLE, Norman
PUCKE, Peter
PUGH, Martin
        Reuben P.
PURKINS, Enoch
PURSINGER, Alexander
PURVIS, James*
PURYEAR, Thomas C.

QUICK, Aaron
        Alexander
        Jacob Sr.
        Jacob Jr.
        Stephen
        Thomas
        William

RAMSDALE, Oliver
RAMSEY, Jonathan
        Josiah Sr.
        Josiah Jr.
RAW, John
REAL, Charles
REED,
REID David
        Gilford D.
        Robert
REVOIR, Joseph
        Joseph Jr.
        Louis
REYNOLDS, George F.
        Huston
        James
        John
        Samuel
RHYNE, Joseph's estate
RIAL, Charles
RICE, William G.
RICHARDSON, John
RIDER, Reuben
RIGHT, Jacob
RIPPER, James
RITTER, Jesse
RIVARD, Alexander
        Joseph
        Robert
ROADS, George
        Henry
ROANSAVILE, Josiah
ROCHE, Bryant
        Peter
RODGERS, Benjamin
        Benjamin D.
ROUNTREE, Turner
ROWE, Benjamin
        John
ROYER, Nicholas
ROY, Baptiste
        Francois
        Louis
        Joseph
        Ruth
RUTHERFORD, Mary

SAILOR, Emanuel
        William
SALLE, Henry
        Isaac*
        John*
SAMPSON, William J.
SARRANT, Patsy
SCOTT, William B.

SHARP, Benjamin
        Jacob L.
        James F.
        Joseph L.
SHAW, James
SHEARMAN, Daniel
        David
SHOBE, Daniel
        Rudolph
SIMPSON, Erasmus*
        Selby
SIPES, Jacob
SKELTON, Miller
        Willis*
SKINNER, Daniel
        Eleanor
        Francis
        Hugh A.
        John Sr.
        John Jr.
        William*
SLAVENS, Steward
        Thomas
        William S.
SMITH, Abraham
        Darling
        David
        George
        Hamilton
        Jerry
        Jonathan
        Moses
        Reason
        Scudder
        Stephen S.
        Jeremiah
        Jonathan
        Thomas
        William
SNETHEN, Alice B.
        John
SNOWDEN, Samuel
SPIRES, George
        Greenberry
SPRY, Enoch
SRUM, John
STARK, STACK, Job
STAGSDALE, Joshua
STAVENS, Henry
STEPHENSON, Edward
        James
        Milly widow
        Sarah
STERIGERE, David
STEWARD, John

STOCKSTILL, Joshua
STOGSDALE
STONE, John
STOTTS, John M.
STRICKLING, Seth
SUBLETT, Hill
SUMMERS, Allen
    Jesse
    Moses
SUTTON, Ezra
    Jeffrey
TALBOT, David G.
    Christopher
    Haile
    James
    Thomas
    William
TANNER, Allen C.
TAYLOR, James W.
    John W.
    Johnson
TAYON, Francis
THEBEAU, Francis
  TEBO Joseph
THOMAS, Benjamin*
    Elisha M.
    Jesse
    Peleg E.
    Solomon
THOMPSON, Aaron
    David
    John F.
    William
THOMAS, Elizabeth widow
THURMAN, Joseph
TICE, John
TINSLEY, William
TITTLE, James
TOOTSON, James
TOULSON, Benne P.
TRIMBLE, John
    William

· · · · · · · · · · · · ·

TURLEY, William O.
TUTT, William
TUTTLE, Nancy
    Nicholas H.
    Nicholas W.
    Pleasant
URNON, Francis
VAN BIBBER, Isaac
    James
    Joseph
VAUGHAN, Martan
VENAN, Low
VINSAM, Louis
WADDLE, Amos
  WEDDLE Elias
    George*
    Robert
WADE, John
WALKER, William
WALLERY, John
WARD, Frazier*
    David*
    Joseph
    John
    Samuel*
    William
WARNER, Winkoop
WATSON, Aaron
WATTS, Anthony B.
WAY, Elijah
    Capt. Henry
WELCH, Henry E.
    John
WELLS, Charles
    James
WHEELER, Chester
WHITESIDES, Francis
    Holland
    James
WIGGINS, Joseph
WILBOURN, John
WILLABY, John

· · · · · · · · · · · · ·

WILLIAMS, Asa
    Caleb
    Eward
    George
    Jared
    Joseph
    Notley
    Olly
    William
WILLIAMSON, Catherine
    Cornelius
    John
    Polly
    Samuel
WILLS, Charles
WRAY, Elijah
WRIGHT, Charles D.
    Christopher
    Francis
    Hardin
    Jacob
    Richard
    William
WYATT, Anthony
    Douglas
    John Sr.
    Joseph's estate
    Capt. John
    John
    Joseph
YATES, Raphael
    Stephen
YEAGER, Abram
YOUNG, Aaron H.
    John Sr.
    John Jr.
    Dr. John
    Benjamin
    Samuel*
YOUNGER, Charles
ZIMMERMAN, James
ZUMWALT, Adam
    Andrew
    Jacob

· · · · · · · · · · · · · · · · ·

SECONDARY: REPUBLICAN AND INQUIRER, ST. LOUIS
AND ST. CHARLES MISSOURIAN

COATES, John stray Cote Sans Dessein   CLARK, Daniel   esta
COLLINS, Simri   "   "   RELF, Richard   esta
CONWAY, Walter and Samuel   estate   WHITEGATE, Francis stray
CHEW, Beverly   estate   Loutre Twp.

· ·

Montgomery County was formed from St. Charles in 1818. It is the parent
county of Warren (1833) and Callaway (1820). Montgomery County records
prior to 1864 are almost totally lost due to a courthouse fire.

NEW MADRID COUNTY: TAX SALES 1820 (from the Jackson *Herald*), DELINQUENTS 1819 (from the *Independent Patriot*) AND MISCELLANEOUS LEGAL TAXES (from the State Archives of Missouri)

ALEAZER, James
ALLEN, Thomas C.
ANDERSON, George C.
ARCHER, Sampson

BAKER, Jesse
BARTRAM, Michael
BOURNOUR, Francis
BROWN, George
      James
BURGIE, Adam
      Andrew
BURT, Willis

CHARTIER, Charles
CHEEK, Nicholas
CHESEAUR, Hugh M.D.
COGNIARD, Louis
COMMINO, Stuart
CORK, Benjamin
CORRONDALET, Collot

DORSAC, John
DUMAY, Peter
DUNN, Phoebe
DUPEA, Nicholas
DUPREE, John

ELIOTT, Benjamin
EVANS, Enoch
      Sarah

FARLON, Alexander M.
FIELDING, Frederick
FRAZER, Alexander

GAFFORD, John
GAYON, Hyacinth
GILBRETH, James
GIBBS, Lucas S.
GIVENS, Dickson
      Joseph R.
GLASS, William H.
GONE, Charles
GUINGOLD, Joseph

HARNISS, Michael
HARPER, Robert
HARRIS, Robert
HEDY, Stilwell
HOGAN, Charles

JANIS, Anthony
     Francois
     Nicholas

JEARDUN, Berthrew
JOHNSON, Thomas

LADANITE, Paul
LAGRIMORE, Charles
LEGARD, John
LINCOLN, John

McGEE, Joseph

MYERS, William

NORRIS, Daniel
NOVIS, James

PARKS, Laborn
PHILLIP,
PHILLIPS Richard
        Thomas
POWERS, Thomas

St. JEAN, Nicholas
SAMSON, Alexander
SANTQUARTIER, Peter
SEVENE, Thomas
SEXTON, Joshua
STEPHENSON, William
SUTTON, William

TALL, John
TAYLOR, Alfred
      Anthony

UNEROUS, George

WAIR, Sherrington
WALKER, Col. J. H.
WATERS, John
WELLS, Anthony
WILLBORN, John
WINCHESTER, John
        William
WORTH, Lewis

= =

New Madrid is one of the original districts, is the parent county of Scott and Pemiscot and by extension of Mississippi. The original archives of New Madrid have been preserved and are at the Missouri Historical Society, St. Louis.

The earthquakes of 1811-12 so severely damaged the area that the number of residents was greatly reduced; many were awarded land in other parts of the state.

69

ABLE, Wilson	Tywapitty Twp.	J.P.
ADAMS, William		stray
ALFORD, George C.		license
BACON, William		license
BALDWIN, Hartwell		lawsuit
BARTLETT, Thomas		license
BECKWITH, Newmand		license
BIGGS, David		estate
BLACK, Samuel		notice
BLEMENS, John		notice
BOGLIOLO, Mattio		license
BOWDEN, Jesse		lawsuit
BRADY, James		lawsuit
BULLARD, Nathaniel		license
BUTLER, Upton C.		license
CARPENTER, Benjamin		estate
DAVIS, Caleb		estate
Emily		"
Ludwell R.		"
DAWSON, Dr. Robert D.		notice
De LARODARIE, A.		license
EDWARDS, William		lawsuit
ELLIS, Alfred P.		estate
Fanny		"
ESSERY, Joseph		stray
FLETCHER, Thomas		stray
Tywapitty Twp.		
GALLIHER, John		estate
Hugh		"
James		"
Frank		"
GAMBLE, Samuel		stray
GILMORE, Robert J.		J.P.
GOALD, Odeal		notice
Thomas		"
GOCLA, Thomas H.		notice
GOLAIR, James		license
HOUTS, Christopher		lawsuit
HUNTER, David		license
KEINY, Abraham		notice
KELTENHOUSE, E. T.		license
KESLIER, Constantine		peddler
LANE, John	Tywapitty Twp.	stray
LARK, John		estate
Precious		"
LAZELL, William		estate
LE SIEUR, Francis		estate
Godfrey		"

LIGGETT, Enoch		
McCOY, Robert		stray
McELMURRY, Absalom		stray
Tywapitty Twp.		
MAULSBY, Lemuel H.		clerk
MIFFLIN, John N.		estate
Nancy		"
MOORE, John		stray
MULLINS, Daniel		lawsuit
MYERS, William	Moreland Twp.	stray
ORMEN, Thomas		license
POWELL, Thomas C.		estate
PUTNEY, James		estate
RAMSEY, Charles T.		lawsuit
REED, John		notice
RENTY, John J.		license
RODGERS, James		estate
ROSS, John F.		license
Philip		lawsuit
Stephen		estate
RUDDE, Andrew		estate
Elizabeth		estate
RUDDLE, George		estate
Isaac		"
RUTTER, Edmund		lawsuit
ST. CLAIR, Pressly		stray
SHAVER, Nathaniel		lawsuit
SHAW, Mary		estate
William		"
SHIELDS, Catherine		estate
John		"
SOJOURNER, Albert Loid		estate
Clarinda Houston		"
Louis		"
Louisiana		"
Maria Ellen Hampton		"
STALLCUP, Mark H.		lawsuit
STORY, Joseph		lawsuit
STIDGER, Mary A.		notice
William B.		"
STORY, Joseph		lawsuit
TANNER, James		notice
Joseph		estate
TAYLOR, William		lawsuit
THOMPSON, Isaac		notice
TUCKER, John		notice
WAIT, Eleanor		estate
Henry		"

WALKER, John H.   estate
WATHEN, Ignatius   estate
     Mary Ann   "
WATSON, Robert G.   license

WINCHESTER, Nancy   estate
     William Jr.   "
WOOD, Robert   stray
     Tywapitty Twp.

Earliest report of the New Madrid
earthquake, from the Louisiana
Gazette, St. Louis, 11 Dec. 1811

(The Gazette was originally,
and subsequently, known as
the Missouri Gazette and
eventually became the
Missouri Republican.)

71

PERRY COUNTY: SECONDARY LIST FROM THE HERALD AND THE INDEPENDENT
PATRIOT, BOTH PUBLISHED IN JACKSON, CAPE GIRARDEAU CO.

ABERNATHY, A.   Apple Creek   stray
          Battee   "   "
ANDERSON, Jane   notice

BAKER, Reuben   pauper   A.S.
BISHOP, R. L.   "
BROVON, Robert T.   "

CALDWELL, David L.   A.S.
CESSELL, Lewis   "

DUNCAN, Joseph   notice
        Matthew   lawsuit

EGGERS, Elisha   A.S.
EVANS, Owen   notice

FENWICK, Ezekiel   stray
          Cape Cinq Hommes
          George   estate
          James J. (Cape C.H.)   J.P.
          Margaret   estate
          Thomas   Apple Creek stray
FLIN, William   A.S.
FOLEY, Thomas   "

GARNIER, C.   pauper   A.S.
GUITAR, John   "

HAMILTON, Eulalie   estate
          Fenwick J.   "
          George   "
          Josiah F.   "
          (also stray, Cape C.H.)
          Leo   estate
          Matilda   "
          Walter   "
HAYDEN, Benedict   estate
        Clement   "
        John   "
        Joseph   A.S.
        Sarah   estate
        Susan   "
        Thomas   A.S.
HORN, John   Cape Cinq Hommes   stray

LANE, J. W. M.   stray
          Cape Cinq Hommes
LAYTON, Bernard   Apple Creek   stray
        John   estate
        Wilford   Apple Creek   stray
LINN, Polly Ann   lawsuit
        (formerly Duncan)
        William   "

McFLATTERY, Cornelius   clerk
          Cape Cinq Hommes

MANNING, Anastastia   estate
         James   "
         John   "

MILES, Edward F.   estate
       Henry   "
MITCHELL, Archibald   estate
          John   "
          Robert   "
MOORE, Bede   A.S.
       Isidore   Apple Creek   stray
       Richard   estate

NARCE, Francis   Apple Creek   stray

RILEY, Ann   estate
       Benedick   "

SHOLTS, John   Cape Cinq Hommes stray

TUCKER, Joseph   A.S.
        Sarah   estate
        William   "

WARREN, Michael   estate
WELKER, Clara   estate
        Joel   estate
WILKINSON, Walter   A.S.

....

Perry County was formed from Cape Girardeau in November, 1820.
No other counties were formed from it.

BLOCK, P.

CALDWELL, Samuel C.
CAMPBELL, R.
CARTER, John R.
CONWAY, Henry
       John
       Joseph S.

DICKERSON, Obadiah
DILLON, P. M.

EMERSON, Edward P.

FRY, Jacob

HALE, John Miller
HOWARD, J. B.

JAMES, David
JOHNSON, James
JONES, James

KELSO, Robert
KNOX, James

LIPPINCOTT, A.R.
          E.E.

MAHON, R.
MANN, Marshall
MERRYMAN, T.F.

NOYES, Michael J.

PHELAN, James C.
PRUITT, John

RIPLEY, Richard
ROSS, Thomas P.

SANDLIN, John
SCOTT, John
SHEARMAN, Oliver P.
SMITHERS, J.

TRABULL, C. Clay

WELLS, Samuel
WHITE, Hugh

....

SECONDARY LIST FROM THE <u>REPUBLICAN</u> AND THE <u>INQUIRER</u> (BOTH
ST. LOUIS) AND THE <u>MISSOURIAN</u> (ST. CHARLES)

ALLISON, Robert   notice
ASHBURN, George T.   stray
     Mason Twp.

BATES, Charles   stray
BECHURST, Samuel   stray
     Calumet Twp.
BENN, Samuel   stray
BILL, Charles   notice
BRYSON, Elizabeth   estate
     John   "
BUCKHANNON, Thomas   stray
      Calumet Twp.
BURNS, Robert   stray
      Calumet Twp.

CALDWELL, Elizabeth   estate
      Samuel R.   "
CAMPBELL, Major John   notice
CARTER, J. R.   license
CROW, Albion T.   stray
     Mason Twp.

DENNIS, Jacob   stray
      Mason Twp.
DENNY, Jonas F.   bankrupt
DeWITT, G.   notice
DULIN, Thaddeus   license

FOURT, Andrew   stray
FRY, Jacob   estate
     James   "

GARNER, Sarah   notice
     Thruston   "
GRIFFITH, Amos   stray
     Joel   "
     John   "
   all of Buffalo Twp. John
    also listed bankrupt.
GRISWOLD, Frederick   license

HEMPHILL, Robert   stray
     Buffalo Twp.
HENDRICK, Thompson   stray
     Cuivre Twp.
HUGHES, John   stray
     Calumet Twp.

IRVIN,
IRWIN   Robert J.P.   Cuivre

JACKSON, Joseph   notice
     Mary   "
JENKINS, Ephraim   stray
     Calumet Twp.
JONES, Dabney   AS

KERR, Richard   stray
     Calumet Twp.
KNEELAND, David   notice

McCOY, James   bankrupt
McPIKE, W.   stray
     Cuivre Twp.

MAGUIRE, John	notice		REBURST, Samuel	stray
MANN, Marshall	AS		Calumet Twp.	
MASE, John	stray			
MEAD, Isaac	estate		SHAW, Joel	estate
Catherine	"		Mary	"
MILLER, Col. John	notice		THOMPSON, James D.	notice
MOORE, Jeremiah	stray		TOMB, Samuel	stray
Vincent	stray		Cuivre Twp.	
NOYES, M.J.	clerk		TRIBUE, C.C.	license
			TURNER, John	lost horse
OYLEAR, Jonathan	stray		WALKER, Daniel	stray
PARKS, Loes	estate		Calumet Twp.	
Reuben	"		John T.	bankrupt
PATTERSON, William	notice		WATTS, John	stray
PHELAN, James C.	JP		WELLS, Hugh	stray
Calumet Twp.			James	"
POTTER, John	notice		Richard	"
PRUITT, John	license		all Calumet Twp.	
			Thomas	bankrupt
			WILLIAMS, John	stray
			Mason Twp.	
			Rebecca	estate
			WILSON, Samuel	stray
			YOKEN, Solomon	AS

....

Pike County was formed from St. Charles in December, 1818. It
is the parent county of Ralls and by extension of Marion, Monroe,
Shelby, Lewis, Knox, Scotland, and Clark.

Port of St. Louis.

STEAM BOAT INTELLIGENCE.

Arrived, on Monday last, steam boat VISTA, capt.
Emmerson, from Cincinnati.

On the same day, the HERO, capt. Honora, in 22
days out from New-Orleans, with freight and passen-
gers for this place.

Sailed, yesterday, steam boat MAID of ORLEANS, for
New-Orleans—and this morning the CUMBERLAND, for
the same place.

RALLS COUNTY: SECONDARY LIST FROM THE REPUBLICAN AND THE INQUIRER,
ST. LOUIS, AND THE MISSOURIAN, ST. CHARLES

BARRETT, BARNETT, J.C.	A.S.	MARKLE, Charles	notice
BATES, M. D.	A.S.	MASSEY, Joshua	license
BLAIR, James	A.S.	MASSIE Theodorick	A.S.
BRACKEN, William	A.S.	MATSON, Enoch	A.S.
BREWER, Richard	notice	Richard	A.S.
BROOKS, William H.	stray	MEANS, Benjamin	license
		MULDROW, William	A.S.
CARSON, William	estate		
CASTARPHEN, Oney	estate	NEWELL, Richard W.	license
CARY, John	A.S.	NOSHALL, James	A.S.
CHITWOOD, James	A.S.		
COCHRAN, James	A.S.	PARKER, Mary	notice
CONWAY, Samuel	A.S.	Peter	"
CRUMP, Daniel	stray	William	"
		PARRIS, Morgan	A.S.
DALE, John	estate	PRUITT, John	license
DAVIS, Joseph	stray		
Shadrach	A.S.	RALLS, Daniel	A.S.
DeWITT, Green	notice	RICHEY, William	A.S.
DRAPER, Zachariah	license	RIGGS, Nathaniel	stray
		RUSH, John	A.S.
ELY, Isaac	A.S.		
		SARGENT, Philip M.	license
FOX, Abraham	license	SCOBEE, John	A.S.
Ezra James C. estate	A.S.	SEELY, Jacob	estate
FRY, Abraham K.	A.S.	SHEPHERD, David	A.S.
FUGATE, James	A.S.	SHANKLIN, Elijah	stray
Josiah	A.S.	SIMS, Roderick	A.S.
		Stark	A.S.
GENTRY, Jesse	A.S.	SMITH, Alexander M.	estate
GERRY, John	A.S.	Elijah	A.S.
GLASCOCK, Ann	notice	Joseph	estate
Jacob	estate	William W.	A.S.
Asa	A.S.	SNIDER, Gabriel	A.S.
Laban	estate	SPARKS, Reuben	A.S.
Stephen	A.S.	STRODE, Thomas	A.S.
GRANT, Peter	A.S.	William	A.S.
Francis	A.S.		
GRASH, Joseph D.	A.S.	TAPLEY, Green	notice
		THOMPSON, Isham	A.S.
IRVING, John A.	license		
		VAUGHN, James S.	license
JAMISON, William	A.S.	VOSHALL, James	A.S.
JONES, R. W.	A.S.		
JOURNEY, Peter	A.S.	WELDON, James	stray
		WILLIAMSON, George	A.S.
KINNEY, Lewis	license	WRIGHT, Joseph	license
LALEFIELD, William	A.S.		
LEWIS, Valentine	A.S.	=+=+=+=+=+=+=+=+=+
LIPPINCOTT, Samuel	A.S.	
LONGMIRE, John	A.S.	Ralls County was formed from Pike

=+=+=+=+=+=+=+=+=+

McGEE, Patrick — license
McGINNES, Achilles — A.S.
McGOWEN, Harvey — A.S.
McRAE, William — A.S.

Ralls County was formed from Pike
in November, 1820. It is the parent
county of Marion and Monroe and by
extension of Audrain, Lewis, and
Shelby. / / / / / /

BLACK, William L.   AS
BRAVO, Henry   ferry license
BRUNT, John   stray
    "on Crooked River"
BURCH, Jonathan T.   clerk
    Missouriton Twp.
CAMRON, Elisha   AS
CARROLL, Ch.   estate
        H.   "
CLEVENGER, Pharis   estate
          Zachariah   "
          Samuel   clerk
COON, William   estate
CUNNINGHAM, Wright   AS

DODSON, John   stray
    "on Crooked River"
DEWALL, Daniel   AS

FINDLEY, James   JP
    Missouriton Twp.

HARRIS, John   AS

JACK, William   ferry license
JOHNSON, Joseph   stray
    Missouriton Twp.

LINVILLE, Richard   notice

McCROSKIE, Andrew   estate
          Isaac   "
          John   "
MARTIN, Isaac   AS
        William B.   AS
MILLER, William   AS
MORGAN, Sally   notice

RIGGS, Timothy   AS

SHIELDS, John   AS
SMITH, William L.   AS
SNOWDEN, James   AS
        Lovell   stray
    "on Crooked River"
STANDLEY, James   JP
         John   stray
    Missouriton Twp.
STONE, John   AS

THORNTON, John   AS
    also shown as John W.   notice
TURNER, William   stray
    Missouriton Twp.

WALLACE, Robert   estate

ADDAMS, John *
ALLEN, Francis
   Ira
   Seth
ALDER, John
ALKIRE, Solomon
ALEXANDER, Martin
ALLISON, Nathaniel J.
AMBROISE, Josaphin
ATCHISON, George M.
   John *
   Pierce
   Solomon *
AUDRAIN, Peter F.
   James H.
AUBURY,
AUBERN Griffith
   Joseph *
   Roland
   Thomas
AYRES, Ebenezer
   Davenport
   Stephen *
   Stephen M. *

BABER, Hiram H.
BAILEY, Robert
   (estate 1823)
   Martha
BALDRIDGE, Daniel
   James
   John
   Robt. Sr.
   Robt. Jr.
   Melkiah
BAMBRIDGE, Absalom
BANKS, Moses B.
BARABO,
BAREBO Francois *
   Louisa
BARCROFT, Elias
   John
BARNETT, Samuel *
BASHMAN, Joseph
   Louis
BAUGH, Benjamin
   Joseph
   Samuel
   Thomas
   William G.
BEAUCHAMP, Isaac B.
   Joshua
BEAUCHON, Louis
   Mary
BEAMON, Walter *

BEAR, Charles
   Charles Jr.
BEAUSE, Joseph *
BECKER, Baptiste
BECKWITH, Gennings *
BELLOND, Michael
BELLOW, Michael
BENDER, Jacob
BENHAM, Robert
BENNETO,
BENNETT Vasquez *
   Widow
BEQUETTE, Baptiste
BERNARD, Akin
   Etienne
   Isadore *
   Paulette
   (Potite?)
BERRY, Caleb
   Francis
   John H.
   Richard
BESSER, John L. (S?) *
BEST, Mary
   Stephen
   Stephen heirs 1826
BEVAN, William
BEVANUE, Akin
   Joseph *
   Charles *
   Louis
BICKERSTAFF, Richard
BIGELOW, Moses
BIGGS, Randolph (Randle) ++
   Travis
BLACK
(BLOCK?) John ++
   Thomas
BLAIR, William
BLANCHETTE, Peter heirs
   (1826)
BLAND,
BLANK Charlot
   Peter
BOARD, John
BOLING, Daniel
BOONE,
BOON James
   John M. (W?)
   Nathan
   Squire ++
BOSHAMA,
BOSHMA Andrew
   Mead
   Peter *
BOUGH, William W.

BOWEN, George
BOWERS, Polly
BOYER, James
BOYIER,
BOYER Isadore *
BROWN, Griffith
   (estate 1823)
   Elijah
   Henry
   John
   Joseph
   Mary
   Squire
   William
BRUGIERE, Baptiste
   (heirs 1826)
BRUIN,
BREUIN Evan
   Timothy
BRUNELLE, Tousant *
BRUMFIELD, James B.
BRUISTRAN, Peter
BRUSSIER, Widow
BRYANT,
BRYAN Abner
   Elijah *
   James
   Jonathan
   Susanna
BUCKLER, Martin
BURBANKS, Moses B.
BURGE, Henry
BURDEANNA, Peter *
BURNS, Kennedy(Canada) ++
   Robert
BURDYNE, Amos ++
   Benjamin *
   Betsy
BUTCHER, James
   Nelson
BUTLER, Elijah

CADOOTH, John B.
CALDWELL, Archibald *
CALLAHAN, Beston
CALLAWAY, John B. ++
   Joseph heirs 1823
   James heirs 1824
   John B heirs 1826
CALLANT, John B. * ++
   (CALUTE?)
CANNON, Jacob H.
   Joseph
CARAFRAIN, G. (or I?)

CARBONO, Louis
CARDINALE, Charles *
      Jean M.
CARR, John H. *
CARTER, Cyrus
      William
CASTLIO, John
      John Jr.
CASHAW, William
CHAMBERS, Alexander
      Joshua
CHAMPAIN, Louis *
CHAPMAN, George
CHAPPELL, Gordon J. *
CHARTRAIN, Joseph
CHAUNCELLIER, M. Louise
CHRISTY, William Jr.
CICAR, Antoine *
CLAMORE, John
      Louis
CLARK, Andrew
      Norman *
      Samuel
CLARE, John D.
CLAREMONT, Francois *
CLARMO   Joseph L.
      Mary Ann
      Peter
CLAY, James
COALTER, David
   (estate 1823)
COCHRAN, Andrew
      George
COFFER, John
   (estate 1823)
COLE, Luther
COLGAN, Daniel
      Robert
COLLIER, Barton
      Catherine
      George
COLLINS, Bern
      William *
COMEGYS, Abraham
      Cornelius
      Jacob *
      Jonathan *
COMLY, Amos
CONNOYER,
CORNOYER Louis
      M. L.
      Peter
      Thomas
COONS, Nicholas
   (estate 1823)
78   Rebecca

COPES, Thomas P.
CORBA,
CORBEY Francis
      Semore
COTE, Baptiste
      Joseph
COTTLE, Alonzo *
      Oliver
      Seloma
      Sylvanus
      Warren
(Warren heirs 1826)
COULTER, David
   (estate 1824)
COURTNEY, Robert H.
      Samuel
COUSOTTE, Simon
CRAIG, James
      John
      William
CRATER, Michael
CRIDER, John
CROW, Henry
      John
      Jonathan
      Lewis
      Michael
      William
CREECH,
CREACH John
CUDAR, Mecham*
CURTIS, Louis

DARST, Abraham
      David Sr.
      David Jr.
      Isaac
DAUFIN, Abraham *
      Akin
      Alex
      Paulette
DAY, Francis
      Nathaniel *
DECHAND, Charles
DeLAPP, Robert *
DeLELIA, Akin
      Catherine
      Charles *
      Joseph *
      Louis *
DENNY, Charles
DERWAY, Michael
DESLOE, Auguste
  Baptiste heirs 1826
DESSHAW, Charles

DETHIER, Dieu Donna
      Louis
DEVORE, Uriah J. *
DICKSON, Henry
DISCON,
DIXON Hiram
      James
DODIER, Rene
DOE, John B.
DOERIF, James S.
DOFA, Abraham *   ***
DORLAC, Auguste
DORWAY, Michael
DOZENG, Arthur N.*
DOUGLASS, Adam
DRACE, Thomas *
DRAPPO, Lewis
DRISKILL, James
DROWDY, John
      William
  heirs of Wm 1823
      William Jr.*
DRUMMONDS, Milton
      Samuel
DUBA, Jacob
      Joseph
DuBOIS, Isaac
      Jacques
      Joseph
      Peter
DUFF, David
DUFFY, Daniel *
DUKEN,
DUNKIN Elijah
DULEN, DULIN, Thaddeus *
DUNKEN,
DUNKIN John
      Richard
DuQUETTE, Mary (Mme.)
DUMO, Abraham
DUROCHER, Antoine
      Bartholomew
      St. Croix *
DURWAY see DORWAY

EASTON, Rufus *
EBARE,
EBERE Charles Sr.
      Charles Jr.
      Joseph
ECKHART, William
EDWARDS, John *
ELLINGTON, John
EMMONS, Benjamin
EVANS, John C.
      Joseph
*** possibly DOZA

FABIA, Josephine
FAGAN, Giles *
FARNSWORTH, Alden *
    Bill
    Enos
    William
FAULCONER, John M.
FARNUM, Russell
FAX, Andrew
FERRY, John *
FILTEAU, Auguste
    (heirs 1826)
    John *
FISHER, Joshua (estate)
    Martha
    Nicholas
FLAUGHERTY, Felix W.
    James (estate)
    Ralph R. *
FOLLIS, Thomas
    William *
FORE (?), Andrew
FOREMAN, Stephen W.*
FOSTER, Robert G.
FRAZIEUR, David
    James Sr.
    James Jr.
    John
FRENCH, Thomas
FULKERSON, Isaac
    James
    William N.

GALERNA,
  GALLERNO Augustus
GARRATY, Joseph M.
GARVIN, Alexander
    Benjamin
    John
    Joseph
GATTY,
  GATY etc George
    George N.
    John
Geo. heirs 1826
GENAUD,
  GENOR' Joseph (estate)
    Joseph 1826
GERRARDINE, Auguste
GIBSON, GIPSON Joseph
GILL, John
GILLET, Benoni R.
    Leonard F.
    Philo
GILLMORE, Thomas
GLASGOW, Ephraim

GLENDAY, James
    Peter
GLOVER, Philip
GODFAR, Louis *
GODFREY, Widow
GODSEY, Burton
GOE, Daniel *
    Noble
GOODRICH,
  GOODRIDGE James
    John
GOODWIN, Mahlon (Millin)*
GORDON, Forbus *
    William
GRAF, Elizabeth
GRATER, John
GRAVIA, GRAVLIN, Joseph
GRAY, GREY, Samuel
GREEN, James *
    James Jr.
    John
    Robert
    Squire
GRIFFIN, St. Clair
GRIFFITH, Daniel (estate)
    Daniel
    Asa
    Sarah
    Samuel heirs 1826
GROCE, Elizabeth
GROSS, John
GUNN, Calvin *
    Lewis
    Sylvester
GURNOE, Peter *
    Sylvester* Lewis
GUTHRIE, Robert

HAINS,
  HANES John
    J. S.
    Joseph*
HALLAWAY, John *
HAMLIN, Gustavus A.
HANLEY, James
HARO(A)LD, Leonard
HARNEY, Henry L.
HARPER, William
HAY,
  HAYS Daniel
    Henry
    William
HEAD, Nathaniel L. *
    Richard L. *
    William A.
HEADRICK, George

HEALD, Jonas *
    Nathan
    Robert A.
HEALFINE, Thomas
    Valentine
HIGH, HIGHT, Henry *
HIGHTOWER, George *
HILL, William
HINDS, Edwin
    Sandy
    Wiley
HO(U)FFMAN, George
    George Jr.
    John
    Peter
HOLBERT, Joseph
HOLMES, L.P.
    Mary
    Samuel
HOLLOWAY, John
HONORY, Francis
    Francis Jr.
HOPPER, Hannah
HORNSHEE, Nicholas
HORTON, John
HOSTETTER, Christian
    John
HOUSTEN, William L. *
HOWELL, Benjamin
    Francis Sr.
    Francis
    James F. *
    John
    Lewis
    Thomas
HOWLAND, Daniel
    Samuel
HURNO, Louis
HUNOE, Louis heirs 1826
    Francis Sr.
    Francis Jr.
HUNT, Ezra
HUNTER, William
HUTCHINGS, Aaron
    Christopher
    Green

ILER, Daniel
    John
    Richard
    William
IMAN, Daniel

JACOBY, Jane
    John (estate)
JAMES, Nicholas
JANIS, Antoine Sr. *
    Antoine Jr.
    Nicholas
JANUARY
  (JOURNEY) Joseph
JENKINS, Eliot (Elihab) *
JOHNS, James
JOHNSON, Andrew *
    Baker
    Daniel
    Evan
    John
    John W.
    Joseph
    Levi
    William H.
JONES, Jonathan
    John
    Robert
JONO, Baptiste *
JOURNEY see JANUARY
JUDAH, Andrew

KEENY, Hardy *
    John *
    Michael *
KEETH, Isaac
KEITHLY, Abraham (estate)
    Abraham (living)
    Absalom
    Daniel
    John
    Samuel
    William
KELLER, John
KELLY, Thomas *
KENNEDY, Armstrong
KENNELL, A.N.
    Akin (Etienne) *
    Amable
KENNY, Michael Sr.
  (for Thomas Piper)
KERSROI,
KESSON Gregoire
KIBBIE, KIBBEK (?), Peter
KIBLER, I.
    George
    Jacob
KING, John *
    Patrick
KIRKPATRICK, Wallis
80

KIRKPATRICK, William
KISTLER, Frederick
KNOTT, KNOTE, Osbourn

LaBARE,
LeBEAR Charles Sr.
     Charles Jr.
LABARGE, Charles
    Louis
LABEAUX, Baptiste
LABO   Charles Jr.
    Joseph
LABRE, Pierre
LABREVAILLE, Gabrielle
LACROISE, Francois
  St. Paul heirs 1826
LADUC, LADUKE, Morris *
LAFABRE, Alexander
    Auguste
    Charles
LAMARCHE, Charles *
LAMASTERS, Benjamin
LAMBO, Joseph
LAMME, Peter *
LAMOT, Michael
LAPEAR, Francis
LAPPRA, Magdeline
LARALY,
LAREVE Joseph
LARAVETTE, Joseph
LARBIC, Vincent
LAROQUE, Bazille
LASOEUR, Francis
LASUZE, John B. *
LATOUR, LATURE, Joseph
LATTO, Belshezzar
LATTRAILLE, Antoine*
      Gabrielle
LEBEAU, see LaBEAU
LEAPLY, Samuel
LEAVE, Morris *
LECLAIR, Antoine Sr.
    Antoine Jr.
    Francis Jr.
    Josette
LEE, Patrick
LeFEVRE, Alexander
    Auguste
    Charles
LeFLEUR, Francis
LENMAN, Patrick *
LEPAGE, Magdeline (Mme)
    Andrew *
LESAGE, John B.
    Michael

LESCHAYES, Michael
LESIEUR, Francis
LEVAN, Joseph
LEWIS, Charles
    Judith
    Martin
    Milton
    Polly
LICK, George *
LILLY, John
LINDSEY, James
    Thomas
LISBET, Samuel
LOUCIER, Baptiste
LOUIS, Goe Charlotte N
    Milton
LOUISE, Baptiste
    Joseph
    Mary
LOUISON, John Bte.
    Peter
LUCIER, John B.
LUCKET, William
LUCKEY, LUCKY, Henry *
LULO (LUBO?), Battier
LYNCH, George *
    William
LYNHAM, Patrick *

McCHAMBERLY, John
McCLAY, Daniel
    David
    William
McCLENNY, Micajah
    William L. (
McCLOUD,
McLEOD Collin
    Robert*
McCONNELL, James *
    John
McCOY, Daniel
    Timothy
    William
McCUTCHEON, John *
McDONALD,
McDANNOLD Baptiste S
     Baptiste
McEVERS, John
McFALL, Lazarus
McFOSTER, McKnight
McKINNEY, S.T. *
McKINZEY, John *
McNAIR, David
  (with Ralph Flaugher)
McPHEETERS, Theophilus
McWATERS, Aaron
    John*

MACHATTE, Charles C.
      James*
MALLERSON, Elijah
MANLY, John *
MANN, John*
MARESCHAL,
MARISCHAL Antoine
      Touissaint*
MARIE, Achine *
      Francis *
      John
MARKER, Francis
MARNIER, Etienne*
      Francis
MARSHALL, William
MARTAIN, Widow
MARTIN, Hiram C.*
      John *
    Mather or Masher
      Walankthur C.
MARTINEAU, Charles
MARTINO Joseph
MASON, Jesse
      Obadiah
MASSEY, Silas
MASHAW,
MASSEAU Alexander
MEANS, David H.
MEC, William *
MECHAM, Denison P.
MENARD, Louis
MILLER, Fleming
      John
      Robert
MILLINGTON, Ira *
      Jeremiah
      Seth
MILLS, Henry I.
MINES, John
MONROE, James *
MOORE, Elisha
      Horatio
      John
      Thomas
      Zachariah
MORA, Baptiste
MORNING, Mary
MORRIS, Edward
      Heber
      John Sr.
      John Jr. *
      Mary
      Richard
      William
MORRISON, Francis *

MORRISON, James
      Jesse
MOTIE, Francis
      Mary
MUDD, Stanislaus
MURDOCK, Alexander
      Hiram
      James
MURKE, Francis
MURRAY, Baptiste
MYERS, John

NATT, NOTT, William B.
NAYLOR, John
NESBIT, Samuel
NICHOLAS, Henry
      Matthias *
NOBLE, James
      John
NOVAL, Francis *
      Joseph *
      Mary

OBUCHON, Louis
      Louiza
OLIVER, Archibald
      John
ONLY, Louis *
OSIA, Joseph *
OVERALL, Nathaniel
      Wilson
ORTON, John
OWEN, Benjamin *

PALLARDY, Peter Sr.
      Peter Jr.
PANTEAU, Claude
      Napis (?) *
PAPIN, Ellionne
PARMER, Charles
PARO (PENO?) Joseph
PASCHALL, Antoine
      Louis
PATCHEN(R), Paul P.
PEARCE, George *
      Thomas
      William
PEARSON, Edward L. *
PECK, Charles
      Otis *
      Ruloff
PEERS, Edward
PENO, PARO, Joseph
PENROSE, Clement B. Sr.
      Clement B. Jr.

++ ONGAY, Nicholas * ++

PEPPER, Akin
PERKINS, Ephraigm
PERO, Joseph
PERRY, Montgomery
PETITE, Francis *
PETTIBONE, Rufus
PETTUS, John
      William G.
PETTY, John
      William
PHILLIPS, Charles
      John Y.
PIERCE, see PEARCE
PIPER, James *
      Robert
      Samuel *
      Thomas
PIT(T)MAN, John
      Richard B.
PITZER, George
PONTON, Narcis
PORTANOY, Amable
PORTER, Benjamin
POSTAL, William
POUGOL, Lewis
POUSHAL, Mary
POWELL, George H.
PRESSEAU, Francis
      Gabrielle *
      Josephine
PRICE, Augustine
      Frederick
      George
      Isaac
      Jacob
      James
      Michael
      Samuel
PRIEUR, Antoine
      Francis Sr. *
      Noel J.
PRUET, Robert
PURSELL, Lucinda
PURSLEY, Jacob

QUARLES,
QUARLS Joanna A.
      Martha L.
      Mary P.
QUEBEC, Peter

RASSIEUR, Francis Jr.
RAU, John
RAY, Lewis
      Margaret

81

RAY, Julian
    Patrick
RAYOR
 ROYER? Henry
REBOLT, Peter
REILHE, Mme.
REPINE, Francis Sr.
    Francis Jr.
REYNOLDS, Antoine
    John
REVAH, Joseph
RICHARD, John *
RICHARDSON,
 RICKERSON George *
RICHEY, Cynthia
    Tamantha
RICKEY, John
RINGO, Henry
ROBBERTS, William
ROBBERTSON, Elizabeth
 ROBERTSON John
ROBBINS, Abigail
    Frederick
    J. W.
    Jefferson
    Moses
    Prospect K.
    Thaddeus
    Thomas G.
    Welcome A.
ROBBINSON,
 ROBINSON Elizabeth
    Charles S.
    Farissa
    Mary
ROBIDEAU, Isadore
ROCHESTER, John
ROSE, Freeland
ROSSINE, Charles *
ROWLEY, Joel
ROY, Alexander
    Andrew
    Charles
    Julia
    Louis
ROYER, Calis
    Richard
RUSSELL, Henry A.H. (K?)
RUTHERFORD, James
RYAN, Henry

ST. CYR, Fonville F.*
ST. FERNOUR, Michael
SABEN, Daniel
SABORIN, Francis *
SAEGAIN, Elizabeth

SAMPSON, William
SAMUELS, Robert
SANCHITTEER, Louis' heirs
SANTAMONT,
 SANTINO Andrew
    Michael
SAUCIER, Baptiste *
    Charles
    Francis
    John B.
    Michael
    Michael Jr.
    Mme.
    Macky
    Mary
    Savory*
SAUNCILLA, Mme.
SCOTT, David
    Elizabeth
    Felix
    James*
    Walter B*
SCROGGINS, Elizabeth
SEYMORE, Chester
SEWART, William
SHAW, Ann
    Samuel (1826)
  Samuel heirs (1826)
SHELLY, John
SHOBE, Abraham
    Archibald*
    Jesse *
SHULLY, John
SHUTTS, William*
SHY, Samuel
SILVEY, James
SIMONDS, Nathaniel
    Oliver *
SINA, a free woman
    of color
SIPIOT, Francis
SLATER, John
SLUMP, Leonard
SMALL, William H. *
SMEAD, Horace *
SMELCER, David
    George
    Peter
SMITH, Childers *
    Daniel
    Darling
    Edward
    Elizabeth
    George
    James

SMITH, John (two)
    William Sr.
    William Jr.*
SMUIER, William*
SORA, Joseph
SOULA, Tousand*
SPALDING, Thomas
SPENCER, George J.
    Robert
SPEERS, George
STEPP, Andrew
    Catherine
STEPHENS, Simeon
STEPHENSON, Thomas D.
STODDARD, Casius
    John
STONE, Benjamin *
    Bluford
    John B.
    Orlington
STORRS, Ishall
STATER,
 STOTER John
STORY, Edward *
    Henry *
    John *
    Littleton *
STOW, Cephas
STUART, William
STUMP, Leonard
SUBLETTE, Pinkney
SUMNER, Jacob
    Jethro
    Joseph
SWANSON, Thomas

TAGGART,
 TAGGERT James
    Richard
TAYLOR, Caleb *
    John
    Joseph
    Roger
    Samuel
    Thomas
    Washington *
    William *
TAYON, Charles
    Francis
    Joseph
    Louis *
    Peter
    Joseph heirs 1826
TEASDALE, Joseph
TEBO sée THEBEAU

TEENY, Andrew
TEETER,
  TEETERS Benjamin
      John *
      Reuben
TERCERO, Gregory
THEBEAU,
  TEBO Antoine
      Joseph
      Theresa
THOMAS, David C.
      James
      Jesse
      Margaretta
THOMPSON, Aaron *
      John
      Joseph
      Margaret
      Sally
  John's heirs, 1826
THORNHILL, Reuben
TIFFIN, Clayton
TIMBERLAKE, Lucinda
TRUNLEY, Paul
TUCKER, Nathaniel
TURNBOUGH, Lewellen
      Steele
      Allen*

UPHAM, Josiah*

VALANCE,
  VALLANCE Howard D.
      William
VANBURKLEO, William
VANSAN, Pierre
VALLEY, Charles
  Mary's heirs 1826
VASQUEZ, Bennett
VOISARD, Joseph

WADE, Greenberry
      John

WALKER, Benjamin
WALL, John *
      Robert Thompson*
WALLACE,
  WALLIS Joseph
      (heirs 1826)
WALLS, Thompson
WARREN, Widow
WATSON, Archibald Sr.
      Archibald Jr.*
      James
      Johnson*
      William*
  Archibald's heirs 1826
WELCOME, Asparus *
      Charles *
      Etienne
      Katherine
      Louis *
WELLS, George M. (W?)
      Robert W.
      Samuel
      Samuel Jr.*
WELTY, John
      William S.
WETMORE, Parson
WHEELER, John J.*
WHITE, Jacob
      John
      Joseph
      Willey
WHITLEY,
  WHILLEY Solomon
WHITTEAR, Thomas *
WILCOX, Preston B.*
WILKERSON,
  WILKINSON Andrew
      Herod *
      James
      John *
      Jochonias
      William

WILLARD, Rowland
WILLIAMS, Austin C.
      Jacob D.
      Thomas
WILSON, Andrew
      James
     . John
      Uel *
      William*
WIZARD,
  WOIZARD Joseph
WOLF, John
WOODRUFF, Wiatt
WOOLEVER, Henry
WOOLFOLK, John A.
WOOTON, Mme.
      William
  William heirs 1826
WRIGHT, Waller

YATES, John*
YARNALL,
  YARNELL John
      Stephen
YEARDLEY,
  YARDLEY Joseph
      William

ZIMMERMAN, George W.
ZUBRA, Francis
ZUMWALT, Aaron
      Adam
      Andrew
      David
      Elizabeth
      George
      Henry
      Jacob
      John
      Jonathan
      Noah
      William

. . . .

St. Charles was one of the five original districts in Missouri and the city of St. Charles was the state's first capital. It is the only county known to have a territorial census (1817) showing heads of household and ages of household members by brackets. The original of this census has disappeared but it has been photocopied and is available at the State Historical Society of Missouri in Columbia.

BEAVEN, John	merchant	REDD, W. J.	attorne:
BECKWITH, Lot	lost mare	ROBINSON, Isaac	notice
BLOCK, Emanuel	merchant	Therese	"
BROUSTRAN, Helen	estate		
BURLEAU, Sylvester	notice	SCOTT, Hiram	bankrupt
		SHEPHERD, David	bankrup'
CHATTAYNE, Victor	merchant	SLONE, John	stray
COLLIER, John	merchant	SMILEY, Dorothea	notice
COTTLE, Ira	notice	Samuel	notice
Nancy	notice	STODDARD, Joseph	estate
DEVORE, James	attorney	TAYON, Louise	notice
DOZIER, James I.	tavern		
		WILLS, Eliza	notice
FARRIS, John	estate	Thomas	"
HAGEN, Hetty	notice	YARNALL, Elizabeth	notice
William	"		

HALL, Everard — attorney
HENRY, George — barber

JONES, Samuel P. — bookbinder

KEITHLY, Elizabeth — notice
KENAIL, Stephen — stray

LENNAN, Francis — estate
LEWIS, Samuel — stray
LOTHROP, Obijah — stray
LYNN, Isaac — a runaway apprentice
James — "

McCHISNEY, John — stray
    Upper Cuivre Twp.

MARTAIN, William — stray
    St. Charles Twp.
MILLER, Charles — merchant
MOODY, Joseph — estate
Judah — "
MORRIS, Thomas — lost horse

NOEL, Reuben — stray
    Upper Cuivre Twp.

PERCIL, George — notice
Lucinda — "
PERKINS, Elisha — merchant
PHELPS, Cephas — estate
PRESTON, John — merchant

(Wm. was a hatter)

--/-/-/-/-/-/--

MARRIED,—On Tuesday evening Nov. 30th, by the Rev. James Craig, Mr. Philip Grover, to Miss Sarah, daughter of Nicholas Kantz, Innkeeper, all of St. Charles county.
—— On Thursday last, Wm. Levy Esq. of St. Genevieve to Miss Duncan of Cape Girardeau County.

ALEXANDER, Corbin *
   Lawson
   William
ALLY, John *
  William*
ANDERSON, John
ANDREWS, John Sr.
   John Jr.
   William H.
ARMON, Henry
AUSTIN, James
   Mary
   Moses

BAILY, James A.*
   Joel H. *
   Montgomery *
   Reuben *
   William *
BAKER, Adam
   Isaac
   John
   Joseph *
BANISTER, Jonathan
   Joseph
   Nancy
BEQUETTE,
BECKIT (?) Benjamin
   John
BERRY,
BARRY Wilson
BERTHO,
BIRTH Louis
BIERS, Daniel *
BLACKWELL, James
   Jesse
   Robert
   William
BOUMER, Bricks D.
BOUNDS, Isaac *
   Jesse
   John Sr.
   John Jr.
BOUNO(s), James
   John Sr.
   John Jr.
   Jesse
BRADSHAW, John
   William
BRADY, William
BROWN, Benasa (Benajah)
   James
  (cont.)

BROWN, James W.M. *
cont. Joseph *
   Samuel
BRUETTE, Joseph *
BRYAN, Emily
   James
  James' heirs 1823
BUFORD, Thomas
BURGER,
BURGIN, Michael *
BURGIT
BURNHAM, Benjamin
BURNAM Isaac (N.)
   John
BURT,
(BUST?) James
BYAN, Guy

CALDWELL, James
   Robert *
CAMEL,
CAMPBELL James Sr.
   James Jr.
   James P.
   George
   Moses *
   William
CANADY, John
   Josephus
CARDER, George
CARNEY, John *
CARREL, Buck Hotstead *
CARTER, John (two) (one*)
   Tandy
   Washington
   William
CHAPMAN, Robert
CLARKSON, _____ *
CLAY, Eleazer
COBB, John
   Richard
COFER, Elliott
   George
COFFMAN, Daniel *
COLE, Watson
CORA, John
CORNELL, John H.
CORNWELL, George
CRAIG, Andrew *
CRAVINS, Jeremiah
CRIDER, Christopher
   Thomas

CRISSUP, John
CRUMP, Benjamin
   Isaac
   John
CUNNING, Matthew
CUNNERY
CUNNINGHAM, Isaac
   James Sr.
   James Jr.*
   L.
   Mathen G.
   William
heirs of unidentified,
   1823
CURRY, J. or James A. *

DAGGETT,
DOGGETT Margaret
DANIEL, Williamson *
DAVIS, Isaac M.
   Luke
DEDRICKSON, Ezekiel *
DELAUNY, W.
DELILL, Alexander
DEMASTERS, Anderson
DENNISON, Lewis C. *
DENT, Absalom
   John *
   Mark
   Walter
DERICKSON, John
DILL, George
DOGGETT,
DAGGETT Margaret
DONALD, Elial
DOUGHERTY, Owen *
DUCKWORTH, Pulaskiel
DUFF, John DUMASTERS,
DUNLAP, James Anderson*
   Thomas
DUNN, Nathan

EADES, Nathan
   Thomas
EASLY, Thomas
EATON, Abraham
   Jesse
   Lazarus
ELLIOTT, Henry
ESTIS, Barnet
   Gani(u)m
   John T.
  (cont.)

ESTIS, Ledford
cont. Mary
    Oney
    Smith
    William
EVANS, William
    David

FARRAR, Joseph
FITZPATRICK, Thomas*
FLANDERS, John
FLEMING, Alexander
 Flemming Bailey
    Lemuel
    Old Mister
FLORA, Isaac*
    John*
    William*
FORCHAND, John
FOSTER, William*
FOYE, Abraham*
FRANCIS, Henry
FRY, Abraham*

GARNER, Thurston
GARRET, Henry
    Leonard
    Wesley
    William
GEORGE, Thomas
GIBSON, Jesse *
GILBERT, Nathan
GILL, John
GILLILAND, Rachel
GILLISPIE, James and mother
 GALASPY William
GIVENS, Alexander
    Alfred
    Samuel
GOZA, Michael
GRIFFIN, James
    Matthew*
    Nathan
    Scott
    Solomon
GRIFFITH, Joseph Sr.
    Robert B.
GULSHER, Henry*
GUTHRIE, Robert

HALE,   Thomas
 HAILE William
HALBERT, James
HAMILTON, James
HAMPTON, Henry
HANES, Ephraim
    Henry

HARLAN, Rice
HARRIS, Samuel P.
HART, Charles
    Michael
HARTON, John Sr.
 HARLON John Jr.
HATCH, James*
HAYES, John D.
HAYS, Joseph
    Robert
HENDERSON, James
HENRY, Joseph F.*
HERLICK, Joseph
HICKS, Russel*
HIGHTOWER, Thomas
HILL, Thomas
    William
HOLLAND, Michael*
HOLMES, James
HOTSTEAD, Lemuel
HOUSE, Adam
    Jacob*
    Matthias
    Michael
    Nathaniel
HUBARDO, Bates
HUBBARD, John*
HUGHES, Joseph
HUNTER, Samuel
HURD, Andrew*
HURRY, Joseph F.
HURST, Joseph*

JEMIMA, Flora
JESSE, Gibson
JOHNSON, Alex*
JONES, David
    Solomon

KANNACK, George O.
KEER, KERR, James
KENNEDY, John
KINCAID, Samuel
 KINKEAD
KING, Andrew
KINSWORTHY, Joshua

LANDOFF, Samuel*
LATCHERIL, Yasante*
LAYHA, Emalah
    Toosan
LEVERAN, Joseph
LEWIS, Samuel
LOWRE, John*
LYON, Asa*

McALISTER, Jesse
McCORMACK,
 McCORMICK Hardy
    Peter
McCOY, Alexander
    James
    John*
McELROY, Samuel
 McILROY
McFARLAND, Jacob
    James
    Jesse
    John
    Reuben
McGAHAN, George
McHENRY, Archibald
    Elam*
    Enos
    John
McILHENY, Robert
McMATH, Ruben*
McMICHAEL, David*
McREE, John Sr.
 (McKEE?) John Jr.

MADISON, George
    Thomas
MANAGEN, George*
 MANAHAN, William
MANCHESTER, David
MARKS, Dan
    Daviess
    George
MARLOW, Ann
    Nancy
MARTIN, Isaac
    Robert
MATKIN, David
 MATKINS Hiram
    James Sr.
    James Jr.
    Leroy*
    William
MAXWELL, John
MEAD, Philander
MEERS, Henry
MENTEER, James
 MINTEER Joseph
    Robert
MILLER, Robert

86

MITCH, Joseph
MITCHELL, Isaac Sr.
        Isaac Jr.
MOORE, Jacob
     James
     Seth H.
     Thomas
MORRISON, William
MORTELLER (?), Jacob
MULLE(I)NS, Matthew*
MURPHY, David
     Dubart
     Isaac
     James
     Jesse
     John (two)
     Joseph
     Richard
     Thomas
     William Sr.
     William Jr.
MYERS, Henry*

NANTS, William
NEU, Francis W.

OBISHAN, Francois
OHARA, Brice*
ORMAN, Henry

PADGET, Abraham*
PALLISANT (?) heirs
*** PANNICK,
   PARRICK Samuel* ***
PATTISON or
PATTERSON, heirs of William
PATRICK, Caleb
PEERS, John D.
PERSHALLS, Samuel H.
PERRIE,
  PERRIL Hezekiah   ++
      (see PURL)
PERRIN, Samuel
PERRY, James
PEYTON, John
     Thomas   ++
PINKERTON, David
     James Sr.
     James Jr.
     John Sr.
     John Jr.*
     William
PINKSTON, David
POLLY, Henry
     James
***possibly PARRISH

POPE, William
PORTON,
  POSTON Henry
      William
POTTS, Henry
PRATE, Antoine
     John H.
     Peter
PROCTOR, Elizabeth
PURL, Hezekiah

RAGLAND, William *
RAMAS, John
RAY, James
     Yilinda
REED, David
     William
REYBURN, Catherine
RHODES,
  RODES Samuel
RIDEN,
  RIDER Joseph
RIKAH, Francis
RINGER, Abraham *
     Mathias P.
RITTER, James
ROBERTSON, George
     John
ROBINSON, George W.
     John Sr.
     John Jr.
     Philip
ROSE, Samuel *
ROSS, Martin
ROSSO, _?_   ++

SANDLIN, John   ++
SEBASTIAN, George
     Martin
SELKIRK, Alexander *
SHAW, William   ++
SHERILL, John
SHULTZ, Joseph
SHUMAKE, George   Wm.*
     William Sr.
SHALINCE (?), Charles ++
SIMMS,
  SIMS George
     Lewis
SIMPSON, Vinson
     William
SISEL, John
SIVINNY, Allen *
SLAM (?), George Jr.
SMITH, Augustus
     Gideon

SMITH,
  cont. James W.
     William
SPAN,
  SPANN Aaron
SPRADLING, William
STAFFORD, Noah
STAM,
  STAMM George Jr.
     George Sr.
STARK,
  STARKE Jeremiah
     Jonathan
STEGAL,
  STEGALL Griffith D.*
     Martin
STEPHENS, George*
STEPHENSON, John *
STEWART,
  STUART Andrew
     Cornelius
     Jacob
SULLOCK
  (TULLOCK?) Henry
     John
SWIFT, Edward

TALENT, James
TARNALER (?), Peter *
TAYLOR, George
     Pendleton *
TERNAND, Peter
TERRY, Robert *
THARTON, William
THOMPSON, Alex
TOSBERG, Lambert
TULLOCK, Henry ++
     John
TROPAH, Rekah ++

VALLE, John B. *
VANCE, Elisha
     John
     Jordan
     Samuel
VAN HORN, Isaac
VILLINS, Dubriel

WALKER, Lakin
WARD, Ezekiah*(Ezekiel)
WATERMAN, William L. *
WILBORN,
  WILBURN Isaac
     James
     Thomas
WILLIAMS, Elias
     Riley

WILMOT, William*   WILSON, Aquilla   WISI(E)R, William
                               George*
                               John   *   YOUNGER, Alex P.
                               Jonathan   James

....

SECONDARY LIST: from the Herald and the Independent Patriot
              (both published in Jackson, Cape Girardeau Co.)

ALEXANDER, Mme.   A.S.   McFARLAND, Jesse   estate
AUSTIN, John   "   Richard   estate
        Joseph   "   SMITH, Joseph W.   A.S.
EVANS, Mme.   A.S.

....

St. Francois County was formed in December, 1821 from parts of
Ste. Genevieve, Washington, and Jefferson counties. A very small
portion of this county was later taken to form part of Iron Co.

St. Francois was apparently very sparsely populated in the early
years. Less than 30 marriages were performed in the county in the
four years 1822-1825 and of these marriages, 90% of the persons
shown had surnames listed here.

Part of the list of taxes on writs, executions, etc. for Ste.
Genevieve Co., July and November terms of the Circuit Court,
1823. Courtesy State Archives of Missouri.

STE. GENEVIEVE COUNTY: COMBINED TAXES, 1821-22-24, AND TAXES
ON WRITS, EXECUTIONS, ETC., 1819-26, STATE ARCHIVES OF MISSOURI

ALBERT, Charles C.*
ALEXANDER, Joseph
    William
ALLEN, Beverly*
ALLEY, John
    William
AMOREAUX, Benjamin C.*
AMOUREUX, Joseph N. *
    Julian M. *
    Michael
ANDREWS, William *
AUBUCHON, Antoine
    August Sr.
    August Jr.
    August Lun (?)
    Baptiste
    Bazil
    Francois Marie
    Francois P.
    Louis
    Pierre, estate
    Pierre August*
    Pierre Jr. *
  see also OBUCHON
AUSTIN, James
    Moses*

BADEAU, Michael
BAILEY, Henry
BARKER, Joseph
BARRET, John Eugene
BASS, Peter by adm.
BAUNSET, Bte. Vital
BAUVAIS, Bte. Vital
    Gemeon
  (Jemeah, Simeon)
    Joseph
    Joseph Vital
BEAUCHAMP, Baptiste*
    Mme. Widow
BELL, John
BELOS, Pierre
BENIT, William* ++
BERK, BIRK, Rachel Widow
BERRY, Wilson
BEUYATE, Antoine
    Bequet
    Widow ++
BEQUET, Augustin
    Jean Bte. Sr.
    Jean Bte. Jr.*
    Francis

BEQUET, Henry
cont. Joseph
    Pierre
BILLON, Pierre
  (BILLOW, Peter)
BIRD, Amos by exrs.
    Gustavus
BISCH, Albert
BLACK, Anderson*
    John *
BLACKWELL, Jesse
    William
BLOOM, Peter
BOGY, Joseph
BOLDUC, Catherine
    Etienne, Widow
    Widow of Louis
    Pierre
    Prudhomme
    Zacharia*
BOND, James
BONNE, Whight *
BOREL, Johnson
BOREN, James Sr.
    James Jr.
    William
BORIS, William
BOSSIER, Jean Bte.
BOUCHANT, Baptiste
    Widow
BOUNDS, Isaac *
    John
    John Jr.*
*** BOYD, William G. ***
BOYER, Antoine *
    Gabriel
    Godefroy
    Jean
    John
    Joseph
BRADY, William
BRASHEARS, Susannah
BRICE, George D. *
BROWN, Benajah
    Francis
    John S.
    Samuel R.
    Scott
    William R.
BRUGERE, Antoine
BRUGERS
*** also BOYD, Roland

BRYAN, Emily
    James
    Jesse
    Timothy
    William
BURNETT, William
BURNHAM, Benjamin*
    Isaac
    John
    Louis by admr.
BURRUS, Ayser
    Josiah
BUTCHER, Sebastian *
BURTSCHER Theodice and
    Benjamin, together

CALDWELL, James
CAMPBELL, James
    Samuel *
CARDER, George
CARON, Joseph
CARR, William C.
CARRICK, George
CARROLE, Martin
CARRON, Atairosse
    Baptiste
    Joseph
    Louis
CARTER, John
    William
CARTIN, Tandy
CERRE', Antoine*
CERRI Mme. Widow
CHALLELIER, ___
CHAPMAN, Robert
CHARLEVILLE, Baptiste
    Joseph *
*** CLARK, James * ***
CLAY, Eleazer
CLEVELAND, Robert
COBB, John
    Richard
COFER, Elliott
    George
COOPER, Henry W.
COUNTS, Gainum
    William
COURTOIS, Antoine
    Jacques Sr.
    Vincent
***also CLARK, Wm. 89

COUSINS, William
COX, Edward
    Zachariah
CRAVENS, Jeremiah
CRIPPS, John
CRISWELL, Michael
CRESALE
CROSS, Harriet
    Joseph
CUNNINGHAM, Isaac
    James

DAGUET, Peter
DALBE, Joseph Sr.
    Joseph Jr.
DANIELS, Williamson
DARBY, Francis
DAVIS, Timothy*
DEGAINIER, Francois*
DEGUIRE, Jean Bte.
    Louis (two) ***
DEIL, Antoine*
DIEL Henry
DELAUNAY, Alphonse
DELBIE, Joseph
DELUZIERE, Camille estate
DEQUET, Peter
DETCHEMENDY, Clement
    Pascal Sr.
    Pascal Jr.*
DEWAL, Joseph *
DIE', Thomas
DIETERLE, Gottlieb
DODGE, Henry
    Thomas
DONOHOE, John
DORICK, Pelaski
DORLAC, Peter
DRYBRIAD, John
DUBREUIL, Antoine
DUBUISSON, Dumas
DUCLOS, Antoine
DUFOUR, Louis
    Parfait
    Pierre
DUNLAP, James ****
DUROCHER, Berthy
    Bartholomy*
DUVAL, Joseph
DYE, Thomas

EADS, Thomas
EDWARDS, Benjamin
    Cyrus
ELLIOTT, Elias A. *
    Henry

ELLIOTT cont.
    Mary L.
    Infant of H.
ERVIN, William
ESTES, Barnet
    John Sr.
    John Jr.
    Robert
    Smith
EVANS, Eliasa*
    Elijah
    George
    William

FARIS, John
FARLEY, George
    Mme. Widow
FLEMING, Alexander
    Bailey
    Patrick
FLOOD, Larry
FOLEY, Thomas
FOREHAND, John
FORTIN, Baptiste
FOXLEY, Jane
FRACHOUX, Peter
    (Pierre)
FRANCIS, Henry
FREEMAN, James
    Richard

GALE, Joseph (two)
GALLASPIE, John*
GARRET, Leonard
    Wesley
GEORGE, Thomas by agent
GIRARD, Joseph
GUIBORD, Mme. Widow
GILMORE, John
GOOCH, John
GOVERO,
GOVEREAU
    Etienne Sr.
    Etienne Jr*
    Francis
    Henry
    Joseph
(one*)   Louis (two)
    Michael
GOZA, Michael
GRAFTON, Joseph P.
GREGOIRE, Charles
    Charles Jr*
GRENOT, Etienne
GRIFFAN,
GRIFFARD
    Charles
    Louis*
    Michael

GRIFFITH, Joseph
    Robert
GUELE, Joseph
GUIBORD, Louis
    Eugene*
    Mme. Widow
GUIGNON, Louis
    Mme. Widow

HALDEMAN, Edmund
HALE, Thomas
    William
HAMMER,
HAMNER Joel
HANY, Charles
HARRI, HARRICK ? *
HARRIS, Samuel
    William
HART, Charles
    Michael
HARTZEL, Nicholas
HAYNE, Charles
HAYS, Robert Sr.
    Joseph
HEBERLY, Joseph
    Nicholas
HENDERSON, James
HENTHORN, James
HERTICK, Joseph
HICKCOX, Elisha C.
HODSDON, Mons.
HOGAN, Walter
HOLBERT, James
HOLLOMOND, Edmund
HOLMES, James
    William
HOLSTEAD, Lemuel
HORN, Thomas   HOWE, Wm.*
HUBARDEAU, Jean Bte. *
HUDSON, Drury
    John
    Mary
HUGHES, Joseph
HUNT, Joseph
    Noah Sr.
HUNTER, Samuel

JACKSON, David E.
    George E.
    Wingate *
JAMES, Clemens
    Somonon
    William
JANIS, Antoine*
    Aurorie
(continued)

*** Louis Jr* & Louis B* *** ****also DUNLAP, Samuel*

JANIS,
  cont. Francois Sr.
    J. B. Sr.
    J. B. Jr.
JESSE, David
JOHNSON, Josiah
JOHNSTON, Burwell
JONES, John A.
    John K.*
    Robert
JONIS, David

KEENER,
KENNER Francis
KENNEDY, John *
    Josephus*
KERR, Henry
    James
KEEL,
KEIL Birch
    Henry*
    Roberts
KEMPH, Peter
KIMMEL, Allen W.
KINCAID, John
    Samuel

LABRAYER,
LABRIERE, Baptiste
LABRUYERE Julian R.
    Paul
LACHANCE, Gabriel Sr.
    Gabriel Jr.*
    Gervais
    Jean Pepin
    Jervin
    John estate
    Pepin *
    Widow
LAHAIS,
LAHAIE Amie, Aimie
LAJEUNESSE, Louis
    McGriffin
LALUMENDIER, Bazil
    Damonique*
    Francois Sr.
    Francois Jr.
  Janis or Janote
    Jean Bte.
Jos. Jr* Joseph Sr.
    Vital*
LAMARQUE, Etienne
LANDOLT, John
LANE, Harvey
LANGELIES,
LANGELINE Francois

LANGLOIS, Widow
    William*
LAPLANTE, Baptiste*
    Louis
    Marianne
    Mme. Widow
LAPORTE, Louis decd.
    Marie adm.
    Mme. Widow
    Pierre *
LAPOURS, Louis
LA ROSE, Christophe
    Jean Bte. Sr.
    Jean Bte. Jr.
LECLERC, Francois*
LECLERE Louis
LEGRAND, John Marie
LEMEILLEUR, Widow Rene*
LESIEUR, Joseph *
LEVANWORTH, Ralph
LEVRARD, Joseph
    Pierre Sr.
Bte.* Pierre Jr.
LEWIS, Samuel
LICK, William *
LINCH, Francis *
LINN, Lewis
LONGSTRETH, Samuel
LORY, James
LUPIN, Benjamin
LYNN, Benjamin*
McCLENAHAN, James
    John
McCOLLISTER, Jesse
McCORMICK, Peter
McCOY, Alexander
    James
McFARLAND, Jacob
    James
    Jesse
    John Sr.
    John Jr.
    John Andw.
    Reuben
McHENRY, Archibald
    Elam
    Enos
McNOE, George
McPIKE, Haley
    Richard
MADDIN, James *
    Richard
Israel* Thomas Sr.
    Thomas Jr. *

MADISON, Elizabeth
MAILLOTE, Nicholas
MARCHALER, _____
MARKS, Azariah
    Davis
    George
MARTIN, Isaac
    Samuel
MASDEN, James
    Thomas Sr.
    Thomas Jr.
    Esrail (?)
MATKIN, Hiram
    James
    Leroy
  James and David
    (together)
MAURICE, Henry Sr.
  Bte.* Henry Jr*
MAXWELLE, Thomas *
MEAGHER,
MIAHERS Ambrose
MEEKS, Azuriah
    John
MENTIER, James
    Joseph
    Robert
MESSIE, Jacques Sr.
*** Philip *
    Nicholas
MEYOTTE, Nicholas
MICHAEL, Isaac
    M. David
MICHEAU, Michael
MILLARD, Alfred
    Henry *
    Jedediah
    Joshua
    Josiah
MILLER, Richard *
    William
MISSIE, Raphael*
MONMOREL, Francois
MONTGOMERY, Edward
    John*
MOORE,
MOOR Joseph
    Robert
    Seth
    William
MOREAU, Jean Bte.
    Josephe
MORSHELLIAM, Jacob
MURPHY, David
    (cont.)
***also Michel*,
Jacques*, Jean Louis*

91

MURPHY, Dubart
cont. Isaac
James
Jesse
Joseph
Richard
William Sr.
William Jr.
MYGUITE, William

NEW, Mme. Widow
NEWFIELD, Abraham
NOAH, George

OBUCHON, Francois P.
exr. of widow Edith
OGE, Baptiste
Francis Sr.
Francis Jr.
Luke
OKLASS, John
OLIVER, Thomas
ONELLE, Antoine*

PALMER, Mary
PATTERSON, Joseph
James
John
Thomas
PAULITE, see POLLETT
PEPIN, Louis
PERRIN, Samuel
PERRY, James
Montgomery
PETERSON, Joseph
PHILIPSON, Jacob
PILLERS, James F.
PINKERTON, John
Samuel
William
PINKLEY, George
PINNEL, Henry
PIRREL
PLACE, Jh. Duquet
PLACEE
Dugay
PLACIDE, Joseph
POLLETT, Paul Sr.
Paul Jr.
Pierre Robert
Pierre Jr.*
POQUEX, Joseph
PORTERIQUE, Antoine
POSTON, Henry
William
POTS, Henry

PRATTE, Antoine's widow
B. (Belleron)
Evariste
Henry (Rev. Henry)
Jean Bte.
Joseph Rosemund*
Pierre B.
PREMER, Samuel
PREMET
PRICE, Euphrase
PROUX, Joseph
PURDON, James

QUICKLY, John*

RABER, Michael*
RAIBURN, Mme. Widow
RANGER, Mme. Widow
Pierre
READ, David *
William *
REDEN, James
REED, Widow
RELFE, James H.
RESINGER, Adam
REYNOLDS, Samuel
RIBEAU, John*
RIBAUT
RICARD, Trope Sr.
Trope Jr*
RICHARDS, Alex.
RICHARDSON, Ephraim
ROBERTS, Edmund
ROBINSON, J. B. Sr.
J. B. Jr.
John
Philip
William *
ROSE, Daniel H. *
ROUQUE, Margaret
ROUSSIN, Etienne
Michel
Mme. Roben
Mme. Widow
Sanchan
ROZIER, Ferdinand
RUDY, John
RUNNEL, Samuel
RUSSELL, William

ST. GEMME, Auguste
Bartholomew
J. Bte.
Raphael *
Vital Bte.*
ST. VRAIN, Felix

SCOTT, Charles*
Thos.* John
Obadiah *
SCRIPPS, John
SEARCY, David
SEBASTIAN, George
SHANNON, William
SHAW, James
William
SHERREL, John
SHOUMAKE, William
SIMONE, Antoine
SIMONEAU Francois
Bazil *
Joseph *
Mme. Widow
SIMPSON, Vexon
William
SLATER, William*
SMITH, Gideon*
James W.
Samuel
SMYTH, Peter*
SPACKMAN, Samuel
SPENCER, William H.
SPERA, William
SPIRA
STAFFORD, Noah
STEGE, Griffith*
STEWART, Cornelius
STILE, David
STOVER, Thomas
STRICKLAND, Titus
SUDS, John * (SEEDS?
SWICK, Martin
SWIFT, Edward

TALLEN, James
TANG, James
TONG
TAYLOR, George
TESSEREAU, Baptiste
Louis
estate of Pierre
estate of Joseph
THOMAS, John
THOMUR, Antoine
TOMUR Charles*
Francis
Gabriel
Joseph
William
estate of ?
++ TILLAROD, William L.
TRIGERE, Pierre
++ TORIQUE, Pierre

92

TRIGERE, Pierre
TRUDEAU, Henry
    Louis Sr.
    Louis Jr.
TUCKER, Riggs*

URNER, Benjamin
    David

VALLE, Charles
    Charles' estate
    Charles C.
    Charles Francois
    Francois
    Francois estate
    Francois Bte.

VALLE, Felix *
    Jean Bte. Sr.
    Jean Bte. Jr.
    Louis
VILLARS, Dubreuil
VILLAN
VILLEMER, Michel
    Nicholas

WAHLMAKER, John
WALSH, Edmund
    Edward
    Nicholas
    Richard
WHITELAW, Eve
WHITES, William

WEEDS, Robert Sr.
WILLIAM, James
WILLIAMS, Mial (Meal) ***
WILMOTT, William R.
WILSON, Daniel
    John * Jonathan
WINSTON, James
WOOLFORD, Frederick

YOUNGER, Alexander
YOWSLEY, Willis

*** WILLIAMSON, Daniel

....

STE. GENEVIEVE: SECONDARY LIST FROM THE REPUBLICAN AND THE
ENQUIRER (ST. LOUIS) AND THE INDEPENDENT PATRIOT AND THE
HERALD, JACKSON

BROWN, Robert T.	estate	HOWARD, Edmund	estate
BUCKNER, A.	A.S.	Polly Whitlow	"
DONNSHAW, John	stray	HUDDLESTON, A.	A.S.
FARLEY, Frances Whitlow	estate	LA PLANTE, N.	A.S.
Thompson	"	LAVERONE, S.	stray
Thomas	"	LOGAN, James	estate
FENWICK, Ezekiel	estate	McARTHUR, John	A.S.
James L.	"	McLEAN, James	estate
Leo	"		
Martin	"	MORELAND, William	bankrupt
Walter	"	STEEN, H. pauper	A.S.
Zeno			
FRACHOUD, Robert	A.S.	URCHUMBEAU, Charles	A.S.
GARNER, George pauper	A.S.	WATSON, Jane	estate
GIRTY, W.	A.S.	WHITELAW, Coleman	estate
GRIFFIN, Benjamin	estate	Henderson	"
Betsy Whitlow	"	WILSON, Jonathan	stray
HAMILTON, Clarissa Fenwick	"		
HART, Elizabeth	notice		
HEARD, Edmund	estate		
Mary	"		

....

Ste. Genevieve was one of the original districts of Missouri, and is
the site of the state's oldest permanent settlement. It is the parent
county of Jefferson, Madison, Perry, St. Francois, and Washington
counties, and, by extension, of Iron, Ripley, and Shannon counties.

(Entire county 1819, city only 1823, both shown on lists of
delinquents for the years 1822 and 1824)

ABERT, Bazil
ABRAHAM, Israel
ADAMS, David
    Sally, widow
    William
ADULY, William
AHEARD, Anthony
AIARDE, Lange, Mme.
ALEXANDER, Walter B.
ALEXIN, Mme.
  ("Courtois daughter")
ALLANDES, Francis
ALLEN, Archibald
    John
    John E.
ALVAREZ, Augustin
    Mme.
    Manuel
AMBROISE, Louis
AMELIN, Alexis
ANDERSON, Garrett
ANDRUZE, A. Revnd.
APPERSOLE, Christian
APPLEGATE, Milton
ARMSTRONG, George
    James
    John
ARNAUD, Bartholomew
ARNOLD, James
ASHLEY, William H.
AUBUCHON, Gabriel Jr.
    Gregoire
AUSTIN, Horace

BACON, Langston
    Ludwell
    Nathaniel
    Reubin
    William
BAIRD, Thomas
BAKER, Alsworth
BALL, Abner
    John
    John S.
BALEY, Robert
BANISTER, Benjamin
BARADA, Antoine
BARETEAU, Auguste
BARNES, James
BARNETT, Andrew
BARRIBEAU, Pierre

BARRY, Joseph
BARTELMY, Francois
BARTHOLOMEW, Tobin
BARTLETT, Francis
    Phineas
BARTON, David
    Kember
    Joshua
    Nathaniel
BARTOW, Aquilla
BATES, Caroline M.
    Frederick
    Moses P.
    Sarah
BAST, George
BATTUT, Henry
BAXTER, Greenberry
BAY (BEY), Samuel
BAYER, James
BEAUCHAMP, Joseph P.
BEAUFILS, Jean Baptiste
BEEBE, Elijah
    Elisha
BELCOUR, Jean Baptiste
BELCOURT, Baptiste D.
BELISLE, Pierre Legries
BELL, John
    Philip
BELLAND, Pierre
BELLFORD, Baptiste
BELLISSIME, Alexander
BELLON, John B.
BELLVILLE, Pierre
BENNETT, Benjamin
    Charles
    William
BENOIST, Conde
    Francois M. est 1823
    Touissant dit Seraphim
BENT, Silas
BENTON, Samuel M.
    Thomas H.
BERTHOLD, Bartholomew
BERTRAND, Michael
BERRY, James
    Samuel
BERRYSFORD, Robert
BESAUNETTE, Bazile Hebert
BETTICK, William
BEY (BAY), Samuel
BEZET, Paul

BIENVENU, Eugene
    Henry
BILLON, Charles est. 1823
BINGHAM, John
BISSELL, Daniel
BISSONNETTE, Joseph
BLACK, Anthony
BLANCHARD, George
BLOCK, Simon Jr.
BOBB, John Sr.
BODOINE, Antoine
    Godfrey
BOID, John M.
BOLAND, David
BOLI, BOLY, John
    Moses
BOLON, Susan
BOMPART, Francis
BONANI, Pierre
BONHOM, Moses
BORDEAUX, Antoine
BOSSERON, Charles
BOSTWICK, Oliver N.
BOTHICK, John
BOTTON, J. B.
BOUCHER, F ancois
BOUIS, Baptiste
    Vincent widow
BOUJENEAU, Vital
BOUJU, Joseph
BOURBENOIS, Auguste
  (BORBONNE)
BOUVETTE, Jean Baptiste
BOWLES, Augustin
    Caleb
    Widow
BOYD, Philip
BOYER, Jean Francis
BOWNY, James
BRADY, Harriet
  (widow of Thomas)
BRATTON, William
BRAZEAU, Auguste
    Joseph
    Louis Sr.
    Louis
    Nicholas
    Therese, widow
BRECKENRIDGE, James
BREEZE, Thomas
BRENLY, John

BREWER, Benjamin
BRICE, John
BRIGHT, George Y.
    Josiah
BROOKS, Thomas
BROTHERTON, James est. 1819
    Rebecca
BROUSTER, Simon
BROWN, James
    Jehu
    John (Prairie)
    John M.
    Edward
    Joseph C.
    Philip
    William
BROWNER, Jeremiah
BRUNETTE, Jacques
BUCHANAN, George
  Polly widow of Robert
BUCHE, Francois
BUCHER, James
    Nelson
BUD, Jacob C.
BUEL, James C.
BUPRON, Charles
BURK, David
    John
BURKHART, Joshua H.
BURNS, Cornelius
BURROWS, Thomas
BURTSTON, Jonathan
BYRD, Edmund
    Jacob
    Thompson
    William
BYRNS, John
BYRON, John

CABANNE, John P.
CADMAN, Francis
CADWELL, John
CAILLOU, Francis
    Louis
CADVER, James
CALDWELL, George
CALLAUM, Joseph
CALLENDER, John
CALVERT, William
CAMP, Celeste
  widow of Jeffrey
CAMPBELL, Jeremiah
    William (two)
CARDAMA, Andrew
CARMAN, Caleb

CARMAN, Samuel
CAPP, George
CARR, William C.
CARRICO, Asa
    Daniel
  Vincent est. 1819
CARTMELL, Maria
CARTER, Edward
    James
CASHMAN, Conrad
CASNER, George
CASON, Edmund
CASTONGA, Francis
CASTROW, William
CATHERWOOD, D.
  ("by Dr. Healy")
CATRALL, John M.
CAULK, Richard
    Thomas
CAW, Peter
CERRE, Pascal
CHAMP, Prove
CHAMPEAU, Pierre
CHANDLER, Thomas
CHAPMAN, John
CHAPPET, Baptiste
CHARLESS, Edward
    Joseph
CHARLEVILLE, Mme.
CHARTRAND, Amable
    Mme.
    Thomas
CHATILLON, John
CHAUVIN, Francois deVins
    Jacques Sr.
    Jacques Jr.
CHENIER, Antoine
CHITWOOD, Richard Sr.
CHOQUETTE, Antoine
    Henry
    Julian
CHOUTEAU, Auguste Sr.
    Gabriel C.
    Paul
    Pierre Sr.
    Pierre Jr.
CHRISTMAN, William T.
CHRISTY, Joseph
    William
CLAMORGAN, Jacques' heirs
CLARCK, Carlton
    John J.
CLARK, William
CLASBY, Ira
CLEMENS, James Jr.

CLEMENT, Francis
COCKRELL, Starkes
COLLARD, Francois
  Widow of F'cis 1824
COLLET, Robert
COLE, Matthew
    Nathan
    William
COLEMAN, Benjamin
COLLINS, Augustavus
    C.
    Roger
    William D.
CONNELL, Michael
CONNOR, Jeremiah
    Nicholas
CONSTANT, Gabriel
  Joseph dit Larimore
    Leon
    Louis
CONWAY, Joseph
COOK, Asher F.
    Oliver R.
COONS, Jean Baptiste
    John
COOP, Samuel
COOPER, Jacob
    John
CORDELL, Arthur
    Hiram
    Steptoe
COSGROVE, Moses
COURTOIS, I. (J?) M.
COUZENEAU, Tousant
COWIE, John
    William
COX, Caleb
COZENS, Horatio
COZINE, John R.
CRAIG, Alexander
    Andrew
CRAWFORD, John
CREELY, Baptiste
    Francois
CRESSER, James
CREVIER, Francis Xavier
CRISWELL, James
    John
    Martha
CRITTEN, Jesse
CRUECHAW, Robert
CRUTZINGER, Alfred
CULVERT, Burwell
    John
CUMMINS, James C.
CUNNINGHAM, John

95

CURTES, Brazell B.
CUYLER, David E.

DABIN, Pierre
DABNY, Auguste
DAGGETT, John D.
DALES, John
DALL, Joel
DALY, Michael
DANJEN, Antoine
DATCHERUT, Adelaide
        Aurora
        Desire
        Elizabeth
        Francis
        Pierre
        Zabel
DAVIS, Daniel
      Isaac
      James
      John
  Ralph est. 1823
DEAN, William
DeCAMP, S. S. G. Dr.
DECKERS, George
       William
DEHETRE, Hyacinthe
DeJARDIN, Paul
DeJERLY, Paul
DeLAURY, David
DeLERCY, Julie
  (free mulatto)
     Louis
DELIADE, Obershaw
DELISLE, Eugene
DeLOIS, Paul
DeLOR, Treget
DeLORIERE, Charles F.
      Henry
DEMERIND, Julius
DEMOISLEM, Auguste
DEMOULIN, Jean Baptiste
DENISON, S. Stern
DENONMOLINE, ?
DENORT, Charles
DENOYER,
  DENOIS Francois
      Joseph
      Louis
      Marien
DENNY, Daniel
DENT, Frederick
DENTON, Thomas
DERBY, John

DERNERY, Henry
DEROIN, John
DEROSIER, Baptiste
DEROUIN, Francois Sr.
      Francois Ginelle
DETANDEBARATZ, Martial
DETHIER, Louis
DEVERS, Moses
DEVOTION, Louis
DEZENTZY, Louis
DIDIER, Pierre
DILLON, Patrick M.
DIXON, Howell
DODSON, Fletcher
DOGY, Joseph
DOLAN, Francois
     Michael
DOMINE, Baptiste
DOMINIQUE, Jean Baptiste
      Donly
      Eugene
      John
DONNER, Samuel
DONOHO, Francis
DORRISS, James
DOTY, William F.
DOUGHERTY, Matthew
      Michael
      Richard
      Simon
DOUGLASS, James L.
     Jesse
     Martin
     Thompson
     William
DOWLER, Thomas
DOWNING, Ezebiel
     Jane
     Samuel
     William
DRAPER, Deborah
DROVEN, Francis Jr.
     John
DRUSLAM, Thomas
DUBRAY, Francis
DUBREUIL, Antoine
      Joseph
      Louis
      Pascal
  Susan, widow
DUBURGH, Bishop Louis
DUCHEN, Joseph est. 1824
DUCHOQUETTE, Baptiste
      Francois
      Henry

DUCHOQUETTE, Pierre
DUEL, Archibald
DUFF, Ebenezer
DUMOND, Charles
DUNCAN, John
     Robert
DUNARD, Rev. J. (I?) M.
DUNEGANT, Francois
DUNLAP, Robert
DUNLAVY, Richard
DUNORD, Joseph
    dit DEPUIX
DUPOTRE, Pierre
DUPRISE, Joseph
DUPUIX see DUNORD
DUROCHER, Auguste
DUTREMBLE, Antoine

EASTER, a negro woman
EASTON, Rufus
EBAIR, Joseph
EDWARDS, Elexis
      Henry
      Ninian
ELLENWOOD, Benjamin
ELLIOTT, Andrew
      Elias
ELLIS, Samuel
ENGLISH, Charles
      Elkanah
ESSEX, Thomas
EUGENE, Dominique
EVENS, Daniel F.
EVERHEART, George

FAAHAN, John
FADHER, Bernard
FAIR, Eliza
FARMER, William
FARRAR, B. G.
FARRIS, Aron
     George
     Robert P.
FAYSOUX, Peter
FERGUSON, George W.
     Peter
FERRELL, Edward
FEVER, Sampson
FICKLIN, John M.
FINE, David
    William
FINNEY, John
    William

FITTER, William
FITZGERALD, Michael P.
FITZWATER, Thomas
FLANDRAIN, Antoine
FLEMING, Robert K.
FLOR, Florence
  a free negro woman
FLORE, Labuche
  a free negro woman
FORD, Benjamin
++ FOUNTAIN, Felix ++
  FONTAIN
FORSYTHE, Thomas
FORTOIS, Michael
FOSSETTE, James
FOUATTE, William
FOUCHER, Francois
++   Michael ++
FOURNIER, Francois
FRANEY, Matthew
FREELAND, William
FREEMAN, Daniel
FRY, Jacob
FUGATE, William C.
FULMORE, John
FURR, Lewis
  Sarah

GAGNION, Jean Baptiste
GALLATIN, Abraham
GAMACHE, Auguste
        Baptiste Jr.
GAMBLE, Archibald
GANNON, Michael
        Timothy
GARDNER, Mary
        William
GARNIER, Joseph V.
GATER, John
GATES, John P.
        Matthias S.
GAY (GORHAVE) Nicholas
GEBERT, Dr. P. M.
GEMBIEN, Henry
GERRONE, Antoine
GEUNELLE, Francis
GEURETTE, Pierre
GEYER, Henry
GIBEAU, Joseph
GIDDINGS, Salmon
GIGAIRE, Baptiste
  GIGUAIRE
GILBERT, Auguste
GILHULY, Bernard
GILLY "of New Orleans"

GIRRARD, Baptiste
  estate 1823
GLAZE, Parson
GODAIR, Antoine
        Baptiste
        Baptiste Jr.
GODON, Francois
GOODFELLOW, John
GOODWIN, David
GORDON, Alexander
        Thomas
        William
GORHAVE see GAY
GOSS, Fenton F.
GOUCHY, Francis
GOULETTE, Louis
GOWEN, Charles
GRAHAM, Alexander
GRANT, William
GRATIOT, Charles

  estate 1823
        Henry
        J. P. B.
GRAVELINE, Joseph
GRAVES, John C.
GRAY, Alexander
GREEN, Duff
        William
GRIFFIN, Gilderoy
GRIFFITH, Isaac H.
        William
GRIGG, George
GRIMAUD, Alexander
GRIMSLEY, Thornton
GUIBORD, Augustin
        Baptiste
GUILLORY, Philip
  GILLORY (free colored)
GUINEL, Francois
        Pascal
GUITARD, Louis
        Paul Sr.
        Paul Jr.
        Vincent Sr.
        Vincent Jr.
GUNSOLLIS, James
GUY, John Francis
        John R.
GUYOL, F. M.
GUYON, Hubert
        Mme.
        Vincent

HABB, Victor
HAGERTY, Patrick
HALDERMAN, Peter
HALE, John
HALL, Benjamin
        Isaac
HAMILTON, Andrew
        Ninian
        Hon. William
HAMMOND, Nancy
        Col. Samuel
HANCOCK, Stephen
HANLEY, Thomas
HANNA, John
  ("son of Mrs. Kaufman")
HARBISON, Archibald
HARMAN, James
HARRIS, Barnabas
        estate 1819
        James
        Jean M.
        Thomas
HARRISON, Daniel
        Johnson
        Thomas Sr.
        William
HASKINS, Thomas L.
  HOSKINS
HAWKIN, Jacob
HAWKINS, William (two)
HAYS, Samuel
HAYWOOD, Andrew
        Francis
        John
HEADRICK, Charles
HEBERT, Mme. Basile
        Joseph
HEELY, Thomas
HELDERBRAND, Christian F.
HEMPSTEAD, Charles
        estate 1823
        Stephen Sr.
        Thomas
HENESMAN, Thomas
HENMELL, Auguste
HERBERT, Thomas
        estate 1823
HERD, Thomas
HERTZOG, Joseph
        William
HIBLER, Samuel Sr.
        Samuel Jr.
HICKMAN, Francis
HICKS, Nathan
HICKSON, Joab
HICKY, John

97

HIGGES, Dennes E.
HIGGINS, William
HILL, Amos
    William B.
HINDERLIGHTER, Jesse L.
HINSMAN, Samuel
HITTLE, Thomas
HOARD, Jesse
HODEMONT, Emanuel D.
HOFFA, John
HOFFMAN, H. L.
HOLBROOK, Nancy
HOLLAND, James
HOLMES, Gorman
HOLSTEIN, John D.
HONORE, Jean Baptiste
HONORIE, Louis Tesson
    Noel
HOOPER, Thomas
    William Sr.
    William
HORNETT, Patrick
HORROCKS, Edward
HORTIZ, Jean Baptiste
    Joseph
    Margaret, widow
HOUGH, Daniel
HOUSE, Peter
HOWARD, John
HOWDERSHELL, John
HUBBARD, Elizabeth
HUCHESON, James
HUDDLESTON, Robert
HULL, John
HUME, John
HUNO, Gabriel
HUNT, Theodore
    Wilson P.
HURBISON, James
HYATT, Frederick

INGRAM, Arthur
IRWIN, James
    estate 1823
JACOBY, John
    estate 1823
JAMERSON, Hugh M.
JAMES, Benjamin
    estate 1819
    Cumberland
    James
    John S.
    Morris
    Phineas

JAMISON, William
JANES, Joseph
JANETTE, free negro woman
JANO, Baptiste
JARRITT, Joseph
JEFFREY, Celeste
    free negro woman
JENKINS, Jeremiah
    John
JENKS, William
JENNING, Clement
JENNINGS John
JOHNSON, C.N.T.
    Francis
    James Sr.
    James Jr.
    John
    Robert
    Thompson
JONES, Benjamin
    Eaton
    John
    John Rice, est.
JOVIAL, Joseph
JOYAL
JUMP, John
    Peter

KARNEY, Philip
KAUFMAN, Sarah
KEATHLEY, Thomas
KEESUCKER, John
KELLS, Thomas
    William D.
KELLY, Robinson
KENEDY, William
KENNERLY, George H.
    Mary by gdn.
    James
KERR, Matthew
KEVERING, Timothy
KIENLEN, Christian
KING, George
KINGSLEY, Jedediah
KINKAID, Andrew
KINKHEAD James
    John Sr.
    Walter
    William
KIRKER, James
KLINGER, Fann
    free negro woman
KLUNK, Joseph
KNAPS, Edward

KNIGHT, John
    widow of Louis
KULING, Timothy

LABADIE, Joseph
    Julia
    Louisa
    Pierre
    Sylvester
LABARGE, Joseph
LABBE, Mme. Jacques
LA BEAU, Baptiste
    Francois
LA BEAUME, Louis
    Susan administrator
LA BLOND, Joseph
LA BROSS, Francis
LA BRUEN, Louis
LA BUCHE, Francois
LA CAISSE, Mme. Margaret
    (widow)
LA COMPTE, Hyacinthe
    Mme. Margaret
LA COUNT, Pierre
LA CROIX, Joseph
LADEROOT, Michel
LA DOISE, Joseph
LADONCEUR, Pierre
LAFLECH, Joseph
LAFLEUR, Louis
LA JOYE, Jean Lambert
    Louis
LAKENAN, James
LALANDE, Mary widow
LALONTRE, Andrew
LAMBEN, John Sr.
LAMBERT, Lajoie fils
    Samuel M.
LAMI DUCHOQUETTE, Baptist
    Francois
    Joseph
    Mme.
LAMONT, Daniel
LANDREVILLE, Andre
LANE, William C.
LANGHAM, Angus
    John L.
LANHAM, Hartley
    Stephen
    Richard
LAPOE, Charles
LAPRISE, Mme. Marie
LARD, Fielding
    John

LARIMORE, see CONSTANT
LA RIVIERE Pierre
LAROUX, Helen
        Sylvestre
LASHARSH, Baptiste
LATIA, John
LATRESSE, John
LAURA, Regnay
LAURENT, Ladonier
        Louis
LAVALETTE, Louis
LAVEILLE, Joseph
    widow of Francis
LAWRENCE, Daniel
        George
        James
LEARNED, Louis
LEATHERBURY, George
LE BRUN, Louis
LEDUC, M. P.
LEE, Mary Ann, widow
        Pat .O.
        Thomas
LE GUERRIERE, Charles
LEITENSDORFER, John
LEMA, John
LE MOND, Louis
LENZELL, James
LE ROUX see LAROUX
LE VEILLE see LAVEILLE
LEWIS, Charles
        James O.
        James W.
        John Sr.
        Martrom
        Warner
LIGGETT, Joseph
LIGHT, Aaron
LILLANED, Thomas
LINDELL, J. G.
        Peter
LINK, Absalom
LISA, Manuel
    estate 1823
LITTELL, James
LITTLE, John
    estate 1823
LITMAN, Antoine
LOISE, Paul
LOLLARD, Archibald
        Reuben
LONG, Gabriel
        James
        John
        Nicholas

LONG, Samuel
        William Sr.
        William Jr.
LONGTEMPS, Pierre
LONGWORTH, James
        Joseph
LOPER, James
LOTHER, Robert
LOUISE, Paul
LOURIE, Waite (by agent)
LOVERING, John
LOWE, Richard
LOWLER, Jacob
LOZIER, Baptiste Sr.
        Baptiste Jr.
LUCAS, Adrian
        Charles
    (estate 1823)
        J. B. C.
LUCIER, Antoine
LYCETT, John
LYONS, Joseph

McALLISTER, John
McCLAIN, Stephen
McCLANAHAN, Josiah by agt
McCLURE, James
McCLUSKY, David
McCONNELL, Robert
McCOURTNEY, Alexander
        John
McCOY, Hugh
        James
        Joseph
McCUE, Bartholomew
McCULLOUGH, Henry
        William
McDONALD, Archibald
        Eneas
        James
        Patrick
McFALL, Hiram
McFARLANE, John
McGIRK, Matthew
McGORIN, Daniel
McGUIRE, Thomas
McGUNNEGLE, James
    estate 1823
McKENNON, Theophilus
McKENNY, Charles
McKEYS, James est 1824
McKNIGHT, James
McNIGHT John est 1824
        Thomas

McLAUGHLIN, Daniel
        John
McLAURIE, Josiah
McMANNUS, Edward
McNAIR, Alexander
McNARY, Thomas
McNUTT, Ewing
        Francis
McREA, William

MACKENZIE, Donato by agt
MACKEY, James
MACORMICK, Jordan
MADDING, Stephen
MAGEE, Barry
MAGILL, Samuel
MAGOON, John
MAJORIE, David
MALLATTE, Pierre
MALLET, Antoine
        Pascal
MALONY estate
MARCH, Clement
MARESCHALL, Francois
        Jean B.
        Mme.
MARGRET, a negro woman
MARIA, Gregory
MARIE, Labin
MARIEN, Jacques
MARKHAM, George
MARLY, Antoine
    Felicite, widow
        Luke
        Michel Sr.
        Michel Jr.
MAROCAY, Peter
MARRION, Beneventure
MARSH, Daniel
MARSTON, Morrill
MARTEL, Joseph
MARTIGNY, Margaret widow
MARTIN, Adam Sr.
        Adam Jr.
        David Sr.
        Jonathan P.
        Lewis Sr.
        Louis (E.)
        Moses
        William
MASON, Henry
        Richard
        Thomas
MASSEY, John
        Joshua
        William   99

MASSON, Ann widow
MAURY, Evariste
MAYHEW, William
MAYOTT, Jacques
MEACHAM, Berry (Negro)
MENARD, Amable
    Joseph est. 1823
    Louis
MERRY, Samuel
METZ, Elias Sr.
MIERS, Stephen
MIGNERON, Solomon
MILES, Josiah
MILLAGEN, Richard
MILLER, James
    John
    Samuel
    William
MILTON, William
MINGO, Peter
MITCHELL, Andrew
    Charles L.
    James
MOCK, George
MOITIE, Antoine
    Louis
MOLLAIRE, Baptiste
MONASTRES, David
MONTAGNE, Joseph
MOORE, Daniel
    Harden P.
    Henry   ++
    James
    N. H.
    Samuel
    Simpson
MOORS, Alfred
MOREHEAD, James
MORIN, Baptiste   ++
    Henry
    Joseph
    Mme.
    Michel
MORRIS, James
MORRISON, James est. 1823
    William
MORTON, George
MOSHER, William
MOTIE, see MOITIE
MOUGRAIN, Noel
MOUNT, Britten
    Samuel L.
MOUNTJOY, William
MOUSET, Baptiste

MOUTRY, Joseph
MUCIER, Charles
MULLANPHY, John
    Terresse
MURPHY, Daniel
    Dennis
    James by agent
    John
    Patrick
    Thomas
MURRY, John
    Thomas
MUSICK, Abraham   ++
    David
    Ephraim
    Eli   ++
    Jonah
    Nancy
    Robert
    Uel
    Uri
    William
MYERS, John

NAILER, Alexander
NASH, Francis
NEAL, Reubin
NEEL, Valentine
NEIL, Francis Revnd.
NESTILL, Samuel
NEWELL, Lewis
    Thomas by agt. ++
NEWHOUSE, William
NICHOLAS, Abner
    Joseph
NOBLE, James
NOISE, Therese
NOLEN, Garvais
NEWLIN, Edward ++
NOZEE, Francis

OAF, George
OBER, Samuel R.
OBERSHON, Gabriel
    Joseph Sr.
    Joseph Jr.
OBRYAN, William
O'FALLON, John
OFFULL, Joseph A.
O'HARA, William
O'ROURKE, John
ORR, John
    William
OSHBURN, Ambrose
OUVRE, Louis

PAGE, Daniel D.
PAIN, B. G. by agent
PALMER, William
PAPIN, Alexander L.
    Hypolite
    Joseph
    Marie Louise
    (estate 1823)
    Pierre D.
    Pierre dit Melicour
    Silvester
    Theodore
PARMLY, Silvanus or   ++
    Sylvester
PARK, Josiah
PARKS, Arthur   ++
PATTERSON, Elisha
    John Sr.
    John Jr.
    Saunders
    William
PATTON, John
    Johnson J.
    Robert
PAUL, Gabriel
    Rene
PAYANT, Peter dit
    ST. ONGE
PAYNE, Benjamin's heirs
PECK, J. H.
PELAR, Peter
PELTIER, Joseph
PEPIN, Joseph
PERAS, John
PERDREVILLE, Rene
PERKINS, Joseph
PERRAS, Jacques
PERRY, Francois
PESCAY, Julius
    Mme.
PETERSON, Henry
PETIT, Louis Lamiere
PETTIBONE, Rufus
PETTIS, Spencer
PETTUS, William G.
PHILIBERT, Joseph
PHILLIPSON, Joseph
    Simon
PICKETT, Isaac Newton
PIGEON, Hyacinthe
PIGETTE, Lowrance
    (estate 1823)
PIGGOTT, John
PINCONNEAU, Stephen

PIQUETTE, John A.
PITZER, George
PORCH, Parson
PORIER, Francis
PORTER, William C.
POSLEY, John
POST, Justus
POTTER, John C.
    Joseph
POURNESS, Josiah
POWELL, George
    Peter
PRATHER, Archibald
PRATT, Bernard
PRESSIE, Joseph
PRESTON, William by agent
PREWITT, Charles
    James
    Osborn
PRICE, Christopher M.
    Risdon
  Vayey or Vescay ?
PRIMM, John S. by agent
    Peter
PRIMON, John Sr. by agent
    Paul
PRUETT, Samuel est 1819
    Laboum
PUIGGOT, Laurent
PURDY, James J.
PURSLEY, John

QUARLES, Prior
    Col. Robert
QUICK, Daniel

RAMY, William
RANKEN, Robert
RANY (RANNEY), Nathan
RAPIER, Richard
RAPIEUR, Louis
RECTOR, Elias
    Stephen
    Thomas
    William
REDMAN, Chukesberry
REED, Jacob est. 1823
    John S.
    Leonard
    Strother
REDER, Elijah
REEVIS, Thomas
REGNIER, Louis
REINO, Ignace
RENARD, Hyacinthe

RENCONTRE, Adrian
    Antoine
REPIEN, Joseph
REVONS, Louis
REYNOLDS, John
REYNOR, Henry
RIAN, Anthony
RICE, Nathan
RICHARDS, Hugh
RICHARDSON, Amos
    Booker
    James
    John
    Skelton
RICHY, George
RIDDICK, Thomas F.
RIGGS, John
RILEY, Robert
RISLEY, Philip
RITCHU, James
RIVIERRE, Antoine
    Baptiste
    Francois
  Mary Ann dit BACANE
RIVILE, Louis
ROBAIR, Antoine
    Charles
  Francois, an old
    negro woman
    Louis
    Paulette
ROBAU, Charles Jr.
ROBB, George H.
ROBERT,
ROBERTS Adinyah
    Michael
ROBERTSON, John A.
    William
ROBESON, James
ROBIDOUX, Antoine
    Francis
    Joseph
    Michael
    Tousant
ROCHEBLAVE, Philip
ROCHFORD, Francis
    (estate 1823)
ROCK, Peter
RODGERS, Joseph
ROGERS, Jesse
ROLETT, Michel dit
    LADEROUT
ROLLENS, Henry
ROSE, Matthias
ROURKE, Michael

ROUSSELL, Francois
ROY, Francois
    Joseph
RULFIELD, Eleakem
RUPLEY, Jacob
RUPRUIX, Joseph
RUSSELL, Nehemiah
    John L.(S?) B.
RUTGERS, Arundt

SABOURAN, Peter
ST. CYR, Hyacinthe
ST. JEAN, Peter
ST. JOHN, Marian Laparch
ST. ONGE, see PAYANT
ST. VRAIN, Charles
    Felicite
SALOISE, Joseph
SALOR, Joseph
SAMUELS, Armistead
SANDLING, Randolph
SANFORD, J. T. A. C.
    Michel
    Nicholas
SANGUINETTE, Charles
    Marie
    Simon
SAPPINGTON, Hartly
    Mark
    Nancy
    Rezin
    Richard
    Thomas
    Zephaniah
SARPY, Gregoire
    John B.
SARRADE, John
SARTIN, Hampson
SAVAGE, William A. (H?)
SCHLATTER, William by agt
SCOTT, Alexander by agt
    Moses
SEELY, Jacob
    Jonas
    J.N. Nicholas
    Rebecca widow
SERGEANT, John
SHACKFORD, John
SHAFFER, Samuel
SHAMPO, Pirre
SHATRON, Baptiste
SHARP, David
SHAW, Nathan
SHEARER, Andrew
SHEPBERAL, Samuel

SHEPHERD, David
SHERMAN, Patrick
SHOMER, John
SHORY, Martin
SHOULTS, John C.
SHOUTTS, Peter
SHUDLEY, David
SHY, Samuel
SIBLEY, George C.
SIFFORD, Nicholas
SIMMONS, A.C.
      William
SIMONDS, John J.
SIMPSON, Robert
SIPP, George
      George Jr.
      Joseph
SLOCUMB, Robert
SMITH, Antoine
      Christian
      Elias
      Elijah
      Eliza widow
      Elizabeth
      Hiram M.
      James
      Jesse
      John
      John B.N.
      J. J. Jr.
      Levi
    Oliver by agent
      Patrick
      Samuel B.
      Stephen
      Theophilus
    William est. 1823
    William living 1824
SNAIL, Pierre
SNOW, Eliza widow
      Henry M.
SNOWDEN, James
SOLOMON, David
      Ezekiel
      Louis
      Samuel D.
SOULARD, Antoine
SPALDING, Josiah
SPATCH, Joseph
SPEARS, George
SPENCER, Harlow
      James
STAEDLY, David
STARK, George
STEEN, John
STEPHENSON, Richard

STODDARD, Amos' heirs
STOKES, William
STONER, Isaac
STOOD, Hoff Stephen
STORRS, Asahel
STOVER, John
STOW, William
STOY, Samuel
STRIKER, Stephen P.
STROTHER, George F.
STUARD, William
STUART, Abraham
      Alexander Esq.
STUL, Samuel
SULLENS, Nathan's heirs
      Reuben
      Richard
SULLIVAN, Daniel
      James
      Hartly
      John S.
      Patrick
    Sarah widow
      William
SUNY, Jacob
SUSSANT, Amable
SUTTON, Irwin
      John L.
SYDNER, Samuel
      Washington

TALBOT, Hale
      William
TARNNIRE, Michael
TARULL, James
TAYLOR, John
      William
TAYON, Ignace
TERRY, Benjamin
TESSON, Albert
      Baptiste
      Francis
      Jean B.
      Louis
      Michael
THARP, Dodson
      William
THIBAULT, Alexis
      Francis
THOLOZAN, John E.
THOMAS, Hiram
      Peter
THOMPSON, Daniel
      George
      John W.
      Margaret

THORNTON, George
      John
TIO, John
TIFFANY, C.
      O.
TILTON, William P.
TIMON, James
TOBIN, Sarah
TODD, Benjamin I.
TOURVILLE, Touissaint
TOWN, Ephraim
TRACY, Edward by agen
TRAYNER, Michael
TRIPLETT, William
TRIXLER, Joseph
TRUDEAU, J. B. A.
    TRUTEAU Louis
TRUESDELL, William
TRUSTY, Fencher C.
TUCKER, N.B.
TURNER, Otis

VACHARD, Charles
VACHASE
VALEY, Joseph
VALLE, Francois
      Michael
VALOIS, Francois
VANBRIGHT, Abraham
VANDIT, Antoine
VARNER, Samuel by agent
VASQUEZ, Antoine
      Baronet
      Bennito
      Hypolite
      John
      Julia
VASSIEUR, Regis
VATTANT, Antoine
VENABLES, Richard B.
VERDIMAN, Amaziah
VERDIN, Nicholas
VICKERS, John
VIEN, Baptiste
      Noel
VILLERY, Antoine
VINCENT, Bouis, Mme.
      Guion
VINING, Mary's heirs
VON PHUL, Henry
VOTEAU, Isaac
      John

WADDLE, Henry est. 1824
WADSWORTH, Nathaniel
WAHRENDORFF, Charles

WALKER, David V.
   John R.
WALL, Simon
WALLACK, William
WALTER, Washington
WALTON, Elizabeth
   George
   Henry
   James
   Joseph
   Taylor
   William
WARBURTON, John
WARD, Frazier
   Giles
   John
WARNER, Jabez
WASH, Robert
WATERS, Isaiah
WATKINS, John est.
WELLS, Joseph
WEST, Simon
WETHEN, Ceder
WHENOM, Charles
WHERRY, Joseph A.
   Mackey Sr.

WHETMORE, William
WHILLEY,
  WILLI   Samuel
WHITE, Frederick
   Isaac W.
WHITESIDES, Adam I.
   James
   John
WHITING, Charles
WICKERHAM, Allen
WIER, John
WIGGINS, Samuel
  Stephen by agent
WIGGS, John W.
WILLARD, Alexander
WILLI see WHILLEY
WILLIAMS, John
   John D.
   Joseph
   Lewis
   Samuel
  Capt. Thomas
   Thompson P.
WILLS, James
WILSON, Major George
WILT, Christian
WINES, William A. D.

WINGFIELD, Owen
WISEMAN, Jonathan
WITHINGTON, John
   Thomas Sr.
WOOD, Joseph
WOODBRIDGE, Henry W.
WOODLAND, John
   Samuel
   William
WOOLFORD, Mary Ann

YARD, Lucinda, widow
YATES, Felix
YOSTI, Theotiste
   Louis
  Mme. Theotiste 1823
YOUNG, Benjamin
   Edward
   Joseph

ZIGLER, Francis
   Matthias

....

St. Louis was one of the five original districts of Missouri.
In 1816 part of its western portion was taken to form Howard
County. In 1818 some of its remaining area went into the
formation of Franklin and Jefferson counties.

The French dit which appears in some of the names above is
roughly translated "also known as." It was more than a nick-
name as it was used frequently by one branch of a family to
distinguish them from another branch. The Chauvins of Illinois,
for example, took two of these dit names. One branch remained
Chauvin, one was Chauvin dit Joyeuse, one Chauvin dit
Charleville; descendants of the latter two branches are now
known as Joyce and Charleville. Riviere and Bacane, as another
example, are the same family; so are Payant and St. Onge. In
checking for a name it is quite possible that the family
might be listed under its dit name instead of the family name.

ST. LOUIS COUNTY: SECONDARY LIST

From the Missouri Gazette-Missouri Republican and the Enquirer,
all published in St. Louis 1819-25

ADAMS, John	bkrpt		CAIN, Daniel	stray
AMES, William H.	"	++	St. Ferdinand Twp.	
ARMETAGE, John	merchant		CARRICO, Walter	estate
ARMSTRONG, John	runaway apprent.	++	CARR, Francis	horse for sale
ATCHESON, Solomon	lost note		CAMPBELL, Johnson	stray
			CARROLL, Lawrence	estate
BACONIER, Francois	bkrpt		" Mary Ann	"
BADGER, J. B.	dentist		CASAVAN, Pierre	bkrpt
BALL, Ann	estate		CASHMAN, Conrad C.	stray
BARTON, Aquilla	merchant		Bonhomme Twp.	
BATES, John	notice		CEYFORD, Mary	notice
" Lavina	"		" Nicholas	"
BEAUCHAMP, Joseph D.	estate		CHAMBERS, Charles	notice
" Nelly	"		CHAPMAN, Absalom	notice
BELCOUR, Nicholas	stray		CHARPENTIER, Joseph	bkrpt
River des Peres			CHEAVELIER, Helene	estate
BENNETT, S. Britton	stray		CHITWOOD, Seth	estate
BENTON, Nathaniel ad, runaway slave			CHRISTMAN, Jonas	estate
BERGMAN, John E.	teacher		CLIFFORD, John D.	notice
BERTRAND, Simon	notice		CLINTON, Robert	stray
BLAINE, Elizabeth	"		CODGE, William	stray
" Silas	"		St. Ferdinand Twp.	
BLOOD, Sullivan	"		COHEN, Thomas clock-and-watch-maker	
BOBKINS, Thomas	estate		COLBURN, Jesse	livery stable
BOFEE, John B.	tavern keeper		COLE, John	stray
BOILVIN, Nicholas	bkrpt		" William	"
BOLTON, Joseph Barnes	baker		Bonhomme Twp	
BONHOM, Moses	stray		COLE, Leven	estate
Bonhomme Twp.			COLEMAN, Robert	notice
BOUDON, John	bkrpt		COLLIN, Owen	stray
BOUNDS, Keziah	notice		Gravois Township	
" William	"		CONNOR, Andrew	estate
BRADY, James G.	"		COSTELLY, William	estate
" Jane	estate		COUZENEAU, Nancy	notice
" Joriah	"		CRANE, Aaron T.	notice
BRAWNER, Jeremiah	estate		CRISWELL, Hester	notice
" Richard	"		CROW, Jonathan	stolen horse
BRIGHT, Eliza	"		CRUMP, George	estate
BROADWELL, Moses	ad		CURRY, James C.	stray
BROCKMAN, Elijah	estate		Bonhomme Twp.	
" Francis	"			
BROWN, Edward	estate		DAIES, Henry	estate
(BROWNE) Samuel P.	"		DALY, Michael Florissant lost horse	
BRUCE, Amos J.	ad		DARBY, John	notice
BUCHANAN, Joseph Sylvester			DAVID, Anthony	music teacher
runaway apprentice			DAVIDSON, Daniel	estate
BUCHANNON, Rosetta	notice		DAVIDSON, E.	livery stable
BURCHMORE, George	estate		DAY, Francis	lost mare
BURGESS, George	estate		DEJARDIN, Emily Derouin	notice
BURTS, Stephen	notice		" Paulet	"
BYRNES, Michael	stray		DELAPLAINE, Helen	estate
BYRNS, James	bkrpt			

DELAUNAY, David	sawmill	GORDON, Prescella	estate
DODIER, Eliza	notice	GOREY, Patrick	lost horse
" Joseph	"	GRAY, Philip	lost books
DOGGET, Jesse	stray	GREEN, John	estate
St. Ferdinand Twp.		" Owen	"
DOLAN, Dennis	tailor	GREER, Nathan	
" Patrick	"	GRIFFITH, Isaac	estate
DONOHO, Francis	stray	" Letitia	"
Bonhomme Twp.		GRIST, John	notice
DOUGHERTY, Matthew	stray	" Phoebe	"
" Owen	"	GROESSAN, Leonard	bkrpt
DRIPS, Andrew	merchant	GULAGER, H. watchmaker & jeweler	
		GUYOR, Devius	notice
ECKSTEIN, J.	tailor		
EDSON, Susan	notice	HAB, Victor	lost mare
" Casper	"	HAINES, William	stray
EDWARDS, John	estate	HAMILTON, Jeremiah	stray
ELLIOTT, Andrew	estate	Merrimac Twp.	
ELLIOTT, Mrs. Mary Lewis	school	HAMTRAMACK, John F. T.	ad
(in Ste. Genevieve 1813-23)		HANORI , Noel	stray
ELLIS, Samuel	dentist	(HONORE)"on the Merrimack"	
ELSTONE, Joseph	stray	HARGIS, Thomas	stray
EMBREE, Elisha	notice	HARRISON, Johnson	stray
EMERSON, Alex H.	stray	"on the Grand Glaize"	
ENOS, Pascal	notice	HARVY, David runaway app. to a	
ESDALE, Tom	stray	carpenter	
River des Peres		HART, Edmund	bkrpt
EVENS, T. D.	tailor	HEBERT, Bazile	bkrpt
EVERITT, Richard	estate	HELDERMAN, Peter whiskey merchant	
EXTINE, Jacob Jr.	estate	HENRY, William	bkrpt
		HERBERT, Charles	stray
FINE, Philip	stray	HINDERLONG, Elizabeth	estate
" Wilson ***	"	HOFF, James	estate
"on the Mississippi"		HOGAN, Elizabeth	notice
FISHER, George ++	stray	" Joseph	"
Merrimac Twp.		HOGAN, Thomas	estate
FITCH, Thomas Bennett	notice	HOGELAND, William	stray
FISHER, S. Rhoads ++	lost mare	HOLMES, Frederick	stray
FITZGERALD, Elizabeth	estate	"on the Grand Glaize"	
" M. F.	stray	HONORIE, John B. Tesson	estate
FLORE, Joseph	bkrpt	HOWDESHELL, Jacob	stray
FORTUNE, John A.	"	HULL, Abijah	notice
FRYER, Thomas	tailor	HUNT, Ezra	notice
FOWLER, Charles	estate++	HUNT, Warren	bkrpt
GALL, Jacob	estate	JACOB, Reuben	estate
" Margaret	"	JACOBS, Adam	estate
GANNON, Timothy	bkrpt	" Catherine	"
GARDNER, Nancy	estate	JACOBS, Leonard	merchant
St. Ferdinand Twp.		JENNINGS, John	tailor
GARVIN, Joseph	stray	JOHNSON, Hanson	stray
GAY, George runaway app. to tailor		" Phineas	merchant
GAY, Stephen	stray	JOHNSTON, Joseph J.	notice
GILLEY, John	notice	JONES, George	estate
GLASCOCK, Asa	notice		
GLOVER, Samuel	notice		105

*** The newspaper gives this name as Wilson but it
probably should be Melsor.

KEENEY, Daniel — estate
KENNADY, William — tavern keeper
KERR, John — notice
KIDD, William — notice
KING, William D. — bkrpt

LACKEY, John M. — stray
LACROIX, Julie — estate
" Michael — "
LAHEY, Thomas — estate
LANE, Joshua — boarding house operator
LANE, Micajah — estate
LARRABEE, Russel — bkrpt
LATEROUT, Josephine — notice
(wife of Michel)
LEDUKE, Morris — notice
" Nelly — "
LEWIS, Frances M. — notice
" Elizabeth Darby — "
" Morton — "
" Russell H. — bkrpt
LINGOW, James — lost mare
LIPPINCOTT, S. — bkrpt
" T. L. — tailor
LOMBAR, John — tavern keeper
LOUIS, Fanny — cleaning and dyeing
LOUISELL, James — tavern keeper
LOVERING, Lawson — stray
. "on the Merrimac"
LOW, John S. dissolution of
partnership with Israel Trask Jr.
Florissant
LUDLOW, N. M. — painter

McCLURE, Elizabeth — estate
" James — "
McCULLOCH, Hugh — estate
McCUTCHEN, William — estate
McDONALD, Elizabeth — estate
" Joshua — "
" Joseph — stray
Bonhomme Twp.
McDONELL, Patrick — lost horse
McDONOUGH, Patrick — bkrpt
McDOWNS, William — stray++
McGIN, Patrick butcher: estate
McDOWELL, Thomas — stray++
McGOLDRICH, Robert — bkrpt
McKENNA, Michael — tailor
McKINNON, Theophilus — stray
Bonhomme Twp.
McMANNUS, Edmund — tavern keeper
McNICKLE, J. K. — ad
106

MACKEY, Isabella — estate
" James — "
MALONE, Patrick — stray
St. Ferdinand Twp.
MALONEY, Matthew — stray
River des Peres
MARCHAND, Joseph — bkrpt
MARINIER, Jacques — bkrpt
MARTEL, Joseph — notice
MARTIN, Dr. John B. — physician
MASON, Jemima — estate
MATTOX, William — stray
MEARA, John — tailor
" " and Catherine — notice
MELLONY, Matthew — tavern keeper
MERCEER, Charles — stray
St. Ferdinand Twp.
MILLANDON, Phillip — stray
MILLS, John — notice
Bonhomme Twp.
" Nathan — lost cattle
MITCHELL, Joseph — estate
MOJIN, Charles — notice
" Emily Beyon — "
MOORE, Laton G. — coppersmith
MOREAU, Charles — stray
St. Ferdinand Twp.
MORIN, Joseph — estate
MOSES, Milo — estate
MURPHY, Mathew — merchant
" Maurice — stray

NAGLES, James — merchant
NEEL (NEILL) Joseph — stray
Bonhomme Twp.
NULL, Joseph see NEEL
NORMAN, Gedeon P.

OBUCHON, Francois — bkrpt
OGDEN, David — livery stable
O'HARA, Susan — estate
(widow of William)
OLDENBURG, Louis — stray
OSBERN, C. — tavern keeper

PAINE, Noah W. — notice
" Polly — "
PARISIEN, Vic. — bkrpt
PAUL, William — stray
PAULET, Eulalie — notice
" John — "
PEGION, Hyacinthe — bkrpt
PELL, Jonathan — bkrpt
PHELPS, John — stray
PHILABAR, Gabriel — tavern keeper

PLATT, A.S.		bkrpt
POLAND, James		bkrpt
POLLOCK, William		estate
PORTER, John		estate
POTTER, Hannah		estate
" Robert		"
POTTS, John St. Louis Twp.		stray
POURIER, Francis tavern keeper		
PREWITT, Osborne		stray
"on the Merrimack"		
PULLMAN, John		stray
QUICK, Aaron		"
" Margaret (wid. of Benj.) "		
Carey's Saline		
- QUIGLEY, Patrick		estate
RANKIN, Hugh		notice
RAWLS, Hays ad for runaway slave		
REED, Chloe		estate
REILLY, Michael		stray
" Robert		"
River des Peres		
RIDGELY, Catherine		estate
RITCHIE, James		stray
Bonhomme Twp.		
ROBERTS, Ann		notice
ROSE, Ellzey H.		estate
" Lewis		"
RUNYAN, Peter Bonhomme Twp.		stray
RYAN, Lawrence		notice
SARTRAM, Harrison		stray
"on the Grand Glaize"		
SCHEWE, Christopher Frederick		
schoolmaster		
SEYMOUR, N.		tailor
SHAW, Henry		merchant
SHEARMAN, Job tavern keeper		
SHORT, Eli Merrimac Twp.		stray
" Samuel " Justice of the Peace		
SLADE, Charles		estate
SLOCUM, Robert M.		estate
SMITH, O.C. tavern keeper		
SOULARD, James G.		notice
SPALDING, Agnes P.		notice
SPENCER, Gideon		stray
Bonhomme Twp.		
SPRINGSTON, Ann		estate
" Moses		"
STAPLES, James		estate
" Samuel		"
STAR, Nathan B. ad for runaway app.		
STEEL, Adam stolen horse		
STEELE, David		estate
STEPHENS, Moses		stray
Bonhomme Twp.		
STINE, Jacob R.		furrier

STRAMKY, John W. runaway app.		
TABOR, Joseph stolen horse		
TAYLOR, Ann		notice
TERRELL, Eben		stray
Bonhomme Twp.		
THOMPSON, Alexander		estate
" Lovel		stray
William		"
St. Ferdinand Twp.		
TIMBERLAKE, Samuel runaway app.		
TINON, Claude		estate
TODD, Joseph		estate
TRASK, Israel Jr. Florissan		
dis. of partnership with		
John S. Low		
TROTIER, Joseph		carter
TUTTLE, Dave W.		merchant
VAUDRY, Mary		notice
WABERTON, John		merchant
WALKER, David H.		estate
" M.H.		"
WALSH, Esther		merchant
WARFIELD, Peter		bkrpt
WALTON, Henry		stray
Bonhomme Twp		
WATERS, Joab Jr.		estate
WALTON, Meschack		estate
WATSON, Nancy		notice
" James		notice
WATT, Robert		doctor
WELCH, Ann		notice
" Thomas		"
WEST, Washington		notice
WHEELER, Amos		estate
WHITESIDES, Thomas		stray
WHITSETT, Thomas		estate
WICKERHAM, Aquilla		estate
WIGGIN, Clarissa		estate
" Joseph		"
WILLIAM, John		notice
WILLIAMS, Theophilus		notice
WILLIS, William		lost note
WILSON, Abiel		notice
" Moses E.		estate
" Nancy		"
WINES, Diannah		notice
WITTERWITCH, Martin		stray
St. Ferdinand Twp.		
WORTHINGTON, John		stray
Bonhomme Twp		
WRIGHT, Charles		teacher
ZEIGLER, Matthias		bkrpt
ADDENDA		
SHEPHERD, Charles & Samuel estate		
VITT, Franklin found horse		
VOS, John H.		bkrpt

SALINE COUNTY: DELINQUENTS 1821 FROM THE MISSOURI INTELLIGENCER AND MISCELLANEOUS TAXES FROM THE STATE ARCHIVES

BAKER, Martin
BAXTER, Stephen
BOWMAN, John
BROWN, Cicero
     James
BROWNLEE, John

CATRON, Christopher's heirs
CHAMBERS, B.
CLEMMENS,
  CLEMMONS Henry
         Joseph
CONWILL, Jacob
COOPER, Francis
     Robert

DAVIS, Cornelius
DUCKWORTH, Samuel

FORT, Spear

GALBRETH, A. H.
GLADDEN, Joseph
GOODEN,
  GOODIN Benjamin
        Joseph H.
GRAGG, Malcolm
     Robert

HARRIS, Abigail
     Thomas
HARSELL, John
HART, G. C.
HOLLON, Benjamin
HUNT, Oliver
HUTCHINGS, Smith

JOB, John
JONES, John D.

KEENING, Thomas
KELLY, Joshua
KELSUM, James
KERKINDALE, James
KIELE, Henry

LAWLESS, Burton
LELAND, Samuel
LINCOLN, Abraham
     John

McCLAIN, John
McCLELLAND, Alexander
McELROY, John
McMACHAN, John's
     two sons
McMAHAN, J.

MAYS, John
     Joseph
     Matthew
MILSAPS, James
MULHOLLON, Edward

NAVE, Jacob

ODELL, Jeremiah
ORSBURN, Jesse

PATE, William

RAMSY, William
ROMINE, B.

SHIPLEY, George
SHIPMAN, Matthew
SHOCKLEY, Sarah
SMITH, Alexander
     Isaac
     John
SMITHERS, Joel
SOUTHWOOD, William
STEEL, A.

TENNILLE, George
     Hugh
THOMAS, Anthony
     Anthony C.
TRAMMELL, Philip

VAUGHN, Harrison
VENABLE, Richard

WALL, John B.
     Robert
WALLACE, John
     Robert
WALTON, Ira
WARREN, David
     James
WILLIAMS, Darling
     Joseph

....

SECONDARY LIST FROM THE MISSOURI INTELLIGENCER, HOWARD COUNTY

BRATAIN, William	stray
EDWARDS, William S.	notice
ESTES, Littleberry	stray
Miami Twp.	
FERRILL, William	stray
FINLEY, Asa	notice
GARRETT, Abel	notice
GITTINGS, Michael D.	notice
HAYS, William	notice
ISH, Jacob	notice
William	"
MONROE, Elizabeth Garrett	notice
Thomas	"

NOWLIN, Peyton	estate
PULLIAM, Ann R.	notice
Drewry	"
THOMAS, John Dennis	estate
WILSON, John	notice

....

Saline County was formed from Cooper in November, 1820. In 1833 part of Saline and part of Cooper were taken to form Pettis County.

....

SCOTT COUNTY: 1826 DELINQUENTS AND MISCELLANEOUS TAXES, STATE ARCHIVES OF MO.

ANDERSON, George C.
ARMOUR, David

BALDWIN, John
BANKSON, William
BROWN, James
BURNHAM, Francis
BURTON, Thomas G.

COCKERHAM, Rezin B.
COOK, John D.

FARMER, James
FRAIND, Andrew
       Jesse

HAWKINS, Benjamin
HOPKINS, Joseph A.

KINGSBERRY, Theodore

LANCASTER, Joseph B.
LARK, John

McBRIDE, P.

MARTI, Henry
MYERS, Jacob Jr.

NORMAN, Reuben

PHILLIPS, Shaply
       Thomas
PIRTH, James P.

RAUVIN, Robert
ROBERTS, John
ROBISON, Allen
RUSSELL, William
RUTTER, John P.

STRINGER, Daniel
STRONG, William

TIPTON, William

VAUGHAN, Sterling

WATKINS, N. W.
WATSON, R. G.
WICKLIFFE, M. H.
       R.
WILSON, Solomon

. . . .

SECONDARY LIST FROM THE HERALD AND THE INDEPENDENT PATRIOT, JACKSON, MO.

ABEL, Wilson   notice
BECKWITH, Newman   notice
CONELL, Charles M.   stray
    Moreland Twp.
HOPKINS, Joseph   notice
HOUTS, Jacob   stray
    Moreland Twp.
    Thomas   notice
HUNTER, Joseph   notice
KEITH, George   notice
    Elizabeth   "
MATTHEWS, Charles   estate
MOORE, Felix   estate
    Isadore   "
MYERS, William   stray
    Moreland Twp.

PAYNE, Daniel Moreland Twp.   J.P.
PURTLE, James   notice
POWELL, Thomas C.   notice
ROBERTS, Mary   estate
    Thomas   "
SHIELDS, Mary   estate
    Thomas   "
SMITH, SMYTH, Joseph   notice
WILBOURN, James   notice

. . . .

Scott County was formed from New Madrid in 1821. It is the
parent of only one county, Mississippi, formed in 1845.

WASHINGTON COUNTY: DELINQUENTS 1819 and 1825 (from the Missouri Republican); MISCELLANEOUS LEGAL TAXES FROM THE STATE ARCHIVES

ALLEY, William & wife
AMBROSE, Mathias
ANTHONY, Benjamin
ARREANDEAU, Antoine
ARIANDEAU   Louis
ASHBROOK, George
AUSTIN, Moses
        Stephen F.

BADEN, John
BAILEY, H. B.
BASNETT, A. S.
BASON, Gabriel
BEAR, Thomas & wife
BELL, Joseph H.
BLACKWELL, Jeremiah
BLAIN, Elizabeth
        Silas
BLES, Joseph
BLOCK, Simon
BORING, Joseph
BOUJU, Joseph
BOYER, Charles
        Glode*
BRECKENRIDGE, George
BRIAN, Morgan
BRICKY, John C.
BRIDGE, Benjamin
        Samuel
BRINKER, Abraham
BROWN, Henry
        Robert T.
BRYAN, James
BUFORD, William
BURNS, James
        John S.
        Zadock
BURTON, Drury

CABASSUR, Antoine
CALVERT, John
CAMPBELL, Moses*
CALVIN, _____
CARSEY, Melzer
CATRON, C.
CEOMICK, George
CHEATHAM, Edward
CHISNEY, John
COLE, Felix
        Vespassing
COLEMAN, Joseph Sr.

CONWAY, William
CONNER, Abner
COOPER, John
COPELAND, Cary*
COTTLE, Robert
COUTOY, Berthan
COVINGTON, Strother
COWICK, Adam
        Julian
CRAIG, Andrew
CRAIGHEAD, Alexander
CRAVENS, Sally
CRAWFORD, Isaac
        Josiah
CROW, Benjamin & wife
        Robert & wife
        Walter & wife

DANNEL, William
DAVIDSON, John
        Peter*
DECOSHA, Lewis
DEGAINIER, Jean B.
DEMUN, Lewis
DENNISON, Lewis C.
DEPESTRE, Mary
DICKSON, George
DOGGET, Jesse
DONAHUE, Alfred S.
DONNELL, James
DREWRY, Windsor
DUKE, Hugh
DUNKLIN, Daniel
        John

EDWARDS, Cyrus
EIDSON, Henry
ELLIOTT, Benjamin
EVANS, Henry
        Richard

FERRY, FERREE, James
FERGUSON, Thomas
FICKLIN, Thompson H.
        William H.
FIGH, Terrance
FITZWATER, Moses
FORD, Ambrose
FOUNTAIN, Francois
        Philip
FRAZIER, George

FREEMAN, _____
FULSON, Eliphalet

GARRET, Hezekiah
GARRITSON, K. B. G.
GEORGE, Catherine
        James
GIVENS, Samuel
GOFORTH, Miles
GOUTY, William
GRAY, William
GRENIER, Francis
        Louis
GRODEN, Joseph
GUYARD, Robert P.

HARKINS, S. C.
HARRISON, Thomas
HARTGROVE, Benjamin
        Jesse
        Lemuel
HATCH, James
HAVERSTICK, Jacob
HAWKINS, George
        Isaac K.
        John
        John F.
HENDERSON, Robert
        Samuel
HENRY, Andrew
HERD, Andrew
HICKS, Charles
        Nathaniel
HIGGINBOTHAM, George M.
        Thomas
HILAND, Barney
HILL, John (two)
        Polly
        William
HINKSON, William
HOPKINS, John W.
HORINE, Benjamin
        Michael
HOUSE, Jacob
        Mathias
HUDSPETH, Abijah W.
        George
HUGHS, Nathan
        William
HUNTER, Charles W.
HUTCHINS, John & wife

110

HUTCHINGS, Charles
HYDE, Henry

IMBODEN, Benjamin
INGE, William

JAMES, Phinehas
JAMISON, George
    Isaac
JOHNSON, Calvin
    Edward
    James & wife
JONES, Augustus
    John

KELLY, Joshua
KENNEDY, Ambrose
    Edward
KEY, Elijah
KILES, John
KINCAID, John

LAIEUR, Bartassur
LAMARQUE, Stephen
LARGE, John
LAROCHELLE, John
    John Jr.
LAWNEY, Jesse
LEE, Nicholas
    Stephen
LEVALLEY, Lewis
LEWIS, Hugh
LIBERTY, Joseph
LINE, Joab
LINKHORN, John
LONG, Nelson
LORE, Peter W.
LOVE, John

McCABE, John
McCLUSKEY, William
McCOY, Ananias
McFADDEN, James
McGREADY, Israel
McGUIRE, John & wife
McILVAIN,
  McILWAIN John
McINTIRE, Hugh
McIRWIN, John
McKEAN, John
McKEE, John & wife
McKEENAN, Daniel
    Hugh*
McKINNEY, John
McMANUS, John
McPEAKE, Matthew

MALOGNE, John
MARROW, Augustus
    Pierre
MASSIE, William
MATHEWS, James
MILLER, Andrew
    Jacob
    John
    Joseph*
MINEY, William
MISPLEY, Christe
    John B.
    Trophey
MOORE, Horatio
MORRIS, Jonathan
    (decd 1825)
MORRISON, Samuel
MOYERS, MOYES, Jacob
MURPHY, William
MURRELL, William
MYOTT, Manual

NOE, Dennis
NORDUFF, Henry

O'BRIEN, James J.
    Michael
    William

PAGE, Denis
PARMER, Samuel M.
PASLE, Peter
PATTERSON, Joseph
    Mary
PAUL, Jesse
    John
    William
PENEY, William M.
PERRY, John Sr.
    John Jr.
    Samuel
    William
PHILLIP, Phillip P.
PILLANWILL, John
PORTENOY, Amable
    Sally & son
PRATTE, Jean B.
PRESLEY, Paul
PRICE, Doaster
PROPHET, David

RAMBO, Jacob
RAMO, Louis
RAY, Elijah L.
RECKNA, Christian
    Samuel

REDICK, James
REED, Joseph
    Robert
RENIER, Abraham
REYBOURN, Joseph
RIANDO, Antoine Jr.
    Lewis*
RICHARDSON, Absalum
ROGAN, Bernard*
ROGUE, Pierce
ROLAND, Robert
ROSS, John B.
    Thomas
ROY, James S.
RUBEDOUX, J. B.
RUGGLES, Martin

SANSANSE, John
SAUCHAGRIN, William
SCOTT, Andrew
    James
    John Sr.
    Thomas
SERAFIN, William
SIMMS, Lewis
SIMON, Thomas
SITES, Charles (two)
SLOAN, Samuel D.
    William
SLOSS, John
SMITH, George B.
    John
    Reuben
SMITH T., John
SNIVELY, Jacob
STAPLES, James
    John
STEINBECK, Daniel F.
STEPHEN, George
STOUT, Jacob
SUMMERS, Richard
SWAN, John

TARPLEY, Thomas*
TAYLOR, John
    Samuel
TEBO, Francis
TODD, Richard V.
TRIPP, Henry
TRUSLER, Jacob
TUMAR, Baziel

VALLE, Bazile
VELAH, Dubeal
VERTEAULE, Simon

WALTON, Robert
WARNER, Nicholas*
WASHBURN, James
WATSON, Walter
WEBER, John H.
WESTOVER, Job
WHITAKER, Thomas
WHITE, John

WILABY, Alexander
WILCOX, James
WILKINS, Timothy N.
WILKINSON, Walter
WILKSON, Anthony & wife
WILLIAMS, James
    Justinian
    Pierre

WILSON, Hardin
WINDES, Enoch
WOODS, Jacob

YATES, Reuben
YOUNG, James C.

ZACHARY, William

=+=+=+=+=+=+=+=+=+=+=

Washington County was formed from Ste. Genevieve in 1813. Part of it was later taken to form parts of Iron, Shannon, and St. Francois.

=+=+=+=+=+=+=+=+=+=

SECONDARY LIST: FROM THE INQUIRER AND THE REPUBLICAN, 1819-1826

ANDERSON, James   stray
    Bellevue Twp.
ANDREWS, John   AS
ARREANDEAU, Pierre   AS
ASHBROOK, Moses   stray
    Bellevue Twp.
ATWOOD, William   stray
    Harmony Twp.

BAKER, John   AS
BEAR, James Bellevue Twp.   stray
    Joseph   notice
BEARDSLEY, Josiah   AS
BEAVENS, William   license
BLACK, David W.   stray
    Bellevue Twp.
BIOTTE, Joseph   estate
    Marie
BOJO, Bazile   AS
BOGGS, Robert W.   license
BOWNDS, William   stray
    Bellevue Twp.
BROOKS, John Union Twp.   stray
BUFORD, John Bellevue Twp.   "
BURASAW, Francis   AS

CARNES, Robert   license
CARR, Thomas   AS
CASEY, Andrew   license
CAREY, John   "
CHAMBERS, Alexander   license
CLARK, John S.   stray
    Bellevue Twp.
CLARKSON, John   AS

DEADERICK, A. W.   estate
    Capt. David S.   "
DEEL, Antoine   license

DELAUNAY, John B.   AS
    Polly   "
  (dau. of Jn. B., minor, cripple)
DEVINE, Thomas   license
DUDLEY, Aaron Richmond Twp.   stray
EATON, Abraham   stray
    Bellevue Twp.
ELLIOTT, Benjamin   notice
    Elias A.   estate
    Eliza Ann   notice
    Henry   estate

FERGUSON, Moses   J.P.
    Richmond Twp.
FLANDERS, John   lisense
FLAUGH, Christian   license
FOSTER, Dabney   notice
    Sarah   "
FROST, Simon Harmony Twp.   stray
FULBRIGHT, Daniel "   "
    John "   "
    Martin   "

GARVIN, Thomas Bellevue Twp.   J.P.
GIBBS, Ezekiel   license
GOFORTH, Willaby BellevueTwp.   stray
GORE, Notley P.   stray
    Osage Fork of the Cutway
GUEST, Jonathan   license
GUY, Francis   license

HAGOOD, William G.   stray
    Bellevue Twp.
HARGIS, Thomas Liberty Twp.   stray
HAYS, William "   "
HENDERSON, Nathaniel   stray
    Osage Fork of the Cutway
HILL, Jesse Liberty Twp.   stray
HINCH, William "   "
HINESLEY, Allen Harmony Twp.   stray

HINKSON, L.   Liberty Twp.   J.P.
    Robert   license
HORINE, Michael   stray
    Liberty Twp.
HUDSPETH, Ayres   "   stray
HUFF, A.   license
    John   stray
HUGHES, John   Liberty Twp.   stray
    Samuel   AS
HUNTER, Samuel   license
HURT, A. B.   license

IMBODEN, David BellevueTwp   stray

JAMISON, James   AS
JOHNSON, John   Bellevue Twp stray
JONES, William   AS

KEPLAR, Catherine   estate
    Jacob   "
KINEMONT, Garrison B.   stray
    Bellevue Twp.

LANE, Thomas   Union Twp.   stray
LATURNO, August   AS

McMURTRY, Joseph   AS
    William B.   "
McNEAL, John   BellevueTwp.   stray

MAXWELL, Robert B.   "   "
MEETRY, James H.   AS
MENEDY, Philip   stray
    Richmond Twp.
MILLUM, William   license
MONDAY, Philip   license
MORRISON, John   license
    Lewis   stray
    Liberty Twp.
MURPHY, William   license
MUSSETT, Hiram   notice
    John   stray

NEAVE, William   Union Twp.   stray

O'NEAL, Dennis   license
OWENS, Turence   license

PERRY, Andrew   stray
    John Jr.   "
    Bellevue Twp.
    James F.   AS
PINKLEY, Henry   AS
PRATTE, Amable   pauper
    Joseph   estate
PREWITT, Gabriel   stray
    Bellevue Twp.

RAMBO, Jacob H. adv for runaway slave
REYBURN, John N.   J. P.
    Samuel W.   stray
    Bellevue Twp.
ROBERTS, Brown C.   AS
ROBINSON, James   AS
RUGGLES, Luman   stray
    Bellevue Twp.
RUSSELL, Moses   "   "

SCOTT, John   AS
    Moses   notice
SHORR, Gilbert   notice
SHURLDS, Henry   J. P.
SLOAN, Fergus   AS
SMITH, Augustus   license
    Hiram   license
    William C.   stray
SNIDER, Henry   stray
    Bellevue Twp.
SPRINGER, Charles Harmony Tp. J.P.
STROLLE, George F.   license
STROTHERS, French   stray
    Bellevue Twp.
STUART, John   Harmony Twp.   stray
SULLIVANT, Stephen   stray
    Liberty Twp.

THOMPSON, Aaron   license
    B. J.   Union Twp.   J. P.
TREAT, A. Leon   AS
TWITTY, Roseha (?)   notice
    William   "

WALKER, Samuel   license
WALTHALL, Jane   estate
    Thomas   "
WARNER, Pliny   license
WHEALY, William   AS
WHEELER, David   AS
WILLIAMS, Hezekiah   stray
    Bellevue Twp.
    Reuel   estate
    Theophilus   "
WOOD, William   AS
WOOLSEY, Stephen   stray
    Thomas   "
    Liberty Twp.
WRIGHT, John   "   stray

=+=+=+=+=+=+=

113

WAYNE COUNTY: DELINQUENTS 1821-25-26 (from the Independent Patriot)

AND MISCELLANEOUS LEGAL TAXES (from the State Archives of Missouri)

ALLEN, Moses
ASHER,
ASHERST   John

BALANCE, Nulass
BARKER, Robert
BARR, James
BEAR, James
BELL, John
BERRY, Solomon
BEVER, Adlarence
BLACKBURN, William
BOREN, John
      Margaret
BRAZIL, Richard Sr.
      Robert
      Valentine
BUCKHART,
BURKHART   Joseph

CAMPBELL, Garrett
CAPEHART, Frederick
CARR, John
      William
CAZEY, Melzee
CHILTON, Robert
      Thomas
CLAYPOOL, John Sr.
      John Jr.
      Reuben
COWAN, Richard D.

DAVIS, Thomas
DENTON, John
DENVIEN, Nathaniel
DOUGLASS, Josiah
DRAPER, Reuben

ESTES, John S.

FINDLY, Thomas
FOWLER, Jeremiah

GARTMAN, George
GARNER, Thomas

HALE, Thomas
HARPER, Matthew
HEDGER, Benjamin
HOBBS, John
HOLDTREE, John
HOLT, Thomas
HOMERLY, James
HOWARD, Charles
114

HUBBLE, Matthew
HUMPHRIES, John
HUNT, John

JAMES, George
JARRAT, Anthony
JOHNSTON, William

KELLY, James
      William
KERSEY, Melzer

LADD, Hollis
LASSLY, John
LINE, William
LINKHORN, Joseph
LITTLE, William D.
LOGAN, James
LOGSDON, Joseph
LOVE, John

McFADDIN, James

MANN, Isaac
MASTERS, Jacob
MAYERS, John
MILLER, John

NEELY, Thomas

PRICE, John
      Rachel
      Robert

RESIGNER, Henry
RIGHT, Nicajah
ROBERTSON, Baldon
      Francis
      Jane
ROW, John
ROWLAND, John

SANDLIN, Prescella
SHEROON, Isaiah
SHOOK, Daniel
SKILES, George
      John
      Moses
SMITH, David D.
      Uriah
SPENCER, Jesse
STORY, Elizabeth
STUART, John
      (collector)

TYLER, Isaac

VANDEVER, Moses

WALLIS, Ruth
WARREN, William E. ++
WELLS, Anthony
      Jacob
WELSON, Priscilla
WHEELER, Alfred
WATSON, Miles ++
      Peter
WILKS, David
WILSON, Leonard
WOOD, Zachariah
      Curtice
WOODWARD, David
WOTSON, George

YOUNGBLOOD, Ambrose
      Polly

ZACHERY, John

Wayne County was formed from
Cape Girardeau in 1818. It is
the parent county of Butler
and Ripley, parts of Iron and
Bollinger, and by extension of
parts of Carter, Reynolds,
Shannon, and Texas.

Virtually all Wayne County
records prior to 1892 were
destroyed in two courthouse
fires. ....

From the Independent Patriot and the Herald, Jackson, Cape Girardeau Co.

ANTHONY, Samuel	notice	MARCUS, James St.Francois Twp	stray
ASHABRANNER, Wilben	stray	MASTERS, Littleton	stray
Jefferson Twp.		Jefferson Twp.	
		MARTIN, Robert	stray
BETTIS, Elijah St. FrancoisTwp.stray		MAY, John Jefferson Twp	stray
Overton	"	MELTON, William Logan Twp	stray
Ranson Logan Twp.	stray		
BIGGINS, Clark Logan Twp.	stray	PAYTON, Chesley StFrancoisTwp	stray
James "	"	PETTIS, Robert Logan Twp	stray
BOLIN, Solomon R.	JP		
St. Francois Twp.		REED, Andrew	estate
Sarah	estate	REESE, David St. FrancoisTwp	stray
BOLLINGER, George	estate	ROBINSON, William	lawsuit
Solomon	"	RUBOTTOM, Ezekiel LoganTwp	stray
John Blocklives Twp stray		RUS, David	AS
CARTER, Benjamin	estate	SEAWELL, Joseph	estate
David	"	SEITZ, George StFrancoisTwp	stray
CATO, Louis Jefferson Twp	J.P.	SIMMONDS, Moses	AS
CLARK, Elizabeth	notice	SMITH, Robert StFrancoisTwp	stray
John S. Logan Twp.	stray	STANLY, John	lawsuit
William	notice	STEEL, William Logan Twp	stray
COLLARD, Joseph	stray	STREET, William	AS
St. Francois Twp.		STROUP, Samuel P.	bankrupt
COWAN, Richard D. "	"	SWAIN, Sherad G.	AS
		SWEASED, Charles Kelly Twp	J.P.
DANLEY, Caleb	estate		
Catherine	"	TRUSTY, T.	stray
DAVIDSON, John	lawsuit		
DAVIS, Green W.	notice	WILLIAMS, Phineles Logan Twp	stray
DONLEY, James	lawsuit	WRIGHT, Stephen Logan Twp	stray
DOUGHTY, Joseph	stray		
		. . . .	
FAUSTER, John	stray		
FISHER, James BlocklivesTwp	stray		
GOLLEHOR, Charles	estate		
HALL, Samuel	stray		
HARRIS, William	lawsuit		
HOBBS, William St. FrancoisTwp stray			
HOLMES, John "	"		
JUSTUS, James Logan Twp	stray		
KELLY, Isaac E. Kelly Twp	stray		
Jacob Logan Twp	J.P.		
KEYS, John	bankrupt		
LANDERS, John StFrancoisTwp	stray		
LANE, Williston	AS		
LEWIS, James W.	stray		
"near McDonald's horsemill"			
LOGAN, David Logan Twp	stray		
John Jr. "	"		
Robert A. "	"		

ADDENDA FROM HOWARD COUNTY LIST, 1819

These names appear on the 1819 tax list of Howard County, but are not found in later years in Howard, Boone, Chariton, Clay, or Cooper. While it is certainly possible that these men may have died or moved on, it is also possible that they were in the area of Howard which subsequently became Cole, Lafayette, Ray, or Saline and for that reason they are included here.

ALLEN, Isaac
ARNOLD, Price Sr.

BARTON, Roger
BEATY, James
       Joseph
BELLACE, George
BEMBRICK, Frederick
BOGGS, Lilburn W.
BROWN, Robert

CAMRON, Ezra
CARPENTER, William
CLEMENS, William
CONNER, Jeremiah

DETHRIDGE, Amos
DOUGLAS, Isham
       Thompson
DULANY, Joseph S.

EVANS, Andoca

FIELD, Ebenezer
FOUT, Samuel
FOSTER, Freeman

GILLS, Samuel

HATTON, Thomas
HOPE, Adam
HYDE, James

KAVANAUGH, Charles
KEENY, Thomas

LAMON, William
LAUGHLIN, John
LAWLESS, Bradford
LUNTE, William

McMAHAN, William

MANCHESTER, John
       Thomas
MARTIN, Isaac
MORGAN, Enos

OWENS, Philip

PERKINS, Jesse
PEVELY, Jeremiah
PULLIAM, Boswell

RAMSEY, William Sr.
RAY, John
RECTOR, Elias
RICHARDSON, Jesse
RIGGIN, James

SAUNDERS, Bryant
SCUDDER, John W.
SMITH, Cornelius
STOKELY, Thomas
STODDY, Joseph R.

THRESHER, Robert
THWEAT
  (THEVEAT?) Thomas
TUTTLE, Jane

WARREN, Martin
WAYNE, Ephraim
WATTS, Ewing
WEVER, Benjamin
WOLFSKILL, George

ZEVELY, Alexander
       James
ZUMWALT, Jacob

INDEX

Berrysford	94	
Bertho, Birth	85	
Berthold	94	
Bertrand	94, 104	
Besaunette	94	
Besore	24	
Bess, Best	12,25,30,54,63,77	
Besser	77	
Bethel	8, 63	
Bettick, Bittick	94	
Bettis	115	
Bettle, Bittle	1	
Beuyate	89	
Bevan	77	
see also Beaven		
Bevanue, Bienvenu	77	
Bever	114	
Bey	94	
Bezet	94	
Bickerstaff, Bigerstaff	25,29,77	
Bickum	12	
Biddick, Biddix	1, 36	
Bienvenu, Bevanue	94	
Biers	85	
Biggins	115	
Biggs	8,41,70,77	
Biglow, Beglow, Bigelow	36, 77	
Biler	30	
Bill	73	
Billingsley	30	
Billon, Billow	89, 94	
Bingham, Bigham	30,42,94	
Binns	22	
Bird	12,36,42,54,58,89	
see also Byrd		
Birdsong	30	
Bisch	89	
Bishop	1,12,22,72	
Bissell	57, 94	
Bissonnette	94	
Biswell	1	
Bittle, Bettle	1	
Bivens	12, 25	
see also Beaven		
Black	1,8,59,70,76,77,89,94, 112	
Blackburn	1, 114	
Blackwell	36,85,89, 110	
Bladenberg	8	
Elaine	104, 110	
Blair	12,36,75,77	
Blakeley	42	
Blanchard	94	
Blanchette	77	
Bland	77	
Blank	77	
Blankenship	36	
Blanset	42	
Blanton	59	
Blasingin	30, 54	
Bledsoe	1	
Blemens	70	
Bles	110	
Blevins	1, 42	
Block	12,59,73,84,94, 110	
Blocker	12	
Blood	104	
Bloom	89	
Blotte	112	
Bloy, Bloyes, Bloice	42, 63	
Bluebough	54	
Blunt	12, 21	
Blythe	8, 42	
Board	8, 77	
Boatright	63	
Bobb	94	
Bobkins	104	
Bodoine	94	
Bofse	104	
Boggs	25, 42, 112,116	
Bogliolo	70	
Bogy	89	
Bohannan, Bohannon	1, 12	
Boilvin	104	
Bojo	112	
Boland	94	
Bolduc	89	
Boles	42	
Boli, Boly	94	
Bolin, Boling, Bowlin	12, 30, 77, 115	
Bollinger	12, 115	
Bolon	94	
Bolton	104	
Bompart	94	
Bonani	94	
Bond	57, 89	
Bonhom	94, 104	
Bonne	89	
Boomer, Boumer	42,85	
Boon, Boons	1,8,42,63,77	
Boone, Boune, Bono	63,85	
Boothe	8, 63	
Boozer	42	
Bordeaux	94	
Borel	89	
Boren, Borond, Boring	12, 57, 89, 110, 114	
Boris	89	
Boshana, Boshma	77	
Bosseron	94	
Bossier	89	
Boston	1	
Bostwick	94	
Boswell, Bogwell	22, 36, 42	
Bothick	94	
Botton	94	
Botts	22, 42	
Boucher	42,63,94	
Boudon	104	
Bough	77	
Bouis	94	
Boujeneau	94	
Bouju	94,110	
Boulware	41	
Bounds, Bownds	1, 58, 85, 89, 104, 112	
Bourbenois, Borbonne	94	
Bournour	69	
Bousfield	30	
Bouvette	94	
Bowden	30, 70	
Bowine, Bowen	42, 63, 77	
Bower, Bowers	63, 77	
Bowler	63	
Bowles, Boles	1,22,30,36,94	
Bowlin	12	
see also Bolin		
Bowman	208	
Bowmer	63	
Bown (?)	12	
Bowny	94	
Boyce	12	
Boyd, Boid	1,12,30,36,57,59, 89, 94	
Bowyer	42	
Boyer, Boyier	1,12,77,89,94, 110	
Boywell	42	
Boz	42	
Bozarth	42, 43	
Bracken	75	
Bradbury	25	
Bradford	8, 22, 43, 63	
Bradhurst	25	
Bradley	1,22,30,43,58	
Bradshaw	85	
Brady	1,12,21,36,70,85,89, 94, 104	
Bragg	8,43	
Braley, Brawley	12, 25,43	
Bram	1	
Brammel, Bramly	36, 43	
Branan	43	
Branham	8	
Brants	12	
Brasfield, Brasefield	22, 43	
Brashear, Brashears	43, 89	
Brattain, Bratton	8, 94, 108	
Bravais	12	
Bravo	76	
Brawdy	63	
Braley, Brawley	43	
Brawner	104	
Bray	36	
Brazeau	94	
Brazil	114	
Breckenridge	94, 110	
Breeding	36	
Breeze	94	
Brenly	94	
Brett	43	
Bretton	30	
Brewer	12, 22, 75, 95	
Brice	61, 89, 95	
Bricky	110	
Bridge, Bridges	12, 43, 110	
Briggs	43, 63	
Bright	63, 95, 104	
Brimager	1	
Brink	1	
Brinker	110	
Brinley	57	
Briscoe (Bristoe?)	30, 41	
Brite	8	
Broaddus	43	
Broadhurst	43	
Broadwater (Broadmaker?)	59	
Broadwell	104	
Brock	12, 30, 36, 40	
Brockman	104	
Broiles	30	
Brook, Brooks	1,8,12,21,22,36,63, 75, 95, 112	
Broom	12	
Brother	63	
Brotherton	95	
Brouster	95	
Brovon	72	
Browder	22	
Brown, Browne	1,8,12,22,25,29,30,36,43, 54,59,63,69,77,85,89,93, 95,104,108,109,110,116	
Browner	95	
Browning	54, 63	
Brownlee	108	
Bruce	104	
Bruette	85	
Bruffee	30	
Brugiere, Brugeres, etc.	77, 89	
Bruin, Breuin	77	
Bruistran	77, 84	
Brumfield	77	
Brummitt	43	
Brundage	43	
Brunelle	77	
Bruner	1	
Brunette	95	
Brunk	59	
Brunt, Brunts	43, 76	
Bruusier	77	
Bryan, Brian	13,63,77,85,89,110	
Bryant	1, 8, 13, 30, 63, 77	
Bryson	73	
Buchanan, Buckhannon, etc.	54, 73, 95, 104	
Buche	95	
Bucher	95	
Buckbridge	25	
Buckler	77	
Buckner	13, 30, 36, 93	
Bud	95	
Budges	43	
Buel	95	
Buford	1, 85, 110, 112	
Bugg	13	
Buis, Buie	13, 54	
Bull	13, 22	
Bullard	1, 13, 42, 43, 70	
Buller	43	
Bullitt	13	
Bunche	43	
Bunds	25	
Bupron	95	

Burasaw 112
Burbanks 77
Burch 36, 43, 63, 76
Burchmore 104
Burdyne, Burdeanna 1, 77
Burgan, Burgin 30, 85
Burge, Burgie 43, 69,77
Burger 85
Burgis, Burgess 57, 104
Burgit, Burgot 63, 85
Burke, Burk, Birk 1, 30, 43, 89, 95
Burkelow 1, 54
Burkett 8
Burkhart, 22, 41, 43, 95,
  Buckhart, Burckhartt 114
Burleau 84
Burlet 54
Burliston, Burleson 1, 36, 43
Burman 63
Burnett 8,25,30,43,63,89
Burney 30
Burnham 43, 85, 89, 109
Burns, Burnes 1,13,21,25,30,36,
  also see 43,59,62,63,73,77,
  Byrnes 95, 110
Burroughs, 13,30,36,43,89,95
  Burrows, Burris, Burrus
Burt, Burts 8,63,69,85,104
Burton 22,43,109,110
Burtston 95
Bush 63
Bust 13, 85
Buster 25, 43
Butcher 30, 63, 77, 89
Butler 13,22,36,43,57,63,70,77
Butterworth 1
Buttes 36
Byan 85
Bybee 43
Byers 13
Byle, Byler 11,30
Bynum 43
Byran 110
Byrd 13, 57, 95
  see also Bird
Byres 21
Byrne, 13,29,43,54,57,95, 104
  Byrnes see also Burns
Byrnside 36
Byron 95

Cabanne 95
Cabassur 110
Cabeen 22
Cabell 22
Cadman 95
Cadooth 77
Cadver 95
Cadwell 95
Cail, Coil 63
  see also Coyl
Caillou 95
Cain, Cane 25, 43, 63, 104
Calbert 63
Calbreath 8
Caldwell 1,13,30,35,36,40,72,
  73,77,85,89,95
Call 36
Callahan 1, 63,77
Callant (Calute?) 77
Callaum 95
Callaway 1,8,43,59,63,77
Callender 95
Callew 1
Callit 1
Calvert, Colvert 30,36,95,110
  (?) Colvin
Calvin, Colvin 29, 110
Cameron, Camron 25,63,76,116
Camp 95
Campbell, 1,13,22,25,30,36,43,
  Camel 54,58,73,85,89,95,104,
  110,114
Cannady, Canady 8, 63, 85
  see also Kennedy

Canner 30
Cannon 13, 43, 59, 77
Canole 43
Cantley 36, 63
Cantriel 59
Capp, Cap 22, 95
Capehart 114
Captain 8
Carafrain 77
Carbono 78
Cardama 95
Carder 85, 89
Cardinale 78
Carey, Cary 7, 25, 30, 58, 75
Carlisle 63
Carlock 13
Carman 36, 95
Carnes 43, 112
Carney 1, 43, 85
Caron, Carron 89
Carpenter, 8, 13, 22, 25,
  Curpenter 30, 70, 116
Carr 36, 78, 89, 95,
  104, 112, 114
Carrick 89
Carrico 95, 104
Carrole 89
Carroll, 25, 36, 40, 43, 54,
  Carrell 76, 85, 104
Carruth 8
Carsey 110
Carson 30, 43, 54, 75
Carter 1, 22, 29, 30, 43, 63,
  73,78,85,89,95, 115
Cartin 89
Cartmill, Cartmell 13, 95
Cartner 30, 63
Carver 63
Casavan 104
Case 8
Casey 29, 43, 112
  see also Cazey, Carey
Cash 43
Cashaw 78
Cashman 95, 104
Casner 55
  see also Cosner, Castner
Cason, Casson 41, 43, 95
Cass 22
Cassedy 30
Castarphen 75
Casteel, Castes 25, 30, 43
Castellos, Castlio 30, 78
  (?) Costelly (?)
Castler, Costler 24
Castles 58
Castner (Casner, Costner) 13
Castonga 95
Castrow 95
Cates 22, 25, 43, 63
Catherwood 95
Cathey 30
Catlett 30
Cato 115
Catrall 95
Catron 30, 58, 108, 110
Cattleman 63
Caulk 30, 36, 95
Cavanaugh 36
  see also Kavanaugh
Cave 1, 2, 44
Cavender 13
Caw 95
Caton, Cayton, Caten 30,43,63
Cazey, Casey 114
Cealy 13
Center 13
Ceomick 110
Cerre, Cerri 89, 95
Cessell 72
  see also Sisel
Ceyford 104
Challas 2
Challelier 89
Chamberlain 21

Chambers 30, 35, 59, 63, 78,
  104, 108, 112
Champ 95
Champain 78
Champeau 95
Champion 44
Chandler 8, 13, 21, 59, 63, 95
Chaney 25, 30, 44
Chapman 2, 8, 25, 36, 44, 54,
  78, 85, 89, 95, 104
Chappell, 24, 44, 63, 78
  Chappal, Chapel
Chappet 95
Charless 2, 95
Charleville 89, 95
Charlton 8, 29
Charpentier 104
Chartier 69
Chartrain, Chartrand 78, 95
Chase, Chace 29
Chatillon 95
Chattayne 84
Chauncellier 78
Chauvin 95
Cheatham 110
Cheavelier 104
Cheek 13, 30, 36, 69
Chenier 95
Cherry 44
Cheseaur 69
Chevis 2
Chevonne 36
  (?) Chewning (?)
Chew 68
Childers 25, 36
Chilton 114
Chinneth, Chinworth 58, 63
  (?) Chenoweth (?)
Chisney 110
Chisum 2, 29, 30
Chitcoat 30
Chitwood 36, 75, 95, 104
Choquette 95
Chouteau 95
Christian 2, 44
Christman 44, 95,104
Christy 54, 78, 95
Chronister 13
Cicar 78
Cirkendoll 44
  see also Kirkendoll
Clamore 78
Clamorgan 95
Clanton 63
Clare 78
Claremont 78
Clark, 2, 13, 21, 22, 24, 25,
  Clarke, Clarck 29, 30, 36, 44,
  54, 59, 64, 68, 78, 89,
  95, 112, 115
Clarkson 44, 85, 112
Clarmo 78
Clasby 95
Clay 30, 57, 64, 78, 85, 89
Claybrooks 22, 29
Claypool 114
Clayton, Cleyton 25, 44
Clemens, Clements, 2,25,40,41,44,
  Clemmons etc. 95, 108, 116
Clemenson 58
Clement 95
Cleveland 8, 44, 89
Clevenger 76
Cleyton, see Clayton
Clifford 104
Clifton 8, 64
Clinard 13
Clindennin, 8, 64
  Clendennon, etc.
Clingingsmith*** 13
Clinton 8, 104
Clippard 13
Clodfellow, Clodfelter 13
Cloop 13
Close 25
  *** also see Klinglesmith

119

DeLill, DeLisle 85, 96
Dellis 31
DeLois 96
DeLor, DeLore 96
DeLoriere (also see DeLaury) 96
DeLuziere 90
DeMasters 85
Demerind 96
Demoislem 96
    also see Demoulin
Demoss 64
Demoulin (Demoislem) 96
Dempsey 14, 44
DeMun 110
Dennison, Denison 85, 96, 110
Denny 2, 44, 73, 78, 96
Denois 96
Denonmoline 96
Denort, Dunord 96
Denoyer 64, 96
Densman 7
Dent 37, 85, 96
Denton 8, 25, 96, 114
Denvien 114
DePestre 110
DeQuet, DuQuette 90
Derbin 25
Derby, Darby 96
Derickson 85
Dernery 96
Deroin, Derouin 96
Derosier 96
Derway 78
Deshay, Deshaw 14, 78
DesLoe 78
Detandebaratz 96
Detchemendy 90
Dethier 78, 96
Dethridge, Deatherage 116
Devault 14
Devens 59
Devers 96
Devine 112
Devore 14, 78, 84
Devotion 96
Dewall 76, 90
Dewey 41
Dewitt 31, 57, 73, 75
Dezentzy 96
Dial (see also Doyle) 14
Dickard 31
Dickerson 73
Dickey 44
Dicons 31
Dicosy 41
Didier 96
Die' 90
Dieterle 90
Diggs 59, 64
Dill 44, 85
Dillar 31
Dillon 2, 8, 29, 64, 73, 96
Dinsmore 22
Dinwiddy, Dinwiddie 22, 44
Dirting 8, 11
Discon 78
Dixon, Dickson 2,21,31,35,78,96,110
Dobbin 64
Dodd, Dodds 2, 40
Dodge 90
Dodier 78, 105
Dodson 37, 44, 76, 96
Doe 78
Doerif 78
Dofa 78
Doggett, Daggett 85, 105, 110
Dogy 96
Dolan 96, 105
Dolton 62
Domean, Domine 8, 96
Dominique 96
Donald 57, 85
Donaldson, Donelson 31, 44, 54

Donley 115
Donnell 110
Donner 96
Donnshaw 93
Donohoe, 22, 90, 96, 105, 110
    Donahue, Dunahoe, etc.
Dooley, Duley 8, 45
Doolen, Dulin 54, 73, 78
Doresmus 14
Dorick 90
Dorlac 78, 90
Dorrell 44
Dorriss 8, 37, 64, 96
Dorsac 69
Dorway (DOZA? 78) 78
Dotson 25
Doty 96
Dougherty, 8, 64, 85, 96, 105
Daugherty
Douglas, 2, 14, 37, 44, 78,
    Douglass 96, 114, 116
Dow 44
Dowlan, Dowlin 45
Dowler 96
Downie, Downey 58
Downing 45, 59, 96
Dowson 45
Dowty, Doughty 14, 21, 115
Doxey 22
Doyle, Doyail, 2, 8, 37
    Doiel, Dial
Dozeng 78
Dozier 45, 64, 84
Drace 78
Drake 22, 45
Draper 59, 61, 75, 96, 114
Drappo 78
Drewry 110
Drinkard 22, 45
Drinkwater 31
Drips 105
Driskill 78
Droom 14
Droven 96
Drowdy 78
Drum 14
Drummonds 78
Druslam 96
Drybriad 90
Duba 78
DuBois 78
Dubray 96
DuBreuil 90, 96
DuBuisson 90
DuBurgh 96
Duchen 96
DuChoquette 96
Duckworth 85, 108
DuClos 90
Duden 64
Dudley 112
Duel 96
Duff 37, 78, 85, 96
Duffy 78
DuFour 90
Duke 64, 110
Dugan 31
Dulaney 116
    see also Delaney
Duken 78
Duley, Dooley 2, 8, 64
Dumaster 58, 85
Dumay 69
Duno 78
Dumond 96
Dunahoe (also see Donahoe) 8
Dunard 96
Dunaway 31
Dunbar 58
Duncan, 8, 14, 37, 41, 45,
    Dunkin, Duken 59, 72, 78, 96
Dunegant 96
Dunham 8, 14
Dunklin 110
Dunlap, 8, 9, 14, 22, 25, 85,
    Dunlop 90, 96

Dunlavy 96
Dunn 2,14,22,31,45,54,69,85
Dunney 45
Dunnica 9, 11, 64
Dunning 14, 59
Dunnington 22
Dunord, Denort 96
Dupea 69
DuPotre 96
DuPree 69
DuPrise 96
DuPuix 96
DuQuette (see DeQuette) 78
Duran 45
DuRocher 78, 90, 96
Durway, Dorway 78
Dusan 45
Duskey 2
Dustin 22
Dutremble 96
Dutton 64
Duval 90
Dye 90
Dyer 9
Dysart 22

Eads, Eades 29, 35, 85, 90
Eaker 14
Eaking 14
Earickson 22, 45
Earl 22
Early 59
Earthman 45
Easley 2, 85
East 2, 45
Easter 96
Eastin, Easton 2, 78, 96
Eaton 2, 45, 85, 112
Ebare, Ebair, Ebere 78, 96
Eckhart 78
Eckstein, Extine 105
Edenor, Edinger 14
Edgar 31
Edmonds 14, 64
Edmondson 2, 41, 58, 64
Edson 105
Edwards 2, 9, 14, 22, 31, 40,64,
    70,78,90,96,105,108,110
Eggers 72
Eidson 110
Eigert 14
Eisenhower, Isenhower 15
Elkins 45
Ellenwood 96
Eller 31
Elliott 2, 22, 45, 69, 85, 90,
    96, 105, 110, 112
Ellingtom 2, 54, 78
Ellis 2, 9, 14, 22, 25, 31,
    45, 64, 70, 96, 105
Ellison 2, 14, 31, 45
    see also Allison
Elmore 45
Elsten, Elstone 2, 64, 105
Elton 64
Ely 25, 58, 75
Embree 45, 105
Emerson 73, 105
Emmans, Emmons 31, 78
Emory 59
Engleheart 2
Enlow 37
English 14, 21, 25, 29, 31, 96
    see also Inglish
Eno 25
Enos 105
Enshell 45
Enyart 45
Eplin (see also Aplin) 64
Erelson 45
Ernart -- see Aerhart & Aheard
Ervin, 14, 22, 31, 58, 59, 64,
    Erwin, Ervine etc. 90
    see also Irvin, etc.
Esdale 105

90

127

67, 87

Seeds 92

=+=+=+=+=+=+=+=+=+=+=

133

www.ingramcontent.com/pod-product-compliance
Lightning Source LLC
Chambersburg PA
CBHW021832020426
42334CB00014B/599